S0-DKM-928

First published in 2002

Kogan Page Limited
120 Pentonville Road
London N1 9JN
UK

Kogan Page US
22 Broad Street
Milford CT 06460
USA

British Library Cataloguing in Publication Data

A CIP record for this book is available from the British Library.

ISBN 0 7494 3710 3

Typeset by Jean Cussons Typesetting, Diss, Norfolk
Printed and bound in Great Britain by Biddles Ltd, Guildford and King's Lynn
www.biddles.co.uk

BUILDING
TOMORROW
COMPAN

A GUIDE TO SUSTAINABLE BUSINESS SUC

PHILIP SADLER

Tomorrow's Company

KOGAN
PAGE

Contents

Foreword

In the early 1990s Charles Handy gave a lecture at the Royal Society of Arts, called 'What is a company for?'. There was such interest in what Handy said that in 1993 the RSA decided to challenge senior business leaders to give their vision of the company of the future.

Twenty-five of the foremost business leaders of the time agreed to support and participate in the ensuing Inquiry. A wide-ranging consultation exercise led by Sir Anthony Cleaver, then Chairman of IBM UK, involved more than 8,000 business leaders and opinion formers. The business leaders who participated in the preparation of the Report were aware that massive changes were taking place in the business world. On the one hand, globalization and revolutionary developments in the technologies of communication and information were transforming the competitive environment. On the other hand, important changes were taking place of a social nature, including growing public concern about the impact of business success on the environment. Such concerns were reflected in the growth in number, size and influence of various pressure groups. Following the collapse of the Soviet bloc and the end of the Cold War it had seemed for a time that democracy and Western-style capitalism were now unchallenged as the bases for a prosperous and just society. Yet challenges were now being mounted from many sides, and not only from those concerned for social justice or environmental conservation. There were also critics who argued that some aspects of the way the markets worked favoured short-term thinking and thus acted against the process of sustainable wealth creation. The realization was growing that whereas profit and the creation of long-term value for investors remain crucial, in the New Economy we needed to find new ways to generate these returns in a sustainable manner that would be supported by society in general.

The findings of the Inquiry were published in 1995 in the RSA report 'Tomorrow's Company: the role of business in a changing world'. Considerable public interest resulted in the report selling over 4,000 copies. The report looked at the changing world and, making reference both to its own research and to other recent evidence, set out the vision of the 'inclusive approach'.

At the heart of the inclusive approach is the belief that understanding stakeholder needs (by that, we mean the needs of customers, employees, suppliers, shareholders and society, and the environment) and incorporating them into business strategy are central to the achievement of sustainable competitiveness.

Inclusive companies have vision in the sense of a shared view of an envisaged future and a clear, inspiring purpose and set of shared values. Inclusive companies have mutually beneficial business relationships. Operating from their purpose and values, they build relationships with stakeholders that are best suited to fulfilling their envisioned future and that also allow the stakeholders to fulfil theirs.

Inclusive companies have a success model: a system for measuring the activities of key importance to achieving their envisioned future within the context of their purpose, values and key relationships. Applying an inclusive approach requires clear leadership and continual measurement of the progress of key relationships. There is no set formula. Each company has to find its own way forward.

In the space of time since the report was published, those original business leaders have seen their expectations of accelerating change exceeded by the pace and scope of what has actually happened. They have also witnessed the fragility of the global economic system as markets reeled following the Asian crisis in 1998.

Fortunately, and due to the vision of a few people, the report was not left to gather dust in the RSA library. Its initial impact was quickly followed by the setting up of the Centre for Tomorrow's Company with the task of developing a practical vision of sustainable business that makes equal sense to shareholders and to society. Its purpose is to explore, with business, the fundamentals of sustainable business success and to develop, throughout business, better ways of achieving it. The Centre's work is supported by a number of Britain's leading companies who are seeking both to apply inclusive principles in their own companies and to promote the approach more widely across industry.

In the five years that have elapsed since the Centre was founded in 1996 the language of inclusiveness has been taken up on a massive scale by British industry. Most companies now acknowledge the importance of stakeholder relationships, and the obligations of directors with respect to the interests of stakeholders will shortly become integrated into Company Law. It is one thing to talk inclusiveness, however; it is something else – and something much more difficult – to practise it. It is very timely, therefore, that Philip Sadler, a former Board member of the Centre, has produced this account of what has happened in the intervening years. His survey of the field is not confined to the UK and the story he tells is of a movement that is global in nature and rapidly gathering strength. I personally find it very encouraging to read of so many companies striving to become more inclusive – and in so many ways. It really does seem that our free market system is capable of learning and responding to the need to change, and that like any organism that learns in a timely way, it will survive.

Sir John Egan

Preface

This book has its roots both in long-term influences and in more recent events. The former began at the London School of Economics, where I read sociology with subsidiary economics. I became interested in the boundaries between these two disciplines, and in particular in the interdependence of technological change, social change and economic development.

I then spent 10 years working as a sociologist in the Scientific Adviser's Department of the Ministry of Defence where these interests at macro level were supplemented by studies of leadership and organizational effectiveness at the level of the military unit. At that time, some of the ablest American social scientists were working on these issues under US government contracts and I learnt a great deal from them.

In 1969, soon after my appointment as Principal of Ashridge Management College, I was profoundly influenced by reading *The Age of Discontinuity* by Peter Drucker. In this work Drucker outlined, with what transpired to be exceptional prescience, the economy of the future in which the knowledge-intensive industries supported by radical improvements in information technology would become the chief sources of wealth creation in the developed countries. A little later, Daniel Bell's *The Coming of Post Industrial Society* (1972) added a sociological perspective to Drucker's economic analysis. I developed, as a result of the insights provided by these writings, what I believed to be a clear vision of the direction in which the Western economies were heading, and some grasp of the social consequences.

At this stage the vision was partial in an important respect, but this was remedied in the mid-1970s by the Report of the Club of Rome, *Limits to Growth*. At a more emotional level I was deeply moved by a film, *The Shadow of Progress*, which showed in striking visual images the process of environmental destruction that was occurring in different ways in different parts of the world.

I now felt that I not only had a clear and balanced vision of some important future trends, but also of their implications for business strategy. In particular, at Ashridge, we began in our educational programmes and research to stress the importance of such things as:

▌ leadership (as distinct from management);

▌ the distinctive skills involved in managing change;

▌ the importance of knowledge as a strategic resource;

▌ the need to align business strategy and human resource strategy;

▌ the need for flexible organization structures.

The programmes we launched in these areas were not commercially successful in the 1970s and early 1980s. At the time, these issues were seen as intellectually interesting but of little relevance to business success. The middle to senior-level managers who attended these programmes received them well, even found them inspiring. Almost without exception, however, they reported that these were not live issues in their companies. With few exceptions, very senior managers and directors of major companies did not attend management development courses, nor did they read many books. They were not, in the main, exposed to these ideas.

In the mid-1980s, however, the climate began to change. Demand for courses aimed at developing leadership effectiveness in particular grew rapidly; in the early 1990s courses in strategic human resource management and strategy and organization were established and soon met with strong demand. Books on knowledge management and the learning organization were entering the best-seller lists; Britain's most successful management guru was neither an accountant nor an information scientist, but a social scientist. It was Charles Handy, whose seminal lecture at the Royal Society of Arts asked the question 'What is a company for?' and started the more recent chain of experiences leading to this current work.

Following Handy's lecture, the Royal Society of Arts instituted a project with the title 'An Inquiry into the Nature of Tomorrow's Company'. The ensuing report strongly recommended that companies should adopt what was termed an 'inclusive approach' to governance and management, an approach which took into account the needs and expectations of all the stakeholders – the employees, the customers, the suppliers, the community and, of course, the investors.

The publication of the report in 1995 was followed two years later by the establishment of The Centre for Tomorrow's Company with the task of conducting research into the factors associated with the achievement of sustainable business success. The Director, Mark Goyder, invited me to join the Board of Trustees and to chair its Research Committee. I served in these capacities for three years and have remained in close contact with the Centre ever since. Over this period of time I became increasingly conscious that the ideas that had seemed revolutionary in 1995 were rapidly becoming accepted within the business community. Indeed, not only were senior figures in industry espousing the inclusive approach (not necessarily using that particular expression), they were putting it into practice:

▌ Increasing numbers of companies were stating their purpose in other than purely financial or bottom-line terms and were publishing statements of the values underpinning their policy decisions. Many of these companies were setting up measurement systems to assess the extent to which they were meeting such goals as environmental conservation or being a good corporate citizen.

▌ Similarly, they were engaging in dialogue with their stakeholders and with the various organizations representing their interests.

▌ Organizations were becoming less centralized, more devolved, more flexible and less hierarchical.

▌ New ideas about leadership and ways of developing future leaders were being actively debated.

Meanwhile, other significant developments were taking place in the business environment, which were having a very powerful influence on the thinking and actions of large companies:

▍ The long-awaited, so-called New Economy emerged into the full light of day and rapidly became a major catalyst for change in business thinking and practice.

▍ There was a huge increase in public awareness of the issues surrounding the sustainability of the planet and of the way of life of the richest countries. The term 'sustainable development' rapidly became part of the language; riots and demonstrations against global capitalism hit the headlines; a whole series of best-selling books indicting the world's major international corporations appeared.

▍ The number of investment funds based on the perceived sustainability or social responsibility of companies began to grow rapidly.

▍ Moves to amend company law so as to improve standards of corporate governance and to require directors to have regard to the interest of all the stakeholders were under way.

It became clear to me that a major change process was under way, one that could profoundly alter the nature of free market capitalism. The ideas on which this movement was based were far from new and in the quest for a new form of capitalism there have been many false dawns. This time, however, it seemed to me, at an impressionistic level, that there were so many forces acting in the same direction that real change was likely to come about. But this was merely an impression, gained from reading, visiting the odd Web site, and attending an occasional conference. I resolved to set about compiling a more adequate body of evidence. I quickly found out that there was more evidence, more going on, than I could possibly cover in a book of this nature. I found that what had been happening in Britain was happening also in the United States and to varying degrees in the other European countries.

My account of this movement, therefore, is a selective one. I have chosen to focus primarily on events and trends in Britain and the United States. I have selected some companies for case studies more on the availability of access to the relevant information than on any stricter basis. I am also conscious of the fact that in trying to cover so many different aspects of the changing world of global business within the pages of a single book, the treatment of any one of them is necessarily far from comprehensive. My defence is that the task of integrating different streams of specialist knowledge in order to present a holistic view of trends and events is both an important and a frequently neglected one.

I have found the material I have gathered convincing, in that it has caused me to be optimistic about the future of capitalism. I do not now believe that corporations rule the world, but I do think that they just might save it.

The book begins by revisiting the original Tomorrow's Company inquiry. (Readers already familiar with the RSA Report and the subsequent activities of the Centre for Tomorrow's Company may wish to skip the Introduction.) Attention then switches to the various external trends and influences that are creating a new framework for business:

- the emerging New Economy;

- the issues around sustainable development;

- changes in the world of investment;

- trends in corporate governance.

This section is then followed by an account of what business has been doing, under the headings of:

- The business response;

- Purpose and values;

- Engaging with stakeholders;

- Business success models, measurement and reporting;

- A licence to operate.

The third section of the book focuses on new thinking and practice in the fields of leadership and organization.

The last chapter attempts to draw the picture as a whole and to reach some conclusions, as well as pointing the way for future action.

Acknowledgements

I am grateful to several people associated with The Centre for Tomorrow's Company who have read drafts of the work and have offered helpful comments. In particular, I would like to thank Sarah Beatty, Tony Berry, Ian Buckland, Richard Bull, Sir Anthony Cleaver, Peter Desmond, Russell Devitt, Robert Koenig, Mark Goyder, Clive Morton, Ashton Shuttleworth, Alison Thomas and David Thomas.

Introduction

THE INCLUSIVE APPROACH REVISITED

In 1993, the UK's Royal Society of Arts (RSA) initiated an 'Inquiry into The Nature of Tomorrow's Company'. The inquiry began by bringing together 25 of the top businesses in the UK under the chairmanship of Sir Anthony Cleaver. The objective was to develop a shared vision of tomorrow's company. The subsequent report, published in 1995, challenged business leaders to change their approach. It focused attention on the issue of how to achieve sustained business success in the face of profound social and economic change. It drew attention to several factors holding UK companies back, including:

▌ complacency and ignorance of world standards;

▌ over-reliance on financial measures of performance;

▌ an adversarial culture.

The report continued: 'As the world business climate changes, so the rules of the competitive race are being rewritten. The effect is to make people and relationships more than ever the key to sustainable success.' The report called for companies to adopt what was termed an 'inclusive' approach. 'Only through deepened relationships with – and between – employees, customers, suppliers, investors and the community will companies anticipate, innovate and adapt fast enough, while maintaining public confidence.'

The report's authors called on business leaders to fulfil a significant role in creating a climate for sustainable success. The suggested actions included:

▌ increasing their participation in national and community-based partnerships;

▌ contributing to the establishment of a more open dialogue and a closer working relationship with government;

▌ putting in place more effective business representation and networking structures;

▌ working cooperatively with others to enhance supply chain performance;

▌ helping remove barriers to the birth and development of smaller business.

The report was widely welcomed and stimulated a considerable debate in business circles and the media. The arguments set out in it were further elaborated and exemplified in Mark Goyder's book *Living Tomorrow's Company* (1998). In 1997, Goyder had become the Director of the Centre for Tomorrow's Company, an independent charity established to carry out research and to 'inspire and enable' British business to develop a more inclusive approach.

This book is an account of what has happened since. It is the story of a tide of opinion that is growing both in strength and in spread. The movement has roots stemming back many years, certainly as far as Robert Owen at the beginning of the 19th century. The early pathfinders in more recent times have included environmental activists (the 'Greens'), management theorists and progressive industrialists. There have been a number of 'false dawns' in the past, but there is obviously a much clearer and more widely understood appreciation of the issues and the need for action today. The activation of the debate and its translation into action has involved a wide range of non-governmental organizations (NGOs), associations of business enterprises and government agencies, both nationally based and globally. The clear message is that if businesses are to succeed – indeed to survive – in the socio-economic climate and environmental and ecological conditions of the 21st century they cannot escape taking into account the interests of all their business partners and of the communities in which their operations are set.

The inclusive approach to corporate governance, however, is not just about developing mutually beneficent relationships with business partners or stakeholders. 'The inclusive approach is quite simple. It is an outlook which helps people in a company or any organization to define what it stands for, what its goals are, who and what could help or hinder the achievement of those goals. That, in turn, enables the people managing the organization to judge what to encourage and what to measure, in order to achieve the best results' (Goyder, 1998).

Inclusiveness involves the following aspects:

▌ A clearly stated, widely communicated and shared purpose or mission, together with a vision of the company's future, couched in other than purely financial or commercial terms. In particular, creating shareholder value is not seen as the sole *raison d'être* of the enterprise.

▌ A set of shared values, which form the basis for the actions and decisions of the company and its agents.

▌ A success model, which is based on a deep understanding of the drivers of long-term business success and a balanced process of measurement of performance, based on this, which is forward-looking, not merely historical.

▌ The building of mutually trusting relationships with the company's business partners and key stakeholder groups, such as investors, employees, customers, suppliers and the community. (The nature and number of stakeholder groups will vary from one company to another.)

▌ Acceptance of the need to win 'a licence to operate' in the context of a society increasingly demanding in terms of ethical standards and corporate social responsibility.

Mark Goyder has set out eight propositions, which are the basis of the inclusive approach:

1. Business is subordinate to society. From this it follows that its freedom to operate is limited both by governmental regulation and by the implicit 'licence to operate' granted by the public.

2. Business exists to meet the needs of human beings. Behind each business relationship is a human need or want. No business can survive for long if it fails to meet the needs of the people who have dealings with it over the whole range from customers to investors.

3. Relationships are the foundations of successful business. For example, Frederick Reichheld and Thomas Teal, in their book *The Loyalty Effect* (1996), have shown the strength of the relationship between business success and the ability to build customer loyalty, and how this, in turn, is a function of employee loyalty.

4. Values are the basis of effective relationships. But these values must be reflected in a company's actions.

5. The most successful relationships are win–win, involving reciprocal benefits and hence reciprocal trust. Goyder quotes the example of a supplier approaching Unipart with a suggested 25 per cent increase in prices due to escalating raw material prices. Unipart put in a team that studied the supplier's costs and recommended ways of avoiding waste and improving processes. The result was a 4 per cent reduction in the supplier's prices, which nevertheless improved the supplier's margins.

6. Sustainable business success is dependent on leadership. Inclusive leaders do not only articulate purpose, values and vision; they exemplify them by their actions and ways of working.

7. Every company is different and must make its own journey. There is no single formula that is right for all companies. The search for universal prescriptions is illusory and disabling.

8. Business success cannot be predicted or explained by any approach limited to purely economic concepts. To understand how narrow and inaccurate is the economic explanation of human behaviour,

one has only to consider the wide range of motives that drive entrepreneurs.

Implementing the inclusive approach involves five stages:

1. defining a company's purpose and values;

2. reviewing key relationships and engaging with stakeholders;

3. defining success and the critical success factors;

4. measuring and reporting performance;

5. rewarding and reinforcing.

MacMillan and Downing (1999) point out that the inclusive approach has some support from some of the recent thinking in the field of strategic management and marketing, and in particular from the resource-based school of thought associated with Hamel and Prahalad, Ghoshal and Kay:

In a world where products look increasingly similar and where outsourcing, joint ventures and alliances make it sometimes difficult to discern where one business ends and another begins, where do the sources of competitive advantage lie? The answer, according to the Resource-Based School, is in a company's ways of doing things that are difficult to copy. Apart from its intellectual capital, which may be patented, other invisible assets may be found in the 'core competencies' of key employees and in the business networks of relationships – its 'social architecture' or 'social capital'. Long-term collaborative relationships with key customers and suppliers and (often implicit) ways of working among key staff are thought to produce distinctive competitive advantages. What all of these ideas have in common is that these competencies or capabilities cannot readily be built on opportunistic, coercive or overly exploitative relationships. Rather, trust and commitment lie at the heart of the most valuable relationships. The arguments stress that trusting relationships are more likely to endure into the long term, to encourage collaboration, experimentation and innovation, and to be resilient to short term shocks or crises.

INCLUSIVE LEADERSHIP

In the work of the Centre for Tomorrow's Company the key role of leadership is encapsulated in the phrase 'One plus five'. 'Five' refers to the five key relationships – with employees, customers, investors, suppliers and the community, and 'one' refers to the central role of leadership in providing a vision and a style of leadership which empowers people in the various stakeholder groups and enables them to focus on how to achieve, and share in, sustainable success. This leadership will need to be found not only in the organization's management but also among employees, customers, investors, suppliers and the community.

The basis for an inclusive approach to leadership is the adoption of a set of values which places human relationships centre stage and which defines the purpose of the enterprise in other than purely financial or commercial terms. Inclusive leaders understand the links between the organization and the wider socio-economic environment and in particular see organizational change in the context of social and technological change.

This deep understanding of the nature of the interdependence that exists between an organization and its dynamic environment provides the basis for a critically important function of leadership, which is to contribute to the development of an inspiring yet achievable vision of the organization's future. Such a vision needs to be one that meets the needs of the key stakeholders and at the same time provides the basis for a strategy to develop and maintain a competitive advantage.

If the vision is to be realized, the cooperation of all the stakeholders must be won. Here the key leadership task is to build strong relationships of mutual trust and respect with all the stakeholders and to strengthen the bonds that link them.

THE INCLUSIVE APPROACH IN PRACTICE

The UK Company BAA, a Foundation Member of the Centre for Tomorrow's Company, provides a good illustration of adoption of the inclusive approach adapted to fit the circumstances of a particular company in a particular industry.

According to its Web site, BAA's purpose or mission is 'to make BAA the most successful airport company in the world. This means:

▌ Always focusing on our customers' needs and safety.

▌ Achieving continuous improvements in the profitability, costs and quality of all our processes and services.

▌ Enabling us all to give of our best.

▌ Growing with the support and trust of our neighbours.'

BAA defines its critical success factors as:

'Safety and security

▌ Provide a healthy and safe working environment by giving safety and security the highest priority at all times. We will systematically assess and manage our risks through audited best practice management systems.

People and leadership

▌ Inspire people to excel through demonstrating the highest levels of personal performance, clear leadership and recognition of significant achievement. We will create an innovative environment which encourages teamwork, sharing and learning, and open communication and which produces measurable performance improvement.

Community and the environment

▌ Work in partnership with local communities, setting challenging environmental targets and auditing our performance against them.

Strategy

▌ Develop our core airport management competencies and our property and retail potential. We will grow the value of our non-regulated business and develop our business worldwide. We will achieve world-class standards in capital investment and will become excellent in the use of information technology. By doing this we will continuously improve the profitability, quality and growth prospects of a prudently financed business which is adept at managing diversity.'

BAA was joint top scorer in the assessment of social reporting practices of 50 companies carried out by the UK consultancy SustainAbility. (SustainAbility, 2000).

The company was also a finalist in the year 2000 Business in the Community Awards for Excellence in the category 'Impact on Society'. Some extracts from the citation are given below.

After wide consultation BAA wrote 'Contract with the Community', recognizing that to grow their business was dependent on stakeholder 'trust and support' as a condition of meeting their overall mission.

As part of its 'Contract with the Community', BAA has:

▌ asked the government to rule out another runway at Heathrow;

▌ produced growth strategies for each airport, integrating business objectives with environmental management, planning and community relations;

▌ listened to and understood the concerns of local communities and other stakeholders, and developed practical programmes of action to address them;

▌ improved their environmental performance through management systems, corporate objectives, targets, key performance indicators (KPIs) and service level agreements;

▌ supported and encouraged environmental improvements by business partners through contracts, price adjustments and other incentives;

▌ where BAA do not have direct influence, they have lobbied for wider environmental improvements through bodies such as Airports Council International (ACI) and the UN International Civil Aviation Organization (ICAO);

▌ proactively engaged in European Union and national government consultations on the sustainable development of the aviation industry;

▌ acted as a responsible corporate citizen and employer;

▌ developed a stakeholder partnership approach to the decision-making process on major capacity and other issues affecting the wider community.

BAA achieved this by:

▌ deciding the extent to which the answers apply to the situation;

▌ monitoring the local community to gain an understanding of opportunities for BAA to improve the local quality of life;

▌ identifying the strategic requirements of external stakeholders;

▌ creating collaborative alliances, relationships and partnerships that produce mutual benefits for existing businesses and their stakeholders;

▌ minimizing any negative effect of change on the local community;

▌ balancing safety with the need to provide quality service to customers in line with best practice and company values;

▌ ensuring that diversity is valued and that bias and intolerance are removed from the culture.

Reporting to internal and external stakeholders, BAA report their environmental, social and economic impact in depth through their award-winning annual corporate and airport sustainability reports.

All this is not to say that BAA is a perfect example of good practice, or to deny that there are controversial aspects of its operations, the very nature of which has a huge impact, both on the environment and on people's quality of life. The point is, however, that the transparency of its activities and decision-making processes, together with its willingness to engage in constructive dialogue, show it to be well in advance of the great majority of large businesses in accepting its responsibilities to groups other than its shareholders.

It does not follow, of course, that a company that claims to have adopted an inclusive approach necessarily acts in a manner consistent with this. There are many companies that profess to be inclusive, but their actions indicate otherwise. There are others that both profess inclusiveness and practise it – or at least are clearly making genuine and valiant attempts to do so. There are companies that claim to be driven exclusively by shareholder value and are, indeed, so managed, and there are companies that profess to take a tough stance on shareholder value in order to impress City investors, but in practice pay a great deal of attention to establishing mutually beneficial relationships with customers, employees, suppliers and the community.

The path to inclusiveness is a journey that is never complete; some companies have travelled far; others have made little progress to date; yet others have not started. It is also possible for a company to damage and even destroy trusting relationships built up previously; this is sometimes the result of a knee-jerk reaction in the face of difficult trading conditions.

THE INCLUSIVE APPROACH AND BUSINESS SUCCESS
Built to last

The most comprehensive and rigorous research showing the strength of the relationship between an inclusive approach and sustained business performance is the Stanford University Business School study *Built to Last* (Collins and Porras, 1995). This is a study of large US businesses that have been more or less consistently successful over 50 years or more, and are today the undisputed leaders in their industries. Characteristics of these companies are compared with those of other companies which have been less successful but which, nevertheless, have also lasted well and have generally outperformed the stock market – the 'silver medallists' as distinct from the 'gold medallists'.

For example, in the pharmaceutical industry the 'gold medal winner' is Merck and the 'silver medallist' is Pfizer. In electronics Hewlett-Packard is the top performer, Texas Instruments the also-ran.

The cumulative stock market returns of $1 invested in the leading companies on 1 January 1926 would have produced $6,356 by 1 December 1990, compared with $955 from an equal investment in the comparison companies and $415 in the general stock market.

How the companies differ

The leading companies and the others were compared on 21 characteristics. The largest differences between the two groups were on the following characteristics:

▌ employees have the feeling of belonging to an elite group;

▌ having a strong ideology or mission statement;

▌ having held strong values consistently over many years;

▌ acting consistently in accordance with these values;

▌ indoctrinating recruits in the values;

▌ continuity of management, with CEOs promoted from within;

▌ willingness to take big risks;

▌ above-average investment in people.

The best of the best

Some of the leading companies scored significantly higher on the criteria than the others. On this basis the companies in the United States that best serve as models for those chief executives who are concerned about sustained growth and profitability over the long run are:

▌ Merck, Hewlett-Packard and Procter and Gamble (10 highs);

▌ Motorola and Marriott (9 highs);

▌ 3M, Boeing, GE, Nordstrom, Sony and Wal-Mart (8 highs).

The relevance to the inclusive approach relates particularly to having a clear ideology, continuity of values, actions consistent with values, investment in people, objectives beyond profit and investment for the long term. Several of the high-scoring companies have explicitly adopted the inclusive approach – often from their earliest years. Hewlett-Packard is typical: over 50 years ago the founders, Dave Packard and Bill Hewlett, set out the company's values and objectives in a document known as *The HP Way*. The Stanford research provides evidence to show that the company's behaviour from that time until the time of the research consistently reflected the inclusive principles set out in that publication. More recently, the company has taken a number of actions, the consequences of which remain to be seen. It has carved out part of the company – the instrumentation division – into a separate business and it has appointed someone from outside, someone not schooled in the HP way, as chief executive. Under the leadership of the new CEO, Carly Fiorina, HP has been seeking to effect a merger with Compaq in the face of opposition from the Hewlett and Packard families.

At least the new CEO appears to be off to a promising start. One initiative she has launched is a new strategy called 'World e-Inclusion', aimed at improving the living standards of people on low incomes in developing countries. Elkington (2001) quotes as an example of this programme in action a Peruvian village where HP has installed a computer, large screen monitor and satellite dish; this facility acts both as a cyber café and as a marketing tool for selling their locally grown organic oranges to markets in Lima. Her efforts to promote sustainability in the outside world may, however, be hampered by Wall Street's hunger for short-term growth, and in the context of the severe downturn in high-tech stocks in the United States she will face difficult times in the next year or so.

Corporate culture and performance

Professors Kotter and Heskett of the Harvard Business School carried out another research project that relates inclusiveness to sustained business performance (1992). They studied 207 firms drawn from 22 different industries. Using a simple questionnaire they constructed a 'Culture Strength Index' for each company. The questionnaire, which was addressed to top management, invited them to rate the firms in their own industry on the degree to which they believed that their managers had been influenced by having a strong corporate culture – for example, to what extent did they speak of their company's distinctive style or way of doing things, to what extent were the values explicit and to what extent had the firms been managed according to long-standing policies and practices, not just those of the current CEO.

They then calculated measures of economic performance for these companies, using three methods:

1. average yearly increase in net income;

2. average yearly return on investment;

3. average yearly increase in share price.

There was a slight tendency for firms with strong cultures to have outperformed those with weak cultures over the previous decade.

A study of 20 of the firms with strong cultures but weak performance – for example GM, Goodyear, Sears and K Mart – indicated that they were companies which had done unusually well in the past but which had held on to cultures which were no longer functional in the face of changed market conditions. GM's dominant financial function and strong adversarial approach to industrial relations are given as a case in point.

Twenty-two companies from 10 different industries were selected for further study. All had strong cultures. They included such firms as Hewlett-Packard, American Airlines, Wal-Mart, Pepsi Co, Xerox, Texaco and Citicorp. Comparing them on an industry basis, 12 were classified as high performers and 10 as low performers. None of the low performers did badly in any absolute sense – they just did not do so well as the others.

Industry experts were invited to rate all 22 companies on how much value they placed on leadership and on stakeholder relations, ie relationships with customers, employees and shareholders. Finally, the researchers compared the performance of the 12 companies that placed strong emphasis on stakeholder relations with the performance of the group of companies, 10 in number, identified as having 'problem' cultures, ie ones that were strong, but not performance enhancing and not adapted to current conditions. The results are shown in Table 0.1. The figures relate to the years 1977–1988.

The top 12 increased their net incomes three times more than the 10 poor performers; their share price rose between 400 and 500 per cent between 1977 and 1988, compared with 100 per cent for the 10. The 12

Table 0.1 *Performance differences – companies valuing stakeholder relations most highly compared with others*

	Valuing Stakeholder Relationships and Leadership ($n=12$)	Other Firms ($n=10$)
Increase in Sales	682%	166%
Increase in Share Value	901%	74%
Growth in Workforce	282%	36%
Profit Growth	756%	1%

achieved a return on invested capital of 11.3 per cent compared with 7.73 per cent for the 10.

SUMMARY

Being 'inclusive' means, in practice:

▌ including objectives other than financial ones in the company's stated goals;

▌ measuring performance in non-financial areas and reporting to stakeholders and the public at large;

▌ including consideration of the long-term health of the company when budgeting and planning;

▌ including the company's business partners in dialogue and policy-making groups and including consideration of their interests when making decisions;

▌ including the impact on the community as a factor to be weighed when making decisions;

▌ including people at all levels in the organization in sharing the rewards of success;

▌ including people in all parts of the organization in opportunities to lead.

In Part II we shall look at ways in which companies are adopting the inclusive approach. First, however, in Part I we shall consider the main changes that have taken place in the environment of business since 1995.

Part I

The changing environment of business

1

The New Economy

WHAT IS THE NEW ECONOMY?

For something that has given rise to millions of words over the past 12 months alone, the 'New Economy' remains a curiously vague term. The phrase has no obvious inventor, no single point of origin. In recent years it has taken the place of other terms, such as 'The Information Economy', 'The Second Industrial Revolution' or 'The Post-industrial Society'. The new economic era, by whatever name we call it, has been heralded for a long time; with the advent of the 21st century we can now be certain that it has finally arrived.

There will always be a demand for a simple label by which to describe complex chains of events, but that should not blind us to the nature and depth of that complexity. What is clear is that the scope of the New Economy encompasses much more than dotcom companies and the Internet. The New Economy, in other words, is not the same as the 'e-economy' or the 'dotcom economy', although these are elements of it. It is the case, however, that the new information technologies that have brought dotcom businesses into being are simultaneously restructuring global markets and whole industry sectors, challenging conventional economic thinking and redefining how business is done.

James D Wolfensohn, President of the World Bank, has emphasized the broad scope and impact of the New Economy (2001):

The New Economy is shorthand for nothing less than a revolution in the way business works, economic wealth is generated, societies are orga- nized, and individuals exist within them. Today's realities are telephone- based service centers in India serving US consumers, and new technologies underpinning extraordinary shifts in everything from food production to the health products addressing long standing tropical diseases. The knowledge and information revolution provides a historic opportunity, a new age with enormous potential in promoting competi- tiveness, new economic growth and jobs, better access to basic services, bigger impacts from education and health interventions and, most importantly, enhanced empowerment of local communities and stronger voices for poor people.

Table 1.1 summarizes the main differences between the 'Old Economy' and the 'New'.

ASPECTS OF THE NEW ECONOMY

Now that the euphoria has died down and the dotcom bubble has burst, it is possible to see the characteristic features of the unfolding economic environment more clearly, and to put its technological aspects into perspective. In my view the key elements are:

▮   the steadily increasing globalization of business;

▮   the invisibility and intangibility of much economic activity;

▮   the impact on business of opportunities created by new technology such as mobile communications, the Internet, the intranet, satellite communications and the like.

The New Economy is global

We are certainly a single global economy compared with thirty years ago, but we can say with equal certainty that we'll be even more global- ized in 2050, and very much more in 2100. Globalization is not the product of a single action, like switching on a light or starting a car

Table 1.1 *Old Economy and New Economy comparisons*

	Old Economy	New Economy
Key Industries	oil, mining, steel, vehicles, railways, shipping	computers and software biotechnology, personal and financial services, professional services, entertainment
Key Resources	energy, labour	information, knowledge and talent
Technology	power trains, machine tools etc	information technology
Product Life Cycles	measured in decades	measured in years or months
Trade Pattern	international	global
Working Day	8 hours	24 hours
Communication Media	letter, telephone, fax	mobile devices, e-mail, Internet and intranet
Organization	centralized, hierarchical, functional	devolved, flat, flexible
Work Force Characteristics	mainly male, semi-skilled or unskilled	no gender bias; high proportion of graduates

engine. It is a historical process that has undoubtedly speeded up enormously in the last ten years, but it is a permanent, constant transformation. It is not at all clear, therefore, at what stage we can say it has reached its final destination and can be considered complete.

(Hobsbawm, 2000)

Manufacturing capacity will continue to shift from Western economies to those countries that offer access to cheaper labour. Equally, technology is allowing more and more knowledge-based work such as software creation to be shipped to the lowest-cost environment. This will bring jobs to emerging economies but will also create severe pressures for unskilled workers in more advanced economies.

Globalization resembles the industrial revolution in at least three respects. First, both sets of changes are deeply rooted in history. They both reflect trends that have come together like tributaries of a stream and merged over time, first into a river, then a flood. The industrial revolution had its roots in the discoveries of the Iron Age, in gradual rises in agricultural productivity, in the accumulation of capital searching for investment opportunities and in a number of technological innovations, among which the harnessing of steam power in the late 18th century was the most significant. Similarly, globalization's roots can be seen in such things as the early trading ventures of the Phoenicians, the opening up to trade of the East Indies and the Americas, the building of empires and the export of capital, while more recently developments in information technology and transportation have played key roles.

Secondly, both processes, however beneficial to humankind in the long run, have imposed, and will continue to impose, suffering on countless millions of people over many generations. This applies equally to the labouring classes whose condition in England was chronicled by Engels in the mid-19th century and to the urban masses of Indonesia, India or Mexico today. In both cases, reforming individuals and societies, labour organizations, charitable foundations, progressive employers and philanthropists have striven to mitigate these consequences; in the 19th and early 20th centuries, considerable success was ultimately achieved. Today these problems exist on an infinitely greater scale. Nevertheless, considerable progress is being made in tackling them.

Thirdly, both processes represent the inevitable outcome of all that has gone before in the spheres of technology and economic development. To be 'anti-globalization' makes no more sense than the actions of the Luddites in the 19th century; to make every effort to mitigate the suffering it gives rise to, however, is both morally and economically desirable.

In recent years globalization has accelerated as a result of the increasing adoption of free trade policies and the deregulation of markets, policies vigorously pursued by the member countries of the Organization for Economic Cooperation and Development (OECD) through the World Trade Organization (WTO).

The OECD/WTO view is that open trade has been a driving force for global economic growth, whereas the existence of barriers to trade in the 1930s was a major factor bringing about worldwide depression. Many activists in the fields of human rights and environmental protection are profoundly sceptical about its benefits. The critique of globalization and arguments in favour will be developed further in the next chapter.

The 'death of distance'

'The "death of distance" that is intrinsic to information networking is among the most important forces shaping society at the beginning of the 21st century' (Cairncross, 1997). Teleworking across the time zones is steadily increasing. The 'working day' has no meaning when communication via electronic mail, voice mail, and facsimile transmissions can be sent or received at any time of the day or night.

Invisibility and intangibility

When it comes to achieving business success, the traditional factors of production – land, labour and capital – are rapidly becoming restraints rather than driving forces. Knowledge or intellectual capital and talent, which generate new knowledge and new products, have become the key resources.

A knowledge economy

One measure of the importance of knowledge is the value of intellectual property. For example, in 1999 copyright became the United States's number one earner of foreign currency, outstripping clothes, chemicals, cars, computers and planes. The United States produced $414 billion worth of books, films, music, television programmes and other copyright products.

Peter Drucker (1992) has drawn attention to a dramatic surge in the value of US manufactured goods exports, beginning in the late 1980s. In the six years from 1986 to 1991 this almost doubled. The boom was unprecedented in the United States and unique in the history of the world economy. The common factor in the range of goods involved was that they were high added-value goods and that what added the value was knowledge. He pointed out also that the kind of foreign investment that transfers knowledge along with capital is vastly more beneficial to the host country than investment that simply involves the transfer of capital. An example of the former is the investment in the UK by Nissan, which involved the transfer of greatly superior production technology; an example of the latter is when a UK textile company builds a factory in India and transfers to it obsolescent plant and machinery surplus to requirements in the UK.

Knowledge, as a factor of production, has a number of distinguishing features when compared with land and capital:

▌ It cannot be used up. If one person or a single organization uses some land or some capital it is not possible for another person or organization to make use of the same resource. Yet in the case of knowledge any number of people can use the same piece of knowledge simultaneously without depleting it. And today, because of the existence of the World Wide Web, millions of people can have access to vast stocks of knowledge at nil or marginal cost.

▌ Knowledge as property is hard to protect. Much of the valuable knowledge that companies possess cannot be protected by patents. Much of it moves from one organization to another as people change jobs.

▌ Traditional accounting practices are not very much use when trying to quantify the impact of knowledge on wealth creation. Company balance sheets can give precise information about the value of a firm's capital assets and land valuations, but it is much more difficult to assess the value of a firm's stock of knowledge. The difference between the value of a company's assets and its market value gives some indication, but the stock market valuation also reflects other factors such as the value of brands and, notably in the case of dotcom companies, expectations of future earnings. It is not only difficult to quantify the value of the stock of intellectual capital, it is even more difficult to measure how efficiently the intellectual capital is being used, despite the fact that it is the major investment expenditure of many 'New Economy' firms as well as their key resource.

A key skill for management in the 'New Economy', therefore, is knowledge management, and this theme will be developed further in Chapter 13. Much of the literature that deals with this focuses on the role of information technology; equally important are the implications for the management of people – of the increasingly valuable and valued knowledge professionals. This brings into focus another important issue – the management of talent.

Perhaps the first public acknowledgement of the key role of knowledge in wealth creation was the address given to the Annual General Meeting of the Anglo-Dutch Company Unilever by the then Chairman, Ernest Woodruffe, in 1972. Unilever, he said, had competitors with similar access to capital, who faced lower taxes and enjoyed government subsidies. What they lacked, however, was the 'immense body of varied knowledge and commercial skills which Unilever has built up over the years.

In every aspect of the business knowledge is vital; and much of the knowledge which is important to a firm like Unilever cannot be found in books; it has to be acquired often expensively, sometimes painfully, by experience and deliberate enquiry.

Knowledge is not cheap. Around the world we spend many millions in acquiring it. But without this expenditure we could not survive against competition.

The economies of using knowledge over and over again, everywhere adapting it to local needs, are very great. Knowledge has no marginal cost. It costs no more to use it in the 70 countries in which we operate than in one. It is the principle which makes Unilever economically viable. The knowledge Unilever has is both extensive and complex. It is the source of your profits and of the main benefits Unilever brings to the peoples of the countries in which it operates.'

The role of talent in the 'New Economy'

Sooner or later all knowledge is obsolete – and today it is likely to be sooner rather than later. Talent is the only remaining scarce resource and as such the true source of competitive advantage. The nature of the typical 'New Economy' enterprise, therefore, is better described as 'talent-intensive' rather than 'knowledge-intensive' (Sadler, 1993).

The economic value of talent is illustrated dramatically by the fact (according to *Fortune* magazine) that in the year 2000, the US basketball player Michael Jordan's personal economic value derived from copyrights and merchandising exceeded the gross national product (GNP) of the Kingdom of Jordan. Much of the talent that creates the wealth of the 'New Economy', as in Michael Jordan's case, is not easily encapsulated by the term 'intellectual capital'. The 'knowledge-intensive industries' such as software writing, pharmaceuticals, computers and aerospace are obviously key industries in the 'New Economy'. At the same time, very rapid growth is taking place in such fields as music, the arts, sport, fashion and aesthetic design.

The term talent embraces the kind of outstanding intellectual skills involved in designing a space probe or a new micro-miniature electronic circuit. It also embraces the kinds of abilities or aptitudes possessed by outstanding sports players, actors, musicians, writers, television presenters, chat show hosts, architects and artists.

Peter Drucker (1992) has remarked that knowledge, like electricity, is a form of energy that exists only when it is being used. The same is true of talent. It follows that economic success will accrue increasingly to those societies and those companies that are most capable in identifying, educating, developing and exploiting the talents of their people. The management of talent will be discussed further in Chapter 13.

The impact of new technology

New technology in the field of telecommmunications is creating a whole new set of threats and opportunities for business organizations. In particular, the watershed years bridging the 20th and the 21st centuries have seen explosive growth in a range of uses of the Internet – as an advertising medium, as a marketing tool that makes possible a greater degree of interaction between supplier and customer, as a means of communication with stakeholders and the public at large, and as a medium for learning.

It has resulted in large numbers of quick-off-the-mark new entrants into markets eating into the market shares of established businesses. Successful organizations now come in all shapes and sizes. A new source of competition could be a multinational corporation with huge financial resources; it could, however, be an enthusiastic young entrepreneur with an idea and a computer, who intuitively understands that it is now perfectly possible to become a one-person global enterprise. There is, in short, hardly a company in existence that is not vulnerable to the Internet's potential to diminish the significance of, for example, size, location, time, distance and physical resources.

In *The Death of Distance*, Frances Cairncross (1997) describes how, by using technology creatively, small companies can now offer services that, in the past, only large corporations could provide. The cost of starting new businesses is declining, and so more and more small companies will spring up. Many existing companies will develop into networks of independent specialists; more people will therefore work in smaller units or alone.

Moreover, the technology is moving so fast, it's all too easy to be either too early or too late. In such a world, the timing of an investment or a product launch is critical and it is how companies deal with this factor that determines who falls by the wayside and who moves through to the next round. The aim is to be ahead of one's competitors, however briefly.

As an example of the speed of change in the technology, in September 2001 Motorola unveiled a microchip that is 40 times faster than existing technology. This will enable applications such as streaming video to mobile 'phones. Motorola's chief technology officer claimed that the discovery had the potential to change the telecommunications and computer industries as radically as the invention of the first chips in 1958.

The old economy is not dead

To keep matters in perspective, these observations do not suggest that the economic order is being completely overturned – the 'New Economy' is an 'add-on' to the traditional economy; it does not take its place, just as the industrialized society was an add-on to the agricultural society that preceded it. The industries of the 'Old Economy' will continue to operate. The fact is that around the world there are more cars and aircraft being constructed than ever, more roads being built, more steel being made. The difference is that in the OECD countries these traditional industrial activities comprise an ever-shrinking share of gross domestic product (GDP) relative to the newer industries providing communication, information, entertainment and professional and personal services.

THE NEW ECONOMY AND SOCIAL RESPONSIBILITY

One of the claims that has been made on behalf of the 'dotcom revolution' is that Internet companies are inherently socially responsible. This is assumed for a variety of reasons, including their perceived low environmental impact, their progressive policies on flexible working and even the relative youth of many of their founders. Preliminary results from a UK government-backed inquiry into the social and environmental impact of e-commerce are now challenging that view.

The Digital Futures Inquiry, which has received financial support from 14 companies, including AOL, Amazon UK, BP Amoco and

Unilever, and which was launched by the UK sustainable development NGO Forum for the Future at the beginning of 2000, has established that while there is some enthusiasm for corporate social responsibility (CSR) measures at management level in dotcom companies, there has been little action to turn that enthusiasm into concrete actions.

'It is clear that we have a tale of two mindsets: a theoretical support for everything that conventional companies may think of in CSR and yet a total practical opt-out,' according to Jonathan Porritt, programme director of Forum for the Future. With more data from the Inquiry's survey of 150 dotcom and information technology companies still to come in at the time of writing, responses from 78 businesses show that the majority of senior managers and chief executives in the companies felt social and environmental issues to be 'important' or 'very important' to their business. Around half also agree that 'companies with a good environmental and social reputation are likely to benefit from improved financial performance'.

Crucially, however, roughly three-quarters of the companies in question had no systems or policies to measure their own social and environment impacts or those of their suppliers. The main reasons given include a perceived lack of social or environmental impact, lack of time or resources and lack of in-house expertise. In this respect the pressures facing dotcoms in this area are similar to those facing other small and medium-sized enterprises, which have also been slow to develop formal social and environmental policies.

AOL UK is one of the few dotcoms to begin to address CSR issues and has appointed a Head of Social Inclusion. This company has begun to help tackle homeless and diversity issues through community investment.

In the United States, the environmental impact of dotcom companies is increasingly coming under scrutiny from pressure groups and investors, while elsewhere things are moving almost as fast. Three new European initiatives have been launched to help Internet businesses become more aware of corporate social responsibility issues.

The first of the three projects is a US $1.45 million (£1 million) scheme, Digital Europe, sponsored by Vodafone and Sun Microsystems. This will study the social and environmental impacts of e-commerce in eight sectors. It will then seek to help firms in those sectors become more sustainable. The sectors will be financial services, music, pulp and paper, food retailing, auto-manufacture, books, PCs and second-hand goods. The venture will be run by Forum for the

Future, the sustainable development body that administered the Digital Futures Inquiry, in conjunction with two European organizations – the Wuppertal Institute in Germany and Fondazione Eni Enrico Mattei in Italy. There will be input from the European Commission, which wants to apply the lessons learnt from the Digital Futures Inquiry 'at a pan-European level'.

In addition to the Digital Europe project, Forum for the Future is also establishing a permanent 'policy laboratory' to carry forward the ideas outlined by the inquiry. It has also teamed up with the UK-based Demos think tank to set up a support network for 'e-entrepreneurs' who want their companies to become more socially responsible. The idea of creating a network was one of the recommendations of the Digital Futures Inquiry, which concluded that many e-businesses 'still have a lot to learn about the basic policies and systems necessary to deliver social and environmental improvements'.

It also recommended that e-businesses should use the Web to 'set new standards for real-time, multimedia reporting and stakeholder dialogue', and said they should extend online assurance schemes for safe e-commerce to cover environmental and social issues.

CONCLUSION

As with any other massive wave of socio-economic change, the 'New Economy' will bring problems as well as benefits. In the words of James D Wolfensohn, the President of the World Bank (2001):

> *The New Economy has the potential to unleash extraordinary development benefits and real social and environmental gains, but to achieve such gains requires participation and intervention at the local, national and global level. The New Economy will most effectively deliver a positive balance of benefits and costs if we ensure that societies are fully able to take advantage of the arising opportunities by encouraging socially and environmentally responsible business conduct. This can often best be achieved through partnerships that bring together, and create synergies in, the competencies of civil society and labor organizations, businesses, governments and international bodies.*

The economic structure of the developed nations now straddles three stages of economic growth – agricultural, industrial and post-industrial. In terms of share of employment and gross domestic product, the post-industrial sector, comprising mainly services of various kinds, is by far the largest. There is a partial correlation, but not a perfect one, between this classification and the distinction between the so-called 'Old Economy' and 'New Economy' in that a great deal of manufacturing and agriculture is 'Old Economy' and much of the services sector is 'New Economy'. Increasingly, however, these distinctions become blurred as new technologies, from satellite communications and computer simulation to genetic engineering, are brought to bear in traditional industries. The conclusion is that Tomorrow's Company, no matter in what industry sector it may be, will increasingly need to manage knowledge and talent and deploy 'New Economy' skills.

Peter Drucker (1969) in *The Age of Discontinuity* pointed out that in an information-based economy the schools are as much primary producers as the farmer, and their productivity perhaps more crucial. Since then, national governments have varied in the extent to which they have understood this and acted accordingly. Certainly, the record of successive UK governments in this respect is far from outstanding. However, the supply of people able and qualified to carry out the myriad specialist tasks that an advanced economy will require in the future is not simply the responsibility of national educational provision in schools and universities. Indeed, given the speed of change, it is only by lifelong learning that these skills can be adapted to emerging technologies. In tomorrow's world, successful companies will be those that take up this challenge and see their organizations as institutions of learning as well as production.

2

Sustainability – the new board agenda

Tomorrow's Company recognizes the critical importance of achieving environmental sustainability in the interests of all stakeholders and accepts the challenge this poses.

(RSA Inquiry, 1995)

INTRODUCTION

The future of humankind on this planet depends on the sustainability of a complex system involving three interdependent, highly fragile sub-systems – the natural environment, the social/political system and the global economy. It is axiomatic that the collapse of any one of these would result in the collapse of the others. Catastrophic failure could arise, either regionally or globally, as a result of a massive environmental disaster, the breakdown of law and order and social cohesion or the meltdown of the world's financial markets.

The organizations that potentially have the power and resources to take action to prevent breakdown in any one of these areas are national governments, acting particularly through international alliances, and business organizations, particularly the huge global corporations.

Individuals inevitably feel powerless in the face of such dreadful possibilities. While increasingly anxious about global warming and its consequences, most people continue to use their cars on every possible occasion on the grounds that one person alone conserving energy can make little difference. Nevertheless, as in other fields, by banding together in associations and non-governmental organizations (NGOs) of various kinds, they can exert a powerful influence on those in possession of power.

What is needed, therefore, is a tripartite alliance of governments, large business organizations and NGOs. In later chapters I will produce evidence to show that such an alliance is slowly but surely taking shape at the present time, reflecting a growing acceptance on the part of leaders in all three spheres that they have to work together if the world's future is to be assured.

THE LANGUAGE OF SUSTAINABILITY

A whole new set of terms has come into the language of business in recent years, the key elements of which are the following:

- *Sustainability, durability*: the extent to which the current activities of a company, a nation, or a region are capable of being sustained in the long term.

- *Sustainable development*: meeting the needs of the current generation without compromising the ability of future generations to meet their needs. In the 1980s and early 1990s, this concept was applied almost exclusively to the impact of humans' activities on the physical and ecological environment. More recently, the term is used in a wider sense and includes their impact on society and the economy. (In 2001, in the UK, the Queen's Award to Industry for environmental management was replaced by an award for sustainable development in this wider sense. Nevertheless, all the award citations related to the physical or ecological environment.)

- *The inclusive company*: as defined at some length in the Introduction.

- *The stakeholder company or society*: in the case of a company, one in which due account is given to the interests of all the various parties with which the enterprise has significant relationships – notably customers, employees, shareholders, suppliers and the community. In the case of society, one in which all classes and groups of citizens feel they have a stake.

▪ *Corporate social responsibility (CSR)*: the obligations towards society that business organizations are expected to acknowledge and to reflect in their actions.

▪ *Corporate citizenship*: the process by which a business acts to fulfil its responsibilities to society.

▪ *Inclusive reporting, social reporting, social audits, social and ethical accounting and triple bottom-line reporting*: various processes by which business organizations report their performance against targets in other than purely financial terms to their stakeholders and to the public at large. The term 'triple bottom line', a term coined by John Elkington (1997), refers to three areas of performance – economic, social and environmental.

THE ORIGINS OF THE MOVEMENT

In the final third of the 20th century, public concern about the activities of business and the sustainability of contemporary patterns of economic growth centred on their environmental impact. John Elkington (1997) credits Rachel Carson's *The Silent Spring* (1962) with having sparked the 'environmental revolution'. She drew public attention to the massive destruction of wildlife caused by the use of chemical insecticides and other biocides. Organizations such as Friends of the Earth and Greenpeace were founded; support for such bodies as the World Wildlife Fund grew rapidly. Yet some 14 years earlier, William Vogt in his prescient work *Roads to Survival* (1948) drew attention to the problems already discernible in respect of humans' relationships with their environment, relationships which 'are inevitably exerting a gargantuan impact upon the human world of tomorrow. Disregarded they will almost certainly smash our civilization.' He went on to challenge the American people:

> *Anyone reading this book should share the author's conviction, deepening ever more as the book was written, of how extremely fortunate we*

are to be Americans. I hope I may help this realization to grow, and that with it there will also grow the recognition of the opportunity and responsibility we all have, not only to be effective members of our own national community, but also of the world community. We have not treated our country well; only its lush bountifulness has made possible the richness of our lives in the face of our abusive wastefulness. We still have much wealth left; and as we prudently husband it to avert our own rainy day, we must, in human decency as well as in self-protection, use our resources to help less well-endowed peoples.

In 1970 a book by a Yale professor of law appeared and topped the US best-seller list for 13 weeks – *The Greening of America* (Reich, 1970). The opening sentence grabs attention with its stark message, 'America is dealing death, not only to people in other lands, but to its own people.' Reich went on to assert:

There is a revolution coming. It will not be like revolutions of the past. It will originate with the individual and with culture, and it will change the political structure only as its final act. It will not require violence to succeed, and it cannot be successfully resisted by violence. It is now spreading with amazing rapidity, and already our laws, institutions and social structure are changing in consequence.

Reich's optimism proved to be premature. As Elkington (1997) points out, enthusiasm for conservation waxed and waned over the next 30 years. He distinguishes three waves. The first lasted from the time of Reich's book, saw the publication of the report of the Club of Rome, *Limits to Growth* (1972), and fizzled out with the OPEC action to raise the price of oil in 1973. The ensuing world recession saw the environment relegated to the bottom of the agenda. The following years saw the Bhopal disaster in India, the discovery of the hole in the ozone layer in the Antarctic, Chernobyl, and the pollution of the Rhine. In 1987 another influential publication helped trigger a new wave of concern. This was *Our Common Future*, produced by the World Commission on Environment and Development, under the leadership of Gro Harlem Brundtland, Prime Minister of Norway. This report brought the concept of sustainable development to the attention of a worldwide audience.

Elkington's second wave of activity, from 1987 to 1990, was signalled by the adoption of policies for environmental protection by world politicians, by the emergence of a 'green' consumer movement and by public outrage at the Exxon Valdez disaster. Once again, however, economic recession pushed such matters into the background. Despite the publicity accorded the UN summit in Rio in 1992, little progress was made. The major focus of attention by activists during this period was Shell and its actions in Nigeria as well as the controversy over the Brent Spar oilrig.

Although Elkington relates the fluctuating interest in CSR to stages in the economic cycle, it is important to bear in mind that until the collapse of the Soviet bloc the greatest threat to sustainability was, in people's minds, the possibility of nuclear war. That danger has receded but may well return as the number of countries armed with nuclear weapons rises. In the interim, sustainability continues to be at risk from armed conflict in parts of the world such as the Balkans and the Middle East and from international terrorism.

Hannah Jones (2001) suggests that following the collapse of the Berlin wall a paradigm shift occurred and a new fear emerged – the fear that our Western way of life is unsustainable. Since then, she argues, there has been a sharp polarization of opinion. On the one hand are those who urge the integration of social responsibility and sustainable development into the processes of production and consumption and on the other there are the advocates of the benefits of unfettered capitalism. Perhaps as a euphoric reaction to the collapse of state communism, there were some extreme cases of speculative activity leading to economic instability in the 1990s, prompting that arch-capitalist George Soros to express his concern that 'unbridled self-interest and laissez-faire policies' might destroy capitalism from within.

Elkington believes, however, that a third wave of concern and activity is now gaining strength. It is marked by a more balanced approach to sustainable development in that the social and economic dimensions of sustainability are being given equal weight alongside the environmental dimension. An important aspect is the extent to which cooperation is beginning to replace conflict and hostility in the relationship between large companies and NGOs and pressure groups. Sustainable development is now part of the Board agenda in an increasing number of the world's most powerful and influential companies. To maintain this through the next downturn in the world economy is a major challenge for the future.

Simon Zadek (2001) sees the recent renaissance of interest in corporate social responsibility as an outcrop of the 'New Economy':

Success in the 'New Economy' is as much about a corporation's ability to build a sense of shared values with key stakeholders as it is about the technical quality of products and services. Corporations that achieve this will extract the maximum premium for their branded, lifestyle products, get the best employees on terms that secure their committed labour to the business, and most effectively offset criticism from increasingly globalized networks of non-governmental organizations.

WHY ATTITUDES ARE CHANGING

The reasons for changing attitudes to sustainability are to be found in a number of trends.

Increasing affluence

Firstly, the increasing affluence of Western society has generated a fundamental shift in values, away from traditional ones which support the struggle for survival in conditions of scarcity and in favour of ones that relate more to the quality of life than to material factors. A community living in conditions of poverty, with high unemployment, will welcome the setting up of a new manufacturing plant in their vicinity because they value the material prosperity and employment it will bring. They are not too concerned about the polluting smoke that comes from its chimneys, the noise from its forges or the fact that its processes are dangerous and toxic. A prosperous community, however, will oppose any development that threatens the purity of the air they breathe or the pleasant views as they take their evening strolls.

Globalization

The second major influence is the very success achieved by many business organizations, which has made them both large and extremely powerful. Of the 100 largest economies in the world, 50 are corporations. General Motors' sales are approximately equivalent to the GDP of Denmark and the largest 200 companies' combined sales make up approximately one-quarter of the world's total economic activity. Through mergers and acquisitions their size continues to grow. Vodafone has merged with Mannesheim, SmithKline Beecham with GlaxoWellcome and AOL with Time Warner.

Recent riots against 'global capitalism' are an example of the growing concern about the way this immense power is wielded. In the writings of John Le Carré (2001), the international pharmaceutical industry has taken the place of Soviet bloc espionage as public enemy number one.

Critics such as David Korten (1996), Naomi Klein (2000) and Noreena Hertz (2001) point out that some of the 'anti-competitive practices' that are being removed were put in place with the aims of protecting people's jobs and ways of life and protecting the natural environment. They argue for 'fair' trade as well as free trade. They see international competition as a major barrier to the implementation of any significant measure to improve today's economic, environmental or social problems, be they in advanced, developing or non-industrialized countries. Global deregulated capital flows and multinational corporations are relatively unrestricted by national boundaries. The corporations, by their ability or threat to move their investments elsewhere, force nations to compete with one another for capital, jobs (and therefore votes) and ever-scarcer natural resources. (See Chapter 6 for a critique of Klein's work.)

It is pointed out that no nation is seeking unilaterally to re-regulate financial markets because such action would cause capital flight, devaluation and inflation if not outright economic collapse. Similarly, policies that address environmental or social problems requiring higher public spending or higher costs for industry are opposed on the grounds of loss of competitiveness, adverse market reaction or the threat of job losses. Global competition is also the reason why international agreements on reducing global warming emissions or other such targets are unlikely to prove successful for, to be successful, they would require far-reaching structural changes to industry across the world; changes which cannot be contemplated under present market conditions.

Furthermore, the WTO, being the one institution with supranational authority in economic matters, has the remit of preserving the free movement of capital and corporations: the very forces that serve to restrict the power of nation states. In deregulating capital markets, nations have therefore unleashed a force they can no longer unilaterally control.

Globalization, it is asserted, has given birth to the 'stateless corporation'; people and assets move and transactions take place regardless of national borders. There is little regulation and tax avoidance is rife. Governments' attitudes are influenced by the imperative need to attract inward investment and to be competitive in their export markets. National fiscal and monetary policies are subject to outside influences and pressures. Globalization of trade and finance is moving ahead much faster than any form of intergovernmental regulation and governance.

The very large corporations are *de facto* wielding political as well as economic power. Increasingly the legitimacy of this situation is being challenged and companies are realizing that to maintain a 'licence to operate' they have to do much more than simply stay within the law.

Many groups and organizations are seeking to challenge the international economic system and to modify its impact on developing countries, using a range of strategies. The demonstrations against the WTO in Seattle, Prague, London and Genoa by organizations including the International Forum on Globalization brought this subject to the attention of the general public and placed it firmly on the international agenda. The United Nations agenda for the 21st century (Agenda 21) has also given rise to a great deal of thinking and local action on environmental issues.

A more moderate view of the costs and benefits of trade liberalization is offered by Adair Turner (2001):

> *Integration into the global economy opens up more choices than it closes. The challenge for developing countries and for the global institutions is to achieve the clear benefits of global free markets while seeking to offset their inherent imperfections. Global capitalism is not the driver of environmental destruction and inequality between nations its opponents claim, but it is not a faultless route to economic nirvana... The potential for a 'capitalism with a human face' remains largely undimmed by the emergence of global economy... We should be confident of our ability to combine the dynamism of the market economy with the needs of an inclusive society and of a preserved and improved physical environment.*

The International Monetary Fund viewpoint is exemplified by a letter to the *Independent* (5 May 2001) from the Fund's Director of External Relations in which he argues that poverty in the developing countries has many causes – war, poor governance, lack of resources and opportunities, and inappropriate economic policies – and asserts that 'per capita incomes in poor countries with IMF programmes had risen faster than in countries without such programmes'.

New technology

A third problem arises from the close link between business growth and technological developments. While people understand the role of technology in human progress, they are also mistrustful of it. Already there is an international boycott on genetically modified foods and growing concern about the health issues associated with intense use of mobile telecommunications equipment.

At the same time, the development of the Internet has made possible the rapid sharing of information about what companies are doing, for good or ill:

> *The Internet is not just an eco-efficient way of moving bits of information around. For one thing it means that reported information is accessible 24 hours a day. As a result, the Internet is transforming expectations in terms of corporate disclosure. We expect stakeholders to be less satisfied with historic case studies; increasingly expecting to be offered virtual 'windows' into the thinking and operations of major companies. At the same time, many companies have realized that the Internet provides NGOs and other critics of business with opportunities to develop and co-ordinate campaigns at warp speed, requiring ever faster corporate reflexes.*
>
> (SustainAbility, 2000)

Increasing litigation

Particularly in the United States, but also elsewhere, individuals and communities are resorting to litigation in response to what are seen as damaging actions on the part of corporations. The awards made by the courts are reaching sums sufficient to threaten the financial stability of even major companies. The example of Texaco (see Chapter 10) is not untypical.

Specific environmental issues

People are now really beginning to worry about the impact of economic growth on the environment. Most people now believe that global warming is taking place; local incidents of pollution impact heavily on particular communities, while recurring oil spillages continue to damage sea and bird life as well as holiday makers' beaches. The recent report of the Intergovernmental Panel on Climate Change is the latest in a whole series of wake-up calls.

Education

For some years now, children's education in many countries has alerted a growing generation of young people to the issues of sustainability – or at least its environmental aspects. This process has been supplemented for older groups by such things as powerful television documentaries and the publicity given to particular environmental disasters.

CONCLUSION

After several false starts, sustainable development is now firmly on the agenda. The term is now embedded in the languages of politics and business and the issues are here to stay. A wide range of different forces have combined to produce a major shift in people's values.

Company statements on sustainability

BP

We welcome the opportunity which sustainable development offers to align industrial and social agendas better. We need to be part of the solution to the complex questions associated with future global energy supplies. We have no wish to be seen as the problem or even as part of the problem. We wish to be engaged on major public policy issues such as climate change, environmental protection and human rights.

INTERFACE

What is sustainability? It's more than environmentalism. It's about living and working in ways that don't jeopardize the future of our social, economic and natural resources. In business, sustainability means managing human and natural capital with the same vigor we apply to the management of financial capital. It means widening the scope of our awareness so we can understand fully the 'true cost' of every choice we make.

NORSK HYDRO

Hydro will be in the forefront in environmental care and industrial safety.

The challenge we face is to find the proper balance between caring for the environment and serving human needs. Hydro's mission is to take care of the environment and the wellbeing of future generations. This will be the basis of our company policy and decision making. Hydro will demonstrate openness in environmental policy. We will develop and publicize information on all significant environmental aspects of our activities.

NOVO NORDISK

Sustainable development continues to be a complex challenge – notwithstanding the difficulties there can be in defining the term and the means by which we can measure progress towards it. For how exactly can we define the 'carrying capacity of the earth', and ensure that we are not 'compromising the ability of future generations to meet their needs'?

Despite problems of semantics the concept of sustainable development has an important advantage in that it recognizes the interdependence of the economic, environmental and social spheres. This highlights the fact that sustainable development is not something that we as a company can achieve by ourselves. Instead, we must work closely with our customers, suppliers and the rest of our stakeholders to ensure that our products are meeting real needs and being produced in an environmentally sound manner.

Ian Wilson (2000) calls the combined impact of all these changes a 'New Reformation', involving eight shifts of emphasis in people's values:

▮ from considerations of quantity (more) to ones of quality (better);

▮ from valuing independence towards recognizing and valuing interdependence (of nations, institutions, individuals, species);

▮ from mastery of nature to living in harmony with it;

▮ from competition to cooperation;

▮ from valuing technical efficiency to concern for social justice and harmony;

▌ from acceptance of the dictates of organizational necessity towards aspirations for self-development and autonomy as members of organizations;

▌ from acceptance of authority to needing to be involved in decision making;

▌ from valuing uniformity and centralization to looking for diversity, decentralization and pluralism.

Evidently these trends vary in strength and consistency, both between communities and over time, but, as Adair Turner (2001) points out, the past quarter of a century has given rise to a whole set of powerful social movements and these in turn have created changed expectations of corporate conduct.

3

The dimensions of sustainability

The three dimensions of sustainability are environmental, economic and social. Each will be considered in turn.

THE ENVIRONMENTAL DIMENSION

The one word 'environment' covers an immense range of complex issues, among which the following (many of which are interrelated) are perhaps the most prominent:

- the emission of 'greenhouse gases' and global warming;

- pollution of rivers and lakes;

- destruction of the rainforests;

- species facing extinction;

- animal rights;

I use of chemical fertilizers and pesticides;

I exhaustion of non-renewable resources;

I disposal of toxic waste and nuclear waste.

Each of these areas of concern has its own group of activists, its own NGOs, intergovernmental agencies and committees, and the field as a whole has been the focus of innumerable international conferences among which the Rio Summit conference of 1992 is the most well known.

At the political level 'Green' parties have made some impact on the continent of Europe and have had a considerable influence on European Community legislation. In 17 European countries there are 'green' members of national parliaments and in France, Belgium, Germany, Italy and Finland they have taken ministerial positions. In the UK the Green Party is very much an outsider – to some degree because of Britain's electoral system which works in favour of the established major parties. As at July 2001, all the UK had to show were two Green Party MEPs, one Green Party member of the Scottish Parliament and three members of the Greater London Assembly.

The global warming controversy

This is a huge subject in its own right and there is no intention to rehearse all the many issues and arguments here. However, this is the issue that at the time of writing is both the one perceived as being of greatest importance for the sustainability of life on earth and also the most controversial. (An excellent short summary of the evidence and its implications is contained in a discussion paper published by the Universities Superannuation Scheme (USS) (Mansley and Dlugolecki, 2001).)

The issue of 'greenhouse gases' emissions, global warming, carries huge implications for the environment as developing nations increasingly claim their share of what Adair Turner (2001) describes as 'probably one of the world's few finite resources – the CO_2 absorption capacity of the atmosphere'. He points out that 'if China catches up to half the US GDP per capita in the next fifty years it will by then be an economy three times larger than America's simply because its population will be six times bigger'. It needs little imagination to visualize the impact of this rate of growth on global warming.

At the beginning of 2001, the Intergovernmental Panel on Climate Change reported on its latest findings. It said that the world's climate is definitely warming and that the burning of fossil fuels is almost definitely responsible. The companies in the front line on this issue are the oil companies. Some of the world's largest, together with many other large corporations, strongly objected to the 1997 Kyoto agreement to reduce greenhouse gas emissions in industrialized countries by 5 per cent from their 1990 levels between 2008 and 2012. They set up an international lobbying organization – The Global Climate Coalition – to counter global warming theories.

One oil company to withdraw support from this group is BP, which has set a target to cut these emissions by 10 per cent of their 1990 levels by 2010. Lord Browne, the BP CEO, has shown himself to be someone who takes the environment, and global warming in particular, seriously. BP has introduced an internal market mechanism as a means of reducing its greenhouse gases (GHG) emissions. Each BP business is given emission 'caps' and allowances which they must meet either by reducing emissions or by buying allowances through the internal market. The price of the allowances is set by supply and demand. If a business more than meets its emissions reduction target it will have allowances to sell. If it fails it will have to buy allowances to close the gap. As the scheme has developed the price of allowances has been falling as more and more companies meet their targets and sellers begin to outnumber buyers. The scheme is seen as having three advantages. It raises awareness of global climate issues; it forges a link between environmental issues and business strategies; and it quantifies the financial implications of these issues. (At the time of writing, there were plans to spread this market-based approach to other companies by establishing a UK carbon trading market by 2002.)

Another oil company, Shell, came top in the fifth annual Corporate Environmental Engagement Index assessed by the UK NGO Business in the Environment (BiE). However, the BiE report stated that the most disappointing area was reporting and target setting in relation to emissions and global warming. Four out of five of the 184 Index participant companies either set no targets or ones that were very low.

In the UK, global warming was linked to the experience of the wettest winter (2000/2001) since records began, accompanied by widespread floods. The subject hit the headlines again in April 2001 when President George Bush announced that the United States would not ratify the Kyoto treaty. Soon afterwards, Anita Roddick called for an international boycott of Esso petrol because of Exxon's support for Bush's action. The boycott was backed in the UK by a number of celebrities, including controversial artist Damien Hurst, comic Rory Bremner, singer Annie Lennox, and Bianca Jagger, the former wife of the Rolling Stones singer.

Meanwhile, there remains a considerable and vocal body of sceptics who argue either that consistent global warming is not occurring or that it is occurring, but is the result of natural forces and that the contribution of man-made emissions is minimal. (See, for example, the article in *The Sunday Times*, 22 April 2001, 'The myth of global warming endangers the planet'.) Yet another viewpoint is that of Professor Philip Stott of the School of African and Oriental Studies, who argues that the billions of dollars which would be spent implementing Kyoto would achieve very little by way of temperature reduction, but could be better spent on clean water for the world or clearing the debt of all 41 of the world's poorest countries (*The Times*, 19 July 2001).

His views are echoed in a recent book by Bjorn Lomberg (2001) who, while putting forward the controversial opinion that current doom-laden predictions are unwarranted, goes on to suggest that actions taken by governments and environmental agencies could actually make matters worse. Global warming, he asserts, will not reduce food production nor increase storms and hurricanes, but the cost of reducing it, estimated at some US $5 trillion will damage world economic development and hit the developing countries hardest in terms of employment, industry and exports.

To add further controversy to the debate, the renowned astronomer the late Fred Hoyle stated that global warming is desirable and that without it we face the prospect of another ice age.

In the face of these conflicting theories there seems little alternative but to accept the opinions of the majority of the scientific community and assume that global warming is happening, that its consequences for life on this planet will be serious and that it is not too late to take action aimed at arresting its progress.

Raising competitiveness through environmental management

The principles of environmental conservation are today being converted into ideas that business can understand and put to work. The result has been a major shift in the way in which corporations approach environmental issues. More specifically, this involves a whole series of attitude changes:

▌ from seeing only costs and difficulties in the concept of environmental management development to seeing savings and opportunities;

▌ from end-of-pipe approaches to pollution to the use of cleaner,
more efficient technologies throughout entire production systems,
and further, to seeing environmental management as integral to
business development;

▌ from linear, 'throughput' thinking and approaches to systems and
recycling approaches;

▌ from seeing environment issues as responsibilities only for technical departments or experts to seeing these issues as company-
wide responsibilities;

▌ from secrecy and cover-up to openness and transparency;

▌ from lobbying to more open discussion with stakeholders.

Using energy and material resources efficiently is an important factor
in competitiveness. Improvements in energy and raw material
productivity go straight to the bottom line because they are direct cost
factors. Increasingly, companies will strengthen their niches or
sectoral positions by maximizing the environmental dimension. This
again can have a direct effect on sales and market share.

For example, when introducing a new line of trucks, Volvo concentrated on publicizing the trucks' lower fuel consumption and lower
emissions. Since then, Volvo's market share in that segment has grown
by 35 per cent in Europe, and operating margins in its truck operations
are twice as great as its five-year average

Negative results are just as important as positive ones in getting a
company to pay attention to the value-creating effect of environmental
drivers. In 1994, a rating of television sets by a Dutch consumer magazine included a review of four environmental dimensions – energy
consumption, recycling, materials and use of harmful materials. The
results placed Nokia well above the traditional market leader, Sony. In
one month, Sony's share of that market sector in the Netherlands fell
by 12 per cent, while Nokia's increased by 57 per cent. Misjudging
how consumers valued environmental considerations cost Sony
nearly US $1 million every quarter for one single product. The

company has now taken the necessary steps to improve the environmental credentials of its sets and win back its market share.

Manufacturing companies have seen a significant improvement in their financial performance (returns on assets, sales and equity) as a result of having reduced their emissions. Du Pont's Safety, Health and Environmental Excellence Award scheme is designed to encourage staff to bring to light opportunities for cutting emissions and waste. Over the past three years, these awards have generated more than US $200 million in annual cost savings and revenue increases at Du Pont and customer facilities, largely through reductions in emissions and wastes.

THE ECONOMIC DIMENSION

At the level of the enterprise, economic sustainability is simply defined as the continuing ability of a business to be competitive and to create sufficient added value to meet the expectations of investors while making adequate investment in its future. There is much more to it than this, as will be discussed in Chapter 14 where the sources of sustainable competitiveness will be reviewed. The question raised here, however, is the sustainability of the global economy.

There are, in fact, two parallel economies. One is the 'real' economy where goods and services are produced and traded; the other is the 'shadow' economy of the global capital and foreign exchange markets in which millions of investors acting in their own self-interest take actions which determine interest and exchange rates regardless of the interests of governments. For example, a staggering £2 trillion is traded in the international foreign exchange markets every day, much of it speculative in nature.

The sustainability of the real economy could be threatened in a number of ways, but clearly one potential threat is the consequence of a 'meltdown' in the shadow economy.

The sustainability of the shadow economy

The shadow economy is probably the more fragile of the two, since in the last analysis the thing that sustains it is confidence, so that whatever might deal a severe blow to that confidence – such as a domino-effect series of failures of major finance houses – could precipitate disaster. Risks arise from volatile currency speculation, sudden flights of capital, leveraged capital from hedged funds leading to overcapacity, and all of these haunted by the twin spectres of corruption and fraud. Bond markets are complicated by the extensive use of derivatives – futures, options and swaps. These are processed by a combination of advanced mathematical techniques and very high-powered computers and are beyond the understanding of almost all small investors.

Peter Warburton (1999) describes how, in the early 1990s, Procter and Gamble did indeed gamble when using derivatives to reduce the company's interest burden. In November 1993, P & G signed up for a deal with the potential to significantly reduce the interest payable on US $200 million of borrowings. By January 1994 the company was losing US $17 million on the deal and by the beginning of March losses had risen to US $120 million. By the time the company was able to get out of the arrangement the cost had risen to US $157 million – enough to destroy a less powerful business. Warburton's point in citing this example is that the treasury executives at P & G were not novices in the field of high finance, but even very experienced and sophisticated operators can be caught out by the sheer complexity of derivatives.

In the autumn of 1998, disaster seemed very close. The so-called Tiger economies of South East Asia had gone into deep recession a year earlier. The Russian government defaulted on its debts. The US stock market fell 20 per cent in August and September and comparisons with 1929 began to occupy the headlines once more. In late September, Long Term Capital Management, a hedge fund run by a group of brilliant young mathematicians, threatened collapse with potential losses of US $14 billion. Pessimistic and critical books appeared, such as Paul Krugman's *The Return of Depression Economics*, George Soros's *The Crisis of Global Capitalism* and Peter Warburton's *Debt and Delusion*. Calls for greater regulation came from all sides – from politicians, central bankers and investment bankers as well as street-level activists. A year or so later the storm had passed; the Asian economies bounced back and confidence was restored; calls for reform were once again voices crying in the wilderness.

Since then the markets have experienced the so-called dotcom boom and bust. For a while dotcoms with no profit track record achieved billion dollar valuations and companies in associated IT and communications sectors were disproportionately valued in all the leading stock markets. Now that realism has reasserted itself, bear markets have returned (at the time of going to press the markets have largely recovered from the sharp falls following the attacks on the United States on 11 September 2001). Nevertheless, crises of the kind that hit

Barings and nearly sank Long Term Capital Management clearly underline the need for more disclosure and openness by the major players in international financial markets and improved oversight of all types of financial institution.

For example, in June 2001 the Bank of England issued a warning that financial regulators around the world should monitor the growing market for credit derivatives. This is a fast-growing area of trading thought to be worth in excess of US $1 trillion (£714 billion). Anxiety was growing that this relatively new form of financial instrument had not been tested during an economic downturn. A typical transaction would involve one institution being paid a fee to underwrite the risk that another institution would not be repaid money it was owed under a credit agreement with a third party. In this way commercial banks can transfer the risks associated with the loans they make to their clients. The exposures created by these instruments naturally increase as credit risk grows within the economy.

Interest has recently been revived in the so-called Tobin tax, first proposed in 1970 by economist James Tobin. This would involve a levy of 0.25 to 1 per cent on all short-term speculative transactions. This would discourage such activity by raising the costs involved. The proceeds of the tax could be used to alleviate Third World poverty. The premiers of France and Germany have spoken favourably about the possibility of introducing such a tax, and the idea is strongly supported by some NGOs such as War on Want. The imposition of such a tax would require the agreement of all the world's developed countries, a practical issue unlikely to be easily resolved.

The sustainability of the real economy

Despite the fact that the economies of the OECD countries today are variously described as post-industrial, knowledge, 'weightless', or information economies, or simply as the 'New Economy' or the e-economy, it remains the case that the most immediate and significant threat to their sustainability is the supply of energy. A sustained stoppage in the flow of oil from one or more of the world's major sources would have very rapid impact on the production and distribution of food and manufactured goods. The resultant unemployment and real hardships experienced by the populations of the main advanced industrial societies would ensure that economic collapse would be rapidly followed by social disintegration. The most likely cause of such disruption is the unsettled political situation in the Middle East, where more than the survival of Israel and the Palestinian State is at risk. President Bush's desire to extend oil exploration in Alaska and the Gulf of Mexico is no doubt fuelled by the anxieties created by this situation. In the context of such a relatively tangible and immediate threat, the longer-term problems posed by global warming are likely to be pushed to one side.

The long-term solution to both global warming and the fragility of oil supplies is of course identical – on the one hand reduction in the remorseless growth in energy consumption and on the other the development of alternative energy sources. The former lies in the sphere of government, using such tools as energy taxes, development of public transport systems, research grants and regulation. The latter task falls mainly to industry – to the oil companies themselves and the automotive manufacturers in particular.

Economic growth and the quality of life

Assuming that Western-style free market capitalism remains the dominant economic system, in the long term, economic growth could, in theory, provide the resources needed to create the conditions for global sustainable development. It could pull people out of the depths of extreme poverty and social deprivation and could provide the investment capital needed to deliver cleaner, more eco-efficient technologies. But does economic growth by itself deliver a better quality of life? Not according to a great deal of the evidence.

David Korten (1996) in his book *When Corporations Rule the World* points out that in 1954 the then UK Chancellor of the Exchequer R A Butler said that a 3 per cent annual economic growth rate would double the national income per capita by 1980 and make every British man and woman twice as rich as his or her father had been at the same age. In 1989 Richard Douthwaite analysed the benefits of British economic growth and found that almost every social indicator, such as chronic disease, crime, unemployment and divorce rates, had deteriorated over the period of time since the 1950s. More recently, the UK government publication *Social Trends* has highlighted the widening gap between rich and poor, the high levels of homelessness amongst single parents and the instability of many relationships. A similar story is told in the United States which, although it has one of the highest average income levels in the world, fares worse than any other industrialized nation in terms of homelessness, infant mortality, drug abuse, murder, percentage of population on welfare and percentage in prison.

In its October 1997 review the UK National Institute of Economic and Social Research listed the 24 richest nations in terms of GDP per head, and then derived a quality of life ranking based on a combination of the level of GDP generated per hour of work and various social factors such as life expectancy, levels of education and degrees of unemployment, plus political and civil rights. Their conclusions quite clearly show a disconnection between quality of life and economic wealth.

Growth or development?

The use of the term 'development' instead of growth is significant. It implies that the process of wealth creation is concerned with broader goals than simply increases in per capita income. Wealth creation in this sense is not to be measured exclusively in financial terms or counted in numbers of cars or mobile 'phones produced; rather, it is to be measured in terms of the satisfaction of basic human needs – for a healthy diet, access to education and medical care, to clean air and non-toxic environments, freedom from political oppression and from crime. It carries with it the implication for nations that the test of successful government should lie in measured increases in the quality of life as perceived by citizens rather than GNP growth. It implies a more equitable distribution of wealth. It implies for industry the kinds of policies that result in resources being allocated to the production of safer, less polluting vehicles rather than simply more vehicles. Undoubtedly there is plenty of room for progress in improving people's quality of life, wherever they live in the world, and it is this rather than economic growth as traditionally and more narrowly defined that is the essence of the economic dimension of sustainability.

> *Development cannot be said to be sustainable if it is not equitable, or if it does not meet the pressing needs of the majority of the inhabitants of the globe.*
>
> (Brundtland Commission)

THE SOCIAL DIMENSION

Concern about the social impact of business well predates concern about its impact on the environment. Reforming industrialists and politicians of the 19th century campaigned against the exploitation of child labour, the employment of women in mines and excessive working hours. It was left to the poets to worry about the erosion of the Arcadian landscape in favour of those 'dark satanic mills'. Although the Brundtland report mentioned earlier incorporated a societal element into the original concepts of sustainable development, the most widely held perspective in recent years has been one of environmental protection and resource conservation. A consequence of this is that, since the Rio Summit, sustainable development has been mostly linked to pending global environmental disasters such as global warming, the loss of biodiversity, resource conservation and so on. Things are now changing and there is a growing appreciation of the social/political dimension of sustainable development. It is evident, however, from much that has been written on the subject, both by company representatives and people in NGOs or pressure groups, that there is considerable lack of clarity regarding what, precisely, is meant by 'social' in the context of sustainable development. There is confusion, too, as to what the implications for business are. It is much more difficult to set targets in the social field than in relation to such concrete issues as disposal of toxic waste or restriction of fishing quotas.

In my view, the focus of concern should be on three things needed by a sustainable society – social cohesion, strong social institutions and a sound social infrastructure.

Social cohesion

A society characterized by an adequate level of social cohesion is one in which individuals and communities can coexist peacefully and, while respecting others' particular beliefs, values and customs, work together to tackle social problems such as crime, drug trafficking and corruption. For social cohesion to be strong enough to support the social fabric within national boundaries, conditions in regard to social justice must be such that individuals and groups see themselves as having a real stake in society and hence are fearful of having something to lose if the social fabric should disintegrate.

Tony Blair, while visiting Singapore as leader of the British Labour Party in 1996, gave a speech in which he set out a vision of what he termed the 'Stakeholder Economy':

> *We need to build a relationship of trust not just within a firm, but within a society. By trust I mean the recognition of mutual purpose for which we work together and in which we all benefit. It is a 'Stakeholder Economy' in which opportunities are available to all, advancement is through merit and from which no group or class is set apart or excluded. This is the economic justification for social cohesion, for a fair and strong society, a traditional commitment of left of centre politics but one with relevance today if it is applied anew to the modern world... The economics of the centre and left of centre today should be geared to the creation of the Stakeholder Economy which involves all our people, not a privileged few, or even a better off 30 or 40 or 50 per cent. If we fail in that we waste talent, squander wealth-creating ability and deny the basis of trust upon which a cohesive society, One Nation, is built. If people feel they have no stake in a society, they feel little responsibility towards it and little inclination to work for its success.*

Although this idea (or at least the language in which it was expressed) was quietly dropped during New Labour's first period in office, the underlying idea relates very closely to the concept of sustainable social development.

At the global level, respect for other people's beliefs, values and customs is a scarce commodity and the sustainability of the way of life of the developed nations is under threat from extremists representing alternative ideologies or religious fundamentalists. As nations hostile to the West gain nuclear capability, the threat of nuclear war may once again overshadow other issues. Groups of terrorists, often with the support of hostile regimes, are capable of carrying out massive acts of sabotage such as the attacks on New York and Washington in September 2001.

Social institutions

Societal sustainability also requires the existence of strong social institutions of which the family and the local community are of key importance. These are the building blocks of a society, and to the extent that they crumble away so will the whole social fabric be in danger of disintegration. These basic institutions link in with trades unions, churches, clubs, voluntary organizations and groups such as Neighbourhood Watch to establish and reinforce the social mores and to work for the achievement of such goals as greater social justice or the preservation of the countryside.

For a society is not made up merely of the mass of individuals who compose it, the ground which they occupy, the things which they use and the movements which they perform, but above all is the idea which it forms of itself.

(Emile Durkheim)

In the past, where there were strong links between a business (usually family owned) and a local community, as in the case of Bourneville or Port Sunlight in the UK, industry was among the social institutions which, at local level, provided important constituents of the 'glue' that held communities together. That era of business paternalism now lies in the past, but for the sake of the sustainability of our society, the links between business and the community may need to be revived.

Social infrastructure

A sustainable society needs also an adequate level of investment in the social infrastructure, in particular in housing, education and training, healthcare, sports facilities, youth clubs and the creation of employment opportunities.

Social capital

All these things, but particularly strong community ties and a 'sense of civic engagement', fall under the heading of what the Harvard sociologist Robert Putnam (2000) calls 'social capital'. 'Whereas physical capital refers to physical objects and human capital refers to properties of individuals, social capital refers to connections among individuals – social networks and the norms of reciprocity and trustworthiness that arise from them.'

He has drawn attention to indicators of the decline of social cohesion in the United States. He cites, as an example, the decline from over 20 per cent in the 1970s to around 12 per cent in the early 1990s in the proportion of adults attending public meetings on town or school affairs. Applying these ideas to the UK, Matthew Taylor (Taylor and Godfrey, 1999) of the Institute of Public Policy Research argues for a richer 'public space' in which, for example, school caretakers and park attendants contribute to a safer society. He welcomes the approach by many progressive police officers who see their role as part of a jigsaw involving parents, schools, social workers and local employers.

Emile Durkheim, the great French sociologist, introduced the concept of 'anomie' in his book *The Division of Labour in Society*, published in 1893. He used the term to describe a condition that was occurring in society such that rules governing how people ought to behave with each other were breaking down and thus people did not know what to expect from one another. Anomie, simply defined, is a state where norms (expectations on behaviours) are confused, unclear or not present. He observed that social periods of disruption (economic depression, for instance) brought about greater anomie and higher rates of crime and deviance and that sudden change also caused a state of anomie. If that process was observable in France in the late 19th century, how much more intensely is it at work today?

Elkington (1997) also uses the concept of social capital and quotes Fukuyama (1995) who describes social capital as 'a capability that arises from the prevalence of trust in a society'. It is a measure of 'the ability of people to work together for common purposes in groups and organizations'. Fukuyama argues that differences in social capital explain wide divergences in wellbeing and economic performance between countries. One way in which this comes about is that, where a country's social values are such that firms can rely on trust to support their business activities, there are large benefits to be gained from lower transaction costs incurred in lawyers', accountants' and auditors' fees. In turn, the state responds to breaches of trust with excessive legislation and regulation. The importance of trust in the relationships a company enjoys with its business partners is central to the inclusive approach.

The fundamental question is what contribution can business make either acting independently or in collaboration with governments and NGOs to the maintenance and improvement of social capital, in terms of social cohesion, strong social institutions and the quality of the social infrastructure. An adequate response calls for very much more than charitable contributions or cause-related marketing. Examples of the kinds of response companies are making to this challenge are given in Chapter 10.

The UK government has launched a fund to support research into ways of improving the sustainability of UK business. Known as the Sustainable Technologies Initiative, this Department of Trade and Industry (DTI) project has £15 million funding over a five-year period. It will steer money towards research on the social dimensions of sustainability, such as reducing impacts on local communities and working with disadvantaged groups.

CSR Europe (formerly the European Business Network for Social Cohesion) is an association of some 35 companies, including US ones such as IBM, Johnson and Johnson and Levi-Strauss, as well as such European majors such as BP, Shell, Volkswagen, L'Oreal and Telecom Italia. CSR Europe publishes accounts of best practice in community development in the larger European countries, under the headings of employee involvement, education and training, regeneration, equal opportunities, ethical principles, ethical investment and cause-related marketing. Their report on the UK gives 77 case studies of action by British companies (CSR Europe, 1999).

CSR Europe recently investigated the attitudes to social cohesion and related policies and practices of 46 European companies (CSR Europe, 2000). The assessments were grouped into the four headings of the European Employment Guidelines first adopted by the European council in 1997 – Employability, Entrepreneurship, Adaptability and Equal Opportunity. One finding was that whereas companies have a strong sense of internal social cohesion, the concept of corporate citizenship is not widespread. The research was carried out locally by nine research organizations working in the field of socially responsible investment. The researchers relied extensively on company sources such as social reports, Web sites and interviews with executives. In general it was found that the level of disclosure of the largest corporations in Europe is notably low in many cases. In some cases the information requested was simply not available, indicating a lack of strategic attention to social cohesion issues.

CONCLUSION

Throughout much of the literature on sustainable development runs an implicit assumption that the objective is to sustain the way of life of the developed nations and in particular those with the kind of culture that we call 'Western'. The ways of life of a number of earlier cultures were destroyed a long time ago but it is not too late to save others that today are threatened by poverty, disease, population growth and climate change. A global business has global responsibilities; its stakeholders include flood refugees in Bangladesh, AIDS victims in Southern Africa and the tribes of the Amazon basin. It is important to remember, too, that the ultimate aim of sustainable development is to sustain life on planet Earth. This overall objective may well prove to be incompatible with sustaining the Western way of life.

4

Fresh perspectives on investment

The first priority is for investors and those who advise them to apply the inclusiveness test in their assessment of companies. The best fund managers and analysts concentrate the minds of company leaders not only on immediate performance but also on future prospects.

(RSA Inquiry, 1995)

THE GROWTH OF SOCIALLY RESPONSIBLE INVESTMENT

Over the past decade or so a major feature of stock markets on both sides of the Atlantic has been the growth of socially responsible or ethical investment.

Socially responsible investment (SRI) aims to combine investors' financial objectives with their commitment to such concerns as social justice, economic development, or a healthy environment. In practice it involves three distinct types of activity:

1. Screening: the inclusion or exclusion of stocks and shares in unit trusts, investment trusts or other investment portfolios on ethical,

social or environmental grounds. Screening is usually divided into 'negative' screening to exclude unacceptable shares from the portfolio and 'positive' screening to select companies on such grounds as superior social or environmental performance, or long-term sustainability.

2. Shareholder influence and engagement: seeking to improve a company's ethical, social and/or environmental behaviour as a shareholder by means of dialogue, pressure, support for responsible management and voting at AGMs.

3. Cause-based investing: supporting a particular cause or activity by financing it by investment. Cause-based investors may seek a financial return at market rates or they may take a lower or zero financial return in order to achieve a particular 'social return' for society from their investment. Unlike making a donation, cause-based investors or the social finance organizations investing on their behalf require that, at a minimum, the original value of the investment can be returned by either repayment (for loans) or trading (for shares). (This term has recently been coined by the Ethical Investment Research Service (EIRIS).) Cause-based investing is also known as community investing and as socially directed investing.)

The origins of SRI

SRI builds on a long tradition of concern for social justice that can be traced back to Victorian social concerns such as the temperance movement and the struggle for improved conditions of employment. The more recent roots can be traced back to the 1920s when the Methodist Church started investing in the stock market but avoided companies involved in alcohol and gambling. The Quakers soon followed, avoiding weapons manufacture. Churches have been avoiding investing in companies linked to tobacco, alcohol, armaments and gambling investments for years.

The first American ethically screened mutual fund predated the launch of ethical unit trusts in the UK by more than a decade. In 1971, the Pax World Fund was set up in response to the demand for investments that did not benefit from the Vietnam War. In the 1980s, opposition to South African Apartheid fuelled the movement both in the UK and in the United States.

Initiatives for a UK ethical unit trust started in the 1970s and finally reached fruition in 1984, with the launch of the Friends Provident Stewardship Fund. EIRIS had been set up the previous year by ethical investment enthusiasts wanting a common source of research on company activities.

Responding to increasing concern about environmental issues and sustainable development, 'green' unit trusts arrived in 1988 with the launch of the Merlin Ecology Fund (now the Jupiter Ecology Fund).

The formation of the UK Social Investment Forum in 1991 brought together key figures across the full range of ethical and socially responsible investment interests to cooperate in sharing knowledge and advancing the agenda.

When the first UK ethical trust was launched in 1984, informed City observers estimated that the ethical investment market in the UK would eventually reach a maximum size of around £2 million. Yet by the spring of 2001, this type of investment (by now usually described as socially responsible investment) had grown in value to reach some £3.7 billion – more than 1,000 times the original estimate – and the growth shows no signs of slowing. In the year 2000 in the UK alone, socially responsible investment accounted for 5 per cent of all funds invested. There were 52 such funds in Britain and 175 in Europe as a whole.

The rise of this type of investment is closely linked to major changes in society since the early 1960s. It follows the growth of key social movements for the environment, human rights (particularly the anti-Apartheid movement), and animal rights. Major economic trends such as globalization and the emerging power of multinationals, the industrialization of developing countries, and the massive increase in share ownership by unit trusts, pension funds and insurance companies have all helped to drive socially responsible investment forward. As these trends increase, so the pressure for SRI will gather strength, making it a rapidly expanding movement with a powerful future.

The Goode Committee on Pension Law Reform endorsed the legality of SRI for pension funds. The committee's report declared that trustees are 'perfectly entitled to have a policy on ethical investment and to pursue that policy, so long as they treat the interests of the beneficiaries as paramount and the investment policy is consistent with the standards of care and prudence required by law'.

From July 2000 the UK government requires pension funds to state their policies towards social, environmental and ethical issues in the Statement of Investment Principles. In January 2001 the German

Bundestag announced a similar disclosure requirement as part of new pensions legislation

Compared with conventional investors, SRI investors are more likely to be female and younger, to work in a caring profession and to belong to at least one major organization promoting conservation, environmental protection or social change. The combined UK membership of Greenpeace and Friends of the Earth grew from 50,000 in 1981 to over 550,000 by 1993. It is therefore not surprising that SRI took off over this period, with a rate of growth outpacing total investment in unit trusts and investment trusts every year except two since 1989.

ACTIVE ENGAGEMENT

Changing company behaviour by shareholder influence is likely to be a key future trend. One turning point was the resolution on social and environmental policy proposed at the 1997 Shell AGM by corporate governance specialists Pensions and Investment Research Consultants (PIRC) and the church-based Ecumenical Council for Corporate Responsibility. Shareholders representing 17 per cent of Shell's share capital withheld their support from the company on the resolution.

In 2000, shareholder resolutions focusing on environmental and social issues were taken at the AGMs of BP and Rio Tinto, and received unprecedented levels of support. This was seen as a watershed for shareholder activism.

In April 2001, holders of about 7 per cent of BP shares voted for a resolution by Greenpeace supported by the World Wildlife Fund and SANE (Shareholders against New Oil Exploration) calling on BP to take seriously the threats to climate change from fossil fuel investment. The BP Board upped the stakes by making it a vote of confidence. The bulk of the votes came from SRI funds.

TIAA-CREF, the largest private pension fund in the United States, with close to US $200 billion in assets held for university staff, negotiates directly with corporations over human rights issues. The trustees of New York City's pension funds, in the region of $63 billion, support shareholder resolutions asking companies to report on the human rights implications of their investments in Myanmar (Burma). A major coordinating body for shareholder activism in the United States is the Interfaith Center on Corporate Responsibility. The Center has issued its own set of principles for corporate behaviour – the Principles for Global Corporate Responsibility.

In the UK, two NGOs, Traidcraft Exchange and War on Want, have carried out a project entitled The Just Pensions Project. The ensuing publication *Just Pensions* includes a toolkit for trustees on getting engaged with companies. This provides guidance to trustees on the decision to engage, the process to be used, selecting the focus areas of activity, developing a programme of activity, dealing with conflicts of interest, and measuring success. The guidance offered includes a list of questions that could be put to companies in relation to sample issues such as corruption, labour standards, conflict, human rights and access to medicines. With regard to each issue it is suggested that the company be asked, 'Has your company considered the implications of this issue for shareholder value?' There are also suggested general questions covering risk assessment, the existence of properly monitored policies, the reporting processes and the allocation of responsibility.

UK EXPERTS' VIEWS

The legal title to the shares of most British companies is vested in a relatively small number of institutions that invest on behalf of pension funds and policyholders. There are about 60 influential fund managers in Britain with significant buying and selling power in the market. They have the potential to exercise that influence in favour of sustainability – both in the narrower sense of the long-term health of the companies in which their investments are made and in the wider sense of building a sustainable society. The opinions they hold about SRI are obviously extremely important.

The Ashridge Centre for Business and Society conducted a series of interviews with nine leading thinkers from among the providers of advice to pensions trustees – investment consultants and legal advisers (Wilson and Gribben, 2000). The results indicated a high level of scepticism about the benefits of SRI.

The starting point was to question them about the relationship between financial performance and issues of social ethical and environmental responsibility. The respondents were extremely sceptical about a positive link between a company's social or environmental policies and its investment value. Many made the point that the time-scale was too short to be able to assess most SRI funds. Other comments were that if such a relationship was found it could simply be due to superior stock selection and that there were many cases of companies with a good reputation for social responsibility, but having poor financial performance.

It was also pointed out that CSR factors would be more likely to be important in determining longer-term performance, whereas investors and trustees were inclined to look for short-term results.

Several interviewees drew a distinction between environmental and social issues. Whereas they could see clear benefits from good environmental performance in such things as reduced costs and reduced risk, they felt that social factors were less easily defined and much more open to subjective interpretation. In relation to environmental matters sectoral differences were relevant – oil companies and the extractive industries being more at risk than financial services companies.

Good corporate governance was mentioned as being a better predictor of performance, although none of those interviewed cited any evidence to that effect. Nevertheless, UK pension funds, which represent one-third of total market capitalization on the London Stock Exchange, were quick to incorporate SRI principles in their investment policies in response to the changes in pension fund regulations of 2000. An ERM survey of the top 25 UK pension funds conducted in 2000 showed that a vast majority would adopt SRI principles. Imperial College, London confirmed these findings with the publication of a detailed survey, with the support of the UK Social Investment Forum (*Response of UK Pension Funds to the SRI Disclosure Regulation*).

The Ashridge report cites five tests that have been developed to guide trustees:

1. The SRI policy must not lower the expected return on the scheme's assets.

2. Restrictions imposed by an SRI policy should not be so constraining that the fund is inadequately diversified.

3. Implementation must not introduce unacceptable risk exposures or burdensome administrative procedures.

4. The policy should be acceptable to members.

5. Trustees should keep proper records of their decisions and the grounds on which they were made.

THE TOMORROW'S COMPANY APPROACH TO INVESTMENT

Tomorrow's Company represents a practical vision of sustainable business success that makes equal sense to shareholders and to society. At the heart of this view of success is the proposition that companies will only deliver lasting returns if they have a clear purpose and values, visionary leadership and healthy relationships with their various stakeholders, and that it therefore pays investors with a long-term interest to ensure that companies are evaluated against these inclusive criteria. When applied to the world of investment, the Tomorrow's Company approach does not, therefore, superimpose specific ethical or social considerations upon business considerations. It does, however, offer an alternative framework to the current methodology of the majority of those who claim to be analysing companies, predicting their capacity for future success, and assessing investment risk. It is about the sources of long-term success, the ability of the investment decision chain to understand these, and the application of this understanding to the benefit of its ultimate customers. This approach is very similar to that adopted as the basis for the Dow Jones Sustainability Index described later in this chapter. (Because of the potential confusion that may arise from use of the term 'sustainability', which can apply both to the long-term viability of a company and to the sustainability of the total socio-economic–environmental context of wealth creation, The Centre for Tomorrow's Company uses the term 'durability' to refer to the long-term maintenance of a company's shareholder value.)

In June 2001, The Centre, in association with KPMG, published a report: *Twenty-first Century Investment: An agenda for change*. This proposed a radical overhaul of the way investment institutions and investment professionals serve the public. Among the most important specific proposals were:

▪ a leadership index to appear alongside other data in company listings by which investors could assess and compare the long-term health or durability of a company in which they might invest;

▪ an inclusive scorecard by which to assess the relative social and political risk of different sectors;

▌ a new charter for judging remuneration policies for directors and senior executives, with less weight given to short-term share price movements;

▌ the use of multiple indices or reference points to reduce the conformity of behaviour resulting from the use of a single benchmark;

▌ changes in the way performance tables are drawn up to enable consumers to form a more balanced view of the quality of different investment houses.

OTHER DEVELOPMENTS

Two leading UK charities, Oxfam and Christian Aid, with combined pension investments of £53 million, have launched an SRI fund.

Research conducted by MORI for SustainAbility, the consultancy specializing in corporate social responsibility issues, reveals that nearly two-thirds of UK pension scheme members want their trustees to actively apply social, environmental and ethical criteria to their investment decisions.

A survey of 171 large UK pension funds with assets totalling over £300 billion carried out by the UK Social Investment Forum, October 2000, showed that 59 per cent incorporate socially responsible investment into their investment strategies. In January 2001 a survey by Deloitte and Touche showed that 62 per cent of investment managers expect there to be increasing interest in SRI and 5 per cent expect it to increase significantly.

The campaign, Ethics for USS, is an example of how fund managers have had to respond to pressure from pension scheme members. Ethics for USS was established in 1998 to persuade the Universities Superannuation Fund (USS), with its £22 billion of assets, to adopt a social and environmental investment policy. The campaign resulted in the recruitment of an SRI adviser to the fund with the task of engaging with companies to promote socially responsible policies.

The BT pension fund (£29 billion) has also adopted a proactive SRI policy.

Approximately one out of every eight dollars under management in the United States is now invested in companies screened for ethical behaviour or is subject to voting policies that incorporate socially responsible criteria. Socially responsible investment now accounts for over US $2 trillion, an increase of over 80 per cent since 1997 – a rate of growth approximately twice that of the market in general.

A taskforce set up by the UK Social Investment Forum recently made a number of recommendations to the UK government aimed at encouraging greater use of SRI funds:

▌ the introduction of a Community Investment Tax Credit;

▌ the setting up of a Development Venture Fund;

▌ disclosure by banks of their lending to under-invested communities;

▌ more flexibility for charities to invest in community development activities;

▌ expansion of Community Development Financial Institutions.

SRI AND PERFORMANCE

For an institutional investor with a diverse portfolio, deciding to open a fund based on socially responsible criteria or sustainability/durability raises a number of questions. What are the most important issues? Where can objective analysis be found? Which companies are affected? What strategies can a shareholder adopt?

Socially responsible investing (SRI) and other approaches to investment that take account of other than purely financial aspects of a firm's activities have always had to fight the perception that they may be better for the soul than for the bank balance. Most investment professionals argue in principle that adding social criteria on top of the other things that investors normally consider when selecting stocks – company financials, brand values and stock valuation – restricts the investable universe in ways that on the face of it are unlikely to improve returns.

If, for example, one started out with a universe of 100 stocks and social screening disqualified 20 of them, only 80 choices would remain available to try to outperform the market and other active investors who have the entire 100 stocks at their disposal. The conventional wisdom might be different if social criteria effectively screened out all the worst-performing stocks, but a lack of social responsibility is not necessarily detrimental to the share value of any particular company, at least in the short term.

The importance of measurement

Measurement standards and data are more prevalent on the environmental side of sustainability than they are on the social and economic sides. This imbalance weakens the triple-bottom-line argument. It leaves the door open for companies to talk sustainability but fail to practise it. The result is reduced credibility. At present the momentum exists on the environmental front and is less apparent on the other two. The financial world is very quantitative in nature. It can never get enough data. But it will work even with primitive data, occasionally devising ingenious methods to squeeze nuances of meaning out of pretty basic raw numbers. The financial world is learning to work with non-financial data, and that alone is a positive development for sustainability. In the absence of data, however, and of measurement standards that produce such data, sustainability won't fully register in the financial world's evaluations.

The track record

However, despite the scepticism of the UK experts cited previously, the news from the United States, where the track record is significant, is encouraging. The US Social Investment Forum is a national non-profit membership association dedicated to promoting the concept, practice and growth of SRI. The Forum is comprised of investment practitioners and institutions from across all fields who seek to use their investment dollars to encourage positive social and environmental change in society. The Forum's Web site contains a wealth of information about the process of social investment, and the returns that are being achieved. The Forum maintains that the returns of socially responsible investments are competitive and that socially aware investors can do very well. A solid and growing body of empirical evidence has conclusively dispelled the myth of under-performance.

According to Morningstar, a respected investment tracking company, two years ago not a single SRI fund in the United States merited a five-star rating. Today, 21 per cent of the SRI funds that have the necessary three-year record sport a five-star rating. That's *twice* the rate of the overall fund universe. Moreover, only 19 per cent of SRI funds find themselves in two-star or one-star territory, while a third of the overall fund universe carries that low rating

The smaller group of SRI funds that have a five-year record (35 in all) is less impressive, though still acceptable. A total of 19 have outperformed their category peers over the trailing five years, while 16 underperformed. That does not prove that SRI funds are superior but it is hard to make the case that they destroy shareholder value.

Even in the turbulent markets of the first half of 2000, socially and environmentally responsible mutual funds continued to perform at the top of their respective categories, according to the non-profit Social Investment Forum. Twelve of the 17 socially and environmentally screened mutual funds with US $100 million or more in assets earned high ratings from either or both of two of the industry's most respected investment tracking firms: Morningstar and Lipper.

A US $1 billion-plus fund is Domini Social Equity Fund, an index fund. 'It's been a standard-bearer in the social investing world. Because of its strong record over a long time, it has challenged the theory that you automatically surrender your wallet if you want to invest according to your values', said Emily Hall, analyst for Morningstar investment research firm. Managed by Domini Social Investments of New York, the fund for nine years has tracked the Domini Social Index, a socially screened alternative to the S&P 500 created by Kinder Lydenberg Domini & Co. While three-year S&P performance was 23.7 per cent, Domini Social Equity topped it, with returns of 25.16 per cent. This fund is composed of approximately 400 companies, mostly large firms, passing multiple social and environmental screens. But Domini Social Investments has done much more. The fund is very involved in shareholder activism, filing or co-filing 10 shareholder resolutions in 2001 and leading a three-year dialogue with Walt Disney over global labour standards. Domini also pioneered the practice of publishing proxy votes.

Citizens' Index is another US large-cap index fund among SRI choices. Managed by Citizens Trust of Portsmouth, NH, it has a three-year average return of 30.57 per cent, more than five points higher than Domini Social Equity. Total returns for the Citizens' Index through to 30 September 1998 were 176.2 per cent compared with the S&P 139.23 per cent. Citizens' uses somewhat looser screens, excluding only 200 stocks from the S&P 500 as opposed to Domini's 250, with a resulting list of 300 holdings. Additional Citizens' screens include animal testing and the AFL-CIOs company boycott list.

Shareholder activism is a high priority for Citizens', which filed or co-filed shareholder resolutions this year on genetically modified foods, board diversity, sexual orientation policy, vendor standards, and the CERES environmental principles (see Appendix A). In a recent innovation, Citizens' gave Corporate Citizenship Awards to 12 companies in areas such as environment, community and diversity.

Research clearly shows that while stock markets may not always reward companies that are socially responsible, they punish those that are accused of ethical wrongdoing. There is strong evidence that following an announcement of a socially irresponsible event, such as an environmental spill or a breach of ethics, a company's stock value goes down significantly. How long prices stay down depends on what the company does to rebuild the trust of its stakeholders (Svendsen, 1998).

Innovest, the US environmental rating agency, claims that share prices of companies who scored highly on their EcoValue 21 scoring system are showing an increasing lead over companies who scored poorly. More recently, a McKinsey survey of the investment community reported that high standards of corporate governance could command a share price premium of up to 20 per cent, thus considerably reducing the cost of capital for these firms.

The increasing gap in shareholder return between the leaders and laggards of sustainability is currently put down to the fact that environmental and social management are good proxies for assessing the overall quality of the management of a company. Financial analysts look at this in order to get a better understanding of companies' capability to financially outperform their peers in the long term, not just over the next three years.

PIRC

In the UK, the PIRC Socially Responsible Investment Service provides information and support for institutional investors to help them pursue practical and effective socially responsible investment policies. The service is based on the key 'stakeholder' relationships at both local and international levels. The issues monitored include:

▓ environment: corporate policies, quality of reporting, management systems, independent verification;

▌ employment: training programmes, consultation procedures, representative structures, participation, equal opportunities;

▌ human rights: overseas labour standards, involvement with repressive regimes, arms industry;

▌ community policy: charitable and political donations, community involvement;

▌ corporate governance: shareholder rights, best practice compliance, board structures, remuneration, investor relations.

EIRIS

Another UK service advising clients in this field is The Ethical Investment Research Service (EIRIS). This was set up in 1983 with the help of churches and charities that had investments and needed a research organization to help them put their principles into practice.

The service provides the independent research into corporate behaviour needed by ethical investors and helps charities and other investors identify the approach appropriate to their requirements. It publishes guides to help investors and advisers identify and choose between funds with ethical criteria and offers services for all types of client, from checking a portfolio to creating and implementing an ethical investment policy

More than 100 unit trusts, charities, pension funds, fund managers and individuals use its services. EIRIS maintains a comprehensive database on over 1,000 UK and 500 European companies.

ALTERNATIVE INDICES

The NPI Social Index

An early development under this heading was the launch in 1998 of the NPI Social Index, a basket of shares in companies selected as leaders in social and environmental performance. The index enables investors to compare the performance of these shares with the performance of the stock market as a whole. It is also a means for institutional investors to combine ethical investment with tracking an index.

The Dow Jones Sustainability Index

In 1998, following a meeting involving John Prestbo, President of Dow Jones, and Reto Ringger and Alois Flatz of what was known then as Sustainable Asset Management, the Dow Jones Sustainability Index was established. In just six months, the Dow Jones Sustainability Group Index created a great deal of attention, and companies were showing great interest, not only in whether they were in or not, but also where they ranked. Companies are selected not on ethical or social responsibility criteria but on the grounds that they are well-managed businesses in which a longer-term view of success is taken. Some companies began undertaking a reassessment of their sustainability programmes as a direct result of the assessment process that is the basis of selecting the components of the index. (Each company in the index receives information showing how it scored in each part of the assessment and how it compares to others in the same industry.) Thus, the index itself is acting as a stimulus to the sustainability movement.

> *Skandia is dedicated to delivering sustained shareholder value. Our motto, 'Security for Generations,' describes our commitment to creating long-term share value. We believe that our objectives can best be achieved through sustainable business processes and products – through a combination of economic and environmental performance, and social responsibility. Our recent inclusion in the Dow Jones Sustainability Group Index (DJSGI) as a global benchmark in our industry can be credited to our commitment to proactive work on environmental, ethical and intellectual capital issues. Consequently, in recent years we have attempted to connect these issues to business logic and the products and services we offer to our customers. We believe that this customer focus, in combination with our goal to be a leading innovator in our industry, will contribute further to delivering sustained shareholder value.*
>
> (Lars Eric Petersson, President of Skandia.
> *Source*: Skandia Web site)

Analysis of the performance of the Dow Jones Sustainability Index compared with the Dow Jones Global Index over the period January 1994 to July 2000 shows a statistically significant outperformance by the former. In the next 12 months, however, The Sustainability Index significantly underperformed the Global Index.

The constituent companies in the Sustainability Index are picked for the quality of their management and the expectation that this will deliver above-average performance. But in this context above-average commercial performance does not always mean stock-market performance, at least not in the short term. Three measures that securities analysts frequently use to assess quality of management are return on equity, return on investment and return on assets. The 236 companies represented in the Dow Jones Sustainability Group Index had significantly outperformed the average of the Global Index on these criteria over the five years up to December 2000.

However, as five-year averages, these figures do not necessarily counter the short-term factors in the stock market. A high-performing company's stock is not necessarily attractive to investors all the time. If the market has fully priced a great company's foreseeable results, that moment is unlikely to be the best time to buy that stock. If something happens to reduce the likelihood that those foreseeable results will materialize – such as economic recession – the share price will fall. This may explain why DJSGI shares fell more than the overall market in 2000/2001. These stocks were perhaps vulnerable when conditions changed.

The FTSE4Good Indices

In February 2001, the FTSE, which creates and manages equity indexes, announced the launch of its FTSE4Good indices as an important step towards setting a global standard in socially responsible investment. The new indices would include companies that have passed eligibility criteria on matters such as the environment, human rights and social issues.

Companies will be assessed in relation to six criteria:

▌ *Awareness*: A company's understanding of how it affects the environment and the society in which it operates, for better or worse.

▌ *Policy*: Companies should establish broad goals and guidelines to steer behaviour relating to social and environmental challenges, and set objectives and targets for improved performance.

▌ *Management systems*: Companies should establish processes and structures at operating level to ensure that policies are implemented effectively.

▌ *Performance monitoring*: Companies should strive to improve their social and environmental performance in line with the objectives and targets set by their policies and should measure their success in doing so.

▌ *Reporting*: Companies should communicate their understanding of their impacts, policies, management systems and performance with regard to social and environmental issues. Reports should be independently verified where practicable.

▌ *Consultation*: Companies should take steps to consult key stakeholders about their views.

Sustainable Investment Research International

In 2001, a consortium of institutions from various countries was formed to provide common profiles of the largest 500 global companies under the headings of environment, employment, customer relations, community involvement, governance and supply chain issues. Led by PIRC in the UK and Kinder, Lydenberg, Domini in the United States, the group includes institutions in France, Switzerland, Sweden, Germany, the Netherlands, Canada, Italy and Spain.

CONCLUSION

Public opinion is beginning to exercise considerable influence on corporate decision making and behaviour via the investment powers vested in their pension funds. This pressure is one of a number of forces that are moving corporate social responsibility and sustainability onto the agendas of the Boards of the world's largest companies. The inclusive approach argues, however, that the sustainability or durability of a company's share price into the future is a function of many other factors besides the company's record in terms of socially responsible behaviour. These include effective leadership, a clear purpose and vision, and mutually trusting relationships with all groups of stakeholders.

5

Governance issues

A CAUSE FOR CONCERN

A narrow view of corporate governance is that it is about board structures and procedures, compliance with Company Law, accountability to shareholders, correct reporting procedures, audit and remuneration committees and the conduct of Annual General Meetings. A broader perspective is that it is also about being clear about the company's purpose, taking into consideration the full set of relationships between a company and all its stakeholders and the issues that arise in the context of these relationships. It is with both perspectives that we are concerned here.

The OECD report on corporate governance published in 1998 pointed out that corporate governance attracts attention as an issue when performance problems and other matters of public concern are apparent.

In the United States during the 1990s there were several high-profile cases of poor performance in large corporations leading to loss of shareholder value – IBM and General Motors being the most outstanding examples. In the UK there were cases of company failure allied to fraud in the cases of Polly Peck, the Mirror Group and BCCI.

The result was a series of committees leading to codes of conduct and new regulations on both sides of the Atlantic, to be followed by similar developments in other parts of the world. A further development has been that institutional investors have become more proactive, using their power to demand not only high performance but also ever-increasing performance and a clear focus on maximizing shareholder value. In the UK the extent of this power is shown by the fact that approximately 11 per cent of the market is controlled by 3 institutions and 25 per cent by 10 institutions.

An OECD report pointed out that this trend might be detrimental to wider societal interests. The OECD view was echoed by Robert Monks (1998) in his book *The Emperor's Nightingale*, where he described the present stock market as a ' profit-seeking missile of unlimited life, size and power, operating under the stealth of human guise... delivering increasingly unacceptable results to the human beings who created it'. He called for pension fund managers to become more accountable to the interests of pensioners so as to ensure that companies were managed for 'long-term economic value rooted in the social good', rather than for short-term profit maximization.

Avoiding the trap of short-termism

A major threat to sustainability at the level of the firm is the tendency, known as short-termism, for company directors to focus on immediate profit, to the neglect of taking actions to ensure the company's longer-term viability.

A clear example of the kind of investment advice that leads to short-termism appeared in the *Independent*, 15 May 2001. The article referred to the fact that, due to the effects of foot and mouth disease on tourism, the number of passengers passing through BAA's seven UK airports 'rose by just 1 per cent to 10.2 million last month compared with April 2000'. There are three points to make here. First, despite the impact of the disease, passenger throughput had not declined; secondly, the disease effect is evidently short-term in its impact on the company; thirdly, the outbreak of the disease was clearly something quite outside the ability of BAA management to control. Over the years BAA has consistently developed its business to become the world's biggest airport operator and has produced excellent value for its long-term investors. The article praises the BAA Board's decision to appoint an heir apparent to the CEO three years before he is due to retire. Yet the *Independent*'s headline was 'Time to bale out as BAA fortunes dive'.

The role of investment

A key factor in determining a company's long-term sustainability is the proportion of added value that is devoted to investment. The word investment, however, covers a range of different types of resource allocation, each of which carries different implications for the future health of the business.

First, there is investment whose purpose is to enable the company to continue to do what it has been doing and to do it on the same scale. This includes purchasing new plant to replace worn-out equipment, or refurbishing hotel bedrooms. This can be described as standing still in order to avoid going backwards. The simple justification is if we don't make this investment we will go out of business.

Secondly, there is investment that increases capacity and allows the organization to grow. A manufacturing company installs a second machine of the same type and doubles its output. A hotel adds a new wing.

Thirdly, there is investment whose aim is to raise productivity or improve quality. A new machine is added, but one with a much faster rate of throughput or that enables a much higher standard of finished product. The hotel does not just add additional bedrooms; it builds a fitness centre at the same time.

Fourthly, there is investment in innovation. This can take the form of Research and Development expenditure as in the case of the pharmaceutical industry or investment in the plant and equipment that will enable a company to produce new products – for example, switching from the manufacturing of VHS cassettes to DVD discs.

Fifthly comes investment in intangibles, such as brands, intellectual capital or human capital. In the case of a company such as Nike this will be by far the major element in its expenditure. Investing in management and leadership development and training at all levels also comes under this heading.

From the viewpoint of the serious investor the long-term prospects of a company are greatly influenced by the type of investment a company is making in its future as well as by the sheer size of the investment budget. Yet information about the nature and purpose of investment is often lacking. Notes to the accounts in annual reports show expenditure on tangible assets such as plant and equipment, but often give no indication of the nature or purpose of these investments. Accounting for investment in intangible assets such as brand building, or additions to intellectual or human capital, is even less well reported.

The current state of opinion

The current state of public opinion about the obligations of company directors can be judged by the findings of numerous surveys. The United States is often seen as having the most favourable attitude to the maximization of shareholder value, yet in a survey by *Business Week* in 2000, 95 per cent of respondents agreed that US corporations should have more than one purpose and that they should owe something to their workers and the communities in which they operate.

Board members cannot afford to ignore the growing public debate about such issues as global warming or the growing power of global business, nor can they escape the need to understand and respond to society's changing expectations about the role of business. At the same time they need to set out what they see as a realistic view of what business can and cannot achieve, acting either at the level of the individual enterprise or collectively. They then need to communicate these views by means of engagement with the interested parties – national governments, NGOs, stakeholders, local communities etc. Sooner or later they will have to accept that profound change is called for if society's concerns are to be adequately addressed. (Some examples of the kind of best practice that will need to become common practice are given later in this chapter.)

Will Hutton, chief executive of the UK's Industrial Society, has argued that the government should force companies to compile and publish ethical performance indicators drawn up in consultation with stakeholders. Hutton says the indicators should then be publicly audited, with 'corrective action' taken when the targets are not met and 'de-listing from the Stock Exchange held in reserve as the ultimate sanction against companies which do not comply with the new standards'. In his view, increasing support for corporate social responsibility from business and the public will compel the government to codify, upgrade and even legislate for changes in company law and audit in a way from which until now it has held back.

On the eve of the 2001 annual dinner in London of the Confederation of British Industries (CBI), the New Economics Foundation (NEF) called on all FTSE 100 companies to introduce a stakeholder council into their corporate governance structure or 'be consigned to the dustbin of history'. *Stakes not shares*, published in May 2001 by the New Economics Foundation, prescribes a radical governance structure that would make corporations more accountable for the power they wield. The NEF report proposes a 'New Model

Company' – one that incorporates the views and interests of stakeholders and shareholders alike by: 1) establishing stakeholder councils representing stakeholder interest groups, such as employees, customers, suppliers and communities, whose lives and livelihoods are bound up with the company, and 2) prioritizing 'stakes' over shares, placing the long-term interests of the company above the short-term, but potentially destructive, drive for profits.

Progressive companies already engage in stakeholder dialogue as a way to understand society's demands of them. New SRI funds now require stakeholder dialogue to be firmly embedded in a company's operations to manage risk effectively. The stakeholder council, as proposed by NEF, is simply a way to formalize this process.

The UK consultancy SustainAbility has set out a framework for guiding boards of directors in exercising their responsibilities in respect of environmental, social and economic sustainability (SustainAbility, 2001). The framework uses the mnemonic LEADER, and these initials stand for:

▥ *Leadership*: Taking ownership of the triple bottom line agenda.

▥ *Engagement*: Entering into dialogue and consultation with stakeholders.

▥ *Alignment*: Aligning policies for sustainability with operational practices and linking executive remuneration to their achievement.

▥ *Diversity*: Engaging with people of diverse nationalities, ethnic groups, gender, age groups etc.

▥ *Evaluation*: Identifying and monitoring a set of key indicators of social, environmental and economic performance.

▥ *Responsibility*: Having a clear policy on the company's responsibility and accountability to different groups of stakeholders.

The leading companies, in incorporating wider responsibilities into their corporate governance structures and processes, have recognized both a moral obligation and a strong business case.

According to a report in *Pensions Week* (No 194, November 2000), shareholders are willing to pay a premium price for companies with good corporate governance, in the expectation that such companies will produce better than average performance. Quoting a study published in *McKinsey Quarterly*, the article stated that investors saw board practice as being just as important as financial performance when evaluating companies for investment purposes. Investors reported that they would be prepared to pay 18 per cent more for the shares of a well-governed US or UK company than for the shares of a company with similar financial performance but poorer governance practices. The report concluded 'companies that fail to reform their governance will find themselves at a competitive disadvantage when they try to obtain capital to refinance growth'.

They will also find themselves at a competitive disadvantage in other areas. An important aspect of the intangible assets of a company is reputation. As companies like Shell, Nestlé, Coca-Cola and Nike have found out in recent times, damage to a hard-won reputation can be extremely costly. As concern for the environment and for such things as human rights grows, companies that fail to take into account their responsibilities in these areas also accept substantial risks. Litigation and claims for compensation are resulting in huge financial losses. Reputation and risk are relatively easily quantified in terms of sales lost or compensation payments and raised insurance premiums. There are other factors affecting competitiveness which are less tangible but no less important. One is the effect on a company's long-term prosperity of building a set of mutually trusting relationships with key business partners – employees, customers and suppliers. Another is the fact that given the changing climate of opinion, those companies seen as most progressive will be winners in the competition to attract and retain the most talented employees.

As we saw in Chapter 4, these pressures are beginning to be felt in the context of the growth of SRI funds and the development of indices such as the Dow Jones Sustainability Index. The present investment culture, however, has deep roots and will not easily give way. The realization of this by some companies has led to their going private so as to be able to pursue strategies for longer-term advantage free of the short-term pressures of the market.

It is also the case that, given Anglo-Saxon notions about leadership as an individual rather than a team attribute, it is very easy for a dominant charismatic individual to gain despotic control of a Board in the way that Maxwell did in the UK. Although the consequences may not be so dire as in the case of the Mirror Group, it is certainly the case that many of the good practice elements of the Combined Code of the UK Committee on Corporate Governance (or its equivalent in other countries) will be bypassed.

Disclosure of directors' remuneration

In this context it is clearly important that the remuneration of the CEO and other executive directors should be linked to the achievement of a wider range of objectives than the creation of shareholder value alone. Examples of companies that are doing this will be given in Chapter 10.

Fifteen leading pension funds and fund management institutions wrote to the UK's 750 largest quoted companies in April 2001, urging them to reform how they award bonuses to directors. They suggested that remuneration committee reports should be put to a shareholder vote. This action was set in the context of the possibility of future legislation that would make it compulsory for companies to have shareholders vote on approving directors' pay.

In March 2001, the UK government proposed changes that would require disclosure of the following matters in companies' remuneration reports:

▍ the company's performance compared with an appropriate index or comparator group;

▍ details and an explanation of the performance criteria for long-term incentive plans;

▍ details and an explanation of the comparator group, including the names of companies and any changes made;

▍ post hoc justification of compensation payments;

▍ the name of each firm of remuneration consultants that has advised the company's remuneration committee.

THE OWNERSHIP ISSUE AND COMPANY LAW

The pretence that shareholders somehow own the company does not stand up. The stock market is mostly a secondary market. If A buys B's shares none of the money goes to the company. Businesses get most of their new money from retained earnings or bank loans. There is no sense of ownership in the secondary market. If dissatisfied, shareholders leave rather than try to change things. Yet these secondary shareholders have the right to sell the business over the heads of its workers.

As for the duty to make profits for their shareholders – which shareholders, today's or tomorrow's? The general assumption is today's but the obligation also applies to the future. There is no way of balancing both under current systems of governance.

Philip Goldenberg (1997) states the legal position as follows. 'Directors' duties are owed to their company, not to any third party group'. In discharging their duty to the company they must have regard to the interests of shareholders (if the company is solvent – if it is insolvent, then creditors take the place of shareholders for this purpose):

> *This obligation to have regard to the interests of shareholders is not related to the actual shareholders at any given moment in time, but to the general body of shareholders from time to time (one may alternatively, as I have said earlier, express this as that it is to the actual body of shareholders but in their capacity as continuing shareholders). Accordingly, the duty of directors is to maximize the company's value on a sustainable basis. There is nothing in law to prevent directors from having regard to the interests of third parties with whom the company has a relationship (sometimes called stakeholders) – employees, customers, suppliers, financiers and the community generally – if they judge, reasonably and in good faith that to do so is conducive to the success of the company. Indeed, for directors not to give appropriate weight to all their company's key relationships may well inhibit them in the proper discharge of their duty.*

The UK's Company Law Review Steering Group issued a consultative document *Modern Company Law for a Competitive Economy* in February 2000. In this, two options were set out – the Enlightened Shareholder Value option and the Pluralist alternative. Under the Pluralist scheme the rights of the various stakeholders would in some way become legally enforceable. Under the Enlightened Shareholder Value approach much more discretion would be left to Boards to decide how to fulfil their obligations.

The Centre for Tomorrow's Company, in giving evidence to the steering group, argued for this latter approach. The following points were made:

▮ The law should be clarified so that directors were clear that their duty was to the company.

■ Directors should continue to be legally accountable to shareholders for the performance of that duty.

■ The law should be clarified so that directors were left in no doubt that not only were they permitted to have regard to the interests of other key stakeholders, but that they were very unlikely to be able to do their duty by the company unless they showed such regard.

■ While boards thereby retained the freedom to exercise their wider accountability to stakeholders in their own way, the framework governing measurement and reporting of their performance should be strengthened to reinforce the 'culture of challenge'.

■ Companies seeking to take over other companies should be required to make clear the likely social, ethical and environmental impacts, and the board of the target company should be permitted to take account of these consequences in deciding whether to recommend such a bid.

■ The legal and regulatory framework should encourage companies to set out their purpose and vision, their values, their success model and their key relationships.

In its publication *The Corporate Reporting Jigsaw* (1998), the Centre put forward eight key questions for evaluating any proposals for reforming company law:

■ At the end of the process, will companies be as free to be entrepreneurial and fast changing as before?

■ Will the process stimulate companies to make and discuss more decisions by reference to their underlying purpose and values?

■ Will the process offer investors and stakeholders a more consistent criterion by which the company can be judged against its own stated purpose, values, strategy and goals?

■ Will the process stimulate companies to measure and disclose more information across all their relationships that are relevant to future performance?

▌ Will the process of dialogue with investor and stakeholder groups be improved, based on a supply of steadily improving and robust information? Will AGMs promote such a dialogue?

▌ Will the process encourage companies to open up to their stakeholders or to produce more 'boilerplate' information in order to comply?

▌ Will the process leave directors clear about the fact that they owe a duty to the company?

▌ What changes will there be in the regime covering take-overs? Will there be any strengthening in the disclosure requirements and will social, ethical and environmental issues start to be assessed as part of the bidding process?

With specific reference to social and environmental issues the Centre raised the following questions:

▌ Do the proposed changes take environmental, social and ethical decision making closer to the heart of business decision making, thereby contributing to an improvement in the environmental and social impact of business?

▌ Will they lead to greater innovation and transparency, or to more 'boilerplate' statements?

▌ Will they increase the likelihood of dialogue between companies and their investors over social, environmental and ethical issues?

▌ Will they increase the opportunity of dialogue and challenge between companies and their other stakeholders on these issues?

▌ Will they contribute to the development of more meaningful comparisons of the performance of different companies?

▌ How do these proposals fit with the emerging international agenda on reporting – for example, the work of the Global Reporting Initiative or standards such as AA1000?

The Turnbull recommendations

UK companies have to take social, environmental and ethical matters into account when they assess business risks and report on them more fully in annual reports, thanks to new guidance from the Turnbull committee.

In the UK, the Institute of Chartered Accountants in England & Wales set up a committee, chaired by Nigel Turnbull, and asked it to come up with ways of implementing the Stock Exchange's Combined Code of the Committee on Corporate Governance, which was published in June 1999. The Committee is seen as the last piece in a jigsaw of corporate governance codes and recommendations drawn up by committees chaired by Sir Adrian Cadbury, Sir Ronald Hampel and Sir Richard Greenbury.

The Committee's report on internal control proposed that company board members should formally consider all relevant risks, not just the narrow financial ones, which face their organizations, and that audit committees should be asked to carry out a 'wider review of internal control' which includes 'reputational and business probity issues' and matters such as 'safety and environmental issues'. A copy of the draft report was sent to every listed UK company.

These recommendations represent a compromise position between the two extremes of full corporate disclosure of risks on the one hand and, on the other, merely printing a few vague lines in an annual report.

The Turnbull committee's final report was endorsed by The Stock Exchange which has written to company secretaries and finance directors of all UK listed companies telling them they will have to implement the Turnbull committee's recommendations.

THE OECD PRINCIPLES

The OECD Council, meeting at Ministerial level on 27–28 April 1998, called upon the OECD to develop, in conjunction with national governments, other relevant international organizations and the private sector, a set of corporate governance standards and guidelines. In order to fulfil this objective, the OECD established the Ad-Hoc Task Force on Corporate Governance to develop a set of non-binding principles that embody the views of Member countries on this issue.

The Principles are intended to assist member and non-member governments in their efforts to evaluate and improve the legal, institutional and regulatory framework for corporate governance in their countries, and to provide guidance and suggestions for stock exchanges, investors, corporations, and other parties that have a role in the process of developing good corporate governance. The Principles are non-binding and do not aim at detailed prescriptions for national legislation. Their purpose is to serve as a reference point. They can be used by policy makers, as they examine and develop their legal and regulatory frameworks for corporate governance that reflect their own economic, social, legal and cultural circumstances, and by market. The principles set out guidelines for the role of stakeholders in corporate governance:

▌ The corporate governance framework should recognize the rights of stakeholders as established by law and encourage active cooperation between corporations and stakeholders in creating wealth, jobs, and the sustainability of financially sound enterprises.

▌ The corporate governance framework should assure that the rights of stakeholders that are protected by law are respected.

▌ Where law protects stakeholder interests, stakeholders should have the opportunity to obtain effective redress for violation of their rights.

▌ The corporate governance framework should permit performance-enhancing mechanisms for stakeholder participation.

▌ Where stakeholders participate in the corporate governance process, they should have access to relevant information.

The principles also emphasize the importance of disclosure and transparency:

▌ The corporate governance framework should ensure that timely and accurate disclosure is made on all material matters regarding the corporation, including the financial situation, performance, ownership, and governance of the company.

▌ Disclosure should include, but not be limited to, material information on:
   1 the financial and operating results of the company;
   2 company objectives;

3 major share ownership and voting rights;
4 members of the board and key executives, and their remuneration;
5 material foreseeable risk factors;
6 material issues regarding employees and other stakeholders;
7 governance structures and policies.

▮ Information should be prepared, audited, and disclosed in accordance with high quality standards of accounting, financial and non-financial disclosure, and audit.

▮ An independent auditor should conduct an annual audit in order to provide an external and objective assurance on the way in which financial statements have been prepared and presented.

▮ Channels for disseminating information should provide for fair, timely and cost-efficient access to relevant information by users.

MONITORING STANDARDS OF GOVERNANCE

The UK National Association of Pension Funds (NAPF) publishes regularly, under the heading 'Governance Watch', a list of forthcoming AGMs and highlights what it regards as the governance issues arising in each case. The issues covered are the following:

▮ composition of remuneration committee;

▮ composition of audit committee;

▮ chairman and chief executive combined;

▮ no majority of independent non-executive directors;

▮ independence of senior independent director;

▮ length of executive directors' service contracts;

▮ NEDs form less than one third of the Board;

▮ dilution limit on share option schemes;

▌ identification of a senior independent director;

▌ payment of special bonuses;

▌ bonuses are pensionable;

▌ no contract information for chief executive;

▌ no explanation for re-election of director over 70;

▌ notice not issued at least 20 working days before AGM;

▌ absence of nomination committee.

In the list published in *Pensions Week*, 23 April 2001, six issues were flagged in respect of Singer and Friedlander and Bookham Technology, and five each in the cases of PSION, Davis Service and Persimmon.

PIRC Ltd provides a Socially Responsible Investment Service that gives assessments of companies under a number of headings, one of which is governance. This category is in turn broken down into sub-categories as follows:

▌ company policy;

▌ accountability and management;

▌ stakeholder engagement;

▌ disclosure and performance;

▌ standards and audit.

For example, ICI is given a rating of 6 out of a possible score of 10 for governance overall, scoring highly on company policy and standards and audit but scoring only 5 or less on the other factors. The summary report states that the company makes a full statement of compliance with the Combined Code and discloses its investor relations policy. The audit and remuneration committees are fully independent, but a committee member does not sign off the remuneration report. The executive chairman sits on the nomination committee. All ordinary shares have equal voting rights, but voting is conducted on a show of hands unless a poll is called. Company strategy is clearly articulated but with little detail provided. Non-audit fees are fully reviewed by the audit committee but it is not stated if any of the non-audit work is put out to tender.

PIRC also makes recommendations to shareholders in respect of voting at company AGMs. For example, in June 2001, PIRC published a report urging shareholders to block the re-election of two non-executive members of the Board of Marks and Spencer, on the grounds that, as members of the Board's Remuneration Committee, they approved a share option scheme, but did not insist that it was related to tough new performance targets. PIRC also recommended that the 2001 executive share option scheme should be rejected, arguing that the options were too slack and not in line with shareholders' interests.

EXAMPLES OF BEST PRACTICE

Among the steps that progressive companies are taking are the following:

▌ Establishing corporate-wide policies on social, environmental and ethical issues.

▌ Creating dedicated Board Committees. Examples include Ford's Environmental and Public Policy Committee, Shell's Social Responsibility Committee, Alcan's Environmental and Corporate Governance Committee.

▌ Bringing 'triple bottom line' issues onto the agendas of Audit, Remuneration and Nomination Committees.

▌ Setting up independent advisory panels. Camelot has such a panel chaired by a non-executive director.

▌ Creating a dedicated internal management team reporting to the Board. Diageo has a Corporate Citizenship Committee chaired by the CEO.

▌ Appointing an executive board director with responsibility for implementing the company's policy on sustainability.

The following are some examples of the varied approaches that companies are taking in their efforts to improve governance.

Pfizer

It is a long-standing tradition at Pfizer that all major decisions are made by the full board of directors. Consequently, the company has limited the number of committees of the board and addresses the majority of CSR issues at the full board level. Pfizer has also made an effort to diversify its board to reflect a broader range of experiences and perspectives and has sought to appoint directors who will raise social issues at the board level. Pfizer's board meets a relatively high nine times a year, which means that it is generally not difficult to get specific social or environmental issues on the board's agenda. Within management, the Corporate Affairs and the Corporate Governance divisions of the company are responsible for making periodic presentations to the board on current and emerging issues, including community involvement, diversity and ethics, and when specific issues arise, management will make special presentations to the Board. The Board also does a periodic review of the company's overall CSR-related policies and practices. Pfizer's board of directors takes an active role in shaping the company's policies and practices on social issues. For example, when the company discovered that one of its drugs was effective at treating Tracoma, a common eye disease in developing countries, the board played a prominent role in the company's decision to launch a programme to donate the drug and educate people on its use.

3M

3M has had a Public Issues Committee of the board for more than 20 years. The committee is responsible for reviewing and evaluating company policies and practices on a range of CSR issues, including community relations and environmental performance. The committee has five members, four of whom are independent directors, and meets quarterly. The board also has a Board Organization Committee that has responsibility for more traditional governance issues such as compensation and nominating. Within management, 3M has a cross-functional 'Issues Committee' that is tasked with identifying current and emerging issues related to social responsibility and for raising these issues with the Board. The Issues Committee meets at least twice a year and develops a presentation for the Public Issues Committee of the board on the top social issues facing the company. The Public Issues Committee then makes a determination about which of the issues it considers the most important and that warrant further discussion, research or action. While the Board committee plays a primarily advisory role and reacts to issues raised by management, in some cases directors raise new issues with management.

Time Warner

The Values and Human Development Committee was established in May 1998. The Committee has the mandate to provide guidance and oversight to the Company's management in its (i) development and articulation of the Company's core values, commitments and social responsibilities; (ii) development of strategies for ensuring the Company's involvement in the communities in which it does business; (iii) establishment of a strategy for developing its human resources and leadership for the future; and (iv) efforts to find practical ways to increase workforce diversity at all levels and to evaluate the Company's performance in advancing the goal of greater workforce diversity.

Berrett-Koehler Publishers, Inc

Berrett-Koehler Publishers uses an innovative stakeholder approach to corporate governance. In addition to its board of directors, the company has developed a formalized mechanism for incorporating the viewpoints of external stakeholders about the company's policies and direction. In 1998, Berrett-Koehler initiated a process to solicit feedback from authors, suppliers, customers, marketers, distributors, employees and others on a new model for the company's governance structure, purpose and objectives. The company sent a survey to some 500 stakeholders proposing the creation of four Berrett-Koehler Stakeholder Councils (Authors; Supply Chain; Customers, Distributors and Marketers; and Community Action), to serve as advisory committees to Berrett-Koehler staff and the company's Board of Directors. In addition, one representative from each council would serve on the Berrett-Koehler board of directors. Berrett-Koehler plans to launch its first two Stakeholder Councils at its 'community dialogue', an annual meeting in which the company brings together stakeholders to discuss 'topics of common interest'. In addition,

Berrett-Koehler plans to expand its Employee Stock Ownership Plan to include a wider range of stakeholders.

Campbell Soup Company

Campbell Soup is regarded as a leader in corporate governance, ranking third on *Business Week* magazine's 2000 listing of the 'Best and Worst Corporate Boards', after having been ranked number one the previous two years. Published in 1992, the company's progressive governance guidelines, which address a broad range of board policies and procedures, are considered some of the most stringent and comprehensive guidelines among US corporations. The board has also received recognition for its innovative management succession practices, with independent directors taking complete control of finding a new CEO. Additionally, the company has initiated a performance evaluation process for the board in which each director must complete an annual self-assessment, and has plans to expand the process to include a full evaluation of the Board's committee system. Based on the results of the evaluations, which are made public, managers from the company make presentations to the board in the areas in which the directors feel they need more information and understanding. In 1999, the board ordered a survey of director pay and, after seeing the results, took the unusual step of reducing their annual compensation by nearly 30 per cent.

Elf Aquitaine

Elf Aquitaine, the largest oil company in France, has distinguished itself as a leader in corporate governance through policies that emphasize long-term shareholder value, as well as the company's responsibilities to its employees, customers and communities. The company is recognized for being one of a small number of companies in France with a strong, independent board of directors. Company employees own a significant portion of the company's stock, and the Board has been recognized for engaging in dialogue with these and other shareholders. In addition, the board includes an employee representative. The company adheres to the recommendations of the country's Vienot Report on corporate governance, having taken steps to eliminate cross-shareholding groups and interlocking directorships. Additionally, the board has developed guidelines addressing board structure and role, including increasing the number of independent directors.

Finally, the board has implemented policies to align management and shareholder interests more closely through director stock-ownership requirements and stock option compensation packages.

BT

The BT Board is responsible for the overall direction and control of the BT Group. It sets the framework to deliver the company's commitment to follow the highest standards of corporate governance throughout the BT Group. BT applies the principles set out in the Combined Code issued by the UK Committee on Corporate Governance and appended to The Stock Exchange Listing Rules and complies with the detailed provisions of the Code. The company's Statement of Business Practice defines the ethical operating principles of the company and the expectations it has of its employees. This has recently been revised to reflect BT's increasing global activity and these revisions were subject to an extensive internal and external consultation process. As part of BT's corporate governance obligations and on behalf of the BT Board, the Company Secretary undertakes annual reviews of all the non-financial controls identified in the Statement.

Rio Tinto

In 1998 Rio Tinto established a board committee on Social and Environmental Accountability. It is comprised of non-executive directors, but the company's executive chairman, CEO and departmental chiefs attend each meeting. The committee meets three times a year, with the remit 'to promote the development throughout the Rio Tinto Group of business practices consistent with the high standards expected of a responsibly managed company, and to develop the necessary clear accountability on these issues'.

CONCLUSION

In this chapter we have reviewed a wide range of governance issues and an equally wide range of models and guidelines for good practice.

It is important to take a realistic view about the possibility of radical reform of corporate governance practice in the majority of companies and accept that, despite the existence of guidelines and models of best practice or even legally enforceable obligations, self-serving practices, sheer incompetence and fraud cannot be entirely eradicated. Power is always vulnerable to abuse and no matter what checks are put into the system, people who abuse their power will find a way round them.

Good governance, therefore, requires two things. First, it certainly does require models of good practice – but the best ones will not come in the form of stock exchange rules or guidelines issued by other authoritative sources, but will be provided by businesses such as 3M or Campbell's Soup with long-term success records. Secondly, it requires leadership with vision, based on sound values and moral principles.

Part II

What companies have been doing

6

The business response

TWO KINDS OF PRESSURE

Business leaders are under pressure from two quite different sources. On the one hand there are the competitive pressures of the marketplace, coupled with pressures from shareholders and their representatives. On the other hand there are the pressures from NGOs and other pressure groups calling for greater corporate social responsibility.

It is evident that, for most businesses, the competitive environment in which they operate has become tougher in the last decade or so as the New Economy has developed. There are several reasons for this. The deregulation of international trade coupled with increasing numbers of global corporations has meant that companies' home markets, which were once relatively protected, are now opened up to new sources of competition. Whereas 10 years ago Tesco could concentrate on competing with Sainsbury for market leadership in the UK supermarket business, today it faces competition from Wal-Mart.

Technological change has broken down many of the traditional demarcations between industries, so that banks find themselves competing with organizations as diverse as Marks and Spencer or General Motors in the field of credit finance. The Internet has provided new channels of distribution and entrepreneurs have in many cases been quicker off the mark than established businesses to exploit these. The rise of Amazon.com is an obvious example.

The growing emphasis on shareholder value and on short-term gains in share prices in the financial markets has added greatly to these pressures. Whereas in the past fund managers and analysts were content to leave it to managers to decide where to invest surplus capital, the prevailing view is that the market knows best and the expectation is that managers should focus on the core business and return any surplus cash to shareholders. This has the effect of increasing the pressure on managers as it makes the short-term performance of the business much more apparent.

At the same time companies are being subjected to pressures of a quite different kind. These are ones that result from changing social values and consequential changes in expectations on the part of society. The most public expressions of these pressures have taken the form of mass demonstrations in several cities throughout the world. The violence accompanying these has been rightly condemned, but there is growing acceptance that the issues raised by the great majority of peaceful protestors are important and worthy of serious consideration. Books such as Naomi Klein's *No Logo* (2000) and Noreena Hertz's *The Silent Take-over* (2001) have become international best sellers, exerting a powerful influence on people's attitudes to business.

No Logo has been described as 'the Bible of anti-corporate Militancy'. In it Klein sets out her thesis under four headings:

▌ no space – an account of the power of global brands;

▌ no choice – concentration of power in retailing leading to restriction of consumer choice;

▌ no jobs – as investment switches from investing in production facilities and labour to spending on marketing, mergers and brand management;

▌ no logo – how and why there is a political reaction against global corporate power.

Klein's work is based on extensive research, including field studies of working conditions in the developing countries. There is no doubt that she gives an accurate account of a great deal of corporate activity.

She begins with a graphic account of de-industrialization as it has affected the garment manufacturing district of Toronto where erstwhile factories and workshops are now being converted into loft-style apartments or workshops and business premises for artists, graphic designers, yoga instructors or film producers. (She evidently regards these occupations as in some sense less worthy than making things. Nevertheless, as in London, New York or Paris, these are the types of occupation being followed by the sons and daughters of those who once worked in the manufacturing industries.) The few workers left in the garment trade are elderly and she contrasts this with the youth of the garment workers in countries like Indonesia who are working for subcontractors of Nike, the Gap or Liz Claiborne, earning less than US $2 a day. Here and elsewhere in Asia she encountered working conditions very similar to those which prevailed in the factories and sweatshops of Britain and the United States around 100 years ago or in countries like Greece, Portugal or Ireland less than 50 years ago. She accuses multinational corporations such as Coca-Cola, Microsoft, IBM, McDonald's and, above all, Nike of being engaged in a process of 'mining the planet's poorest back country for unimaginable profits'.

The migration of much manufacturing from the developed to the developing world has undoubtedly led to the exploitation of labour markets characterized by low wages, poor working conditions and the suppression of trades unions, and the campaign inspired by Klein's work to improve these conditions is to be applauded. Nevertheless, it must be recognized that the companies involved have had to face the stark alternative – either move manufacturing to areas of low-cost labour or go out of business, as has indeed happened in the case of many clothing manufacturing companies. Poor working conditions in Europe and the United States in the past did not improve overnight. It took many decades of economic growth, productivity gains, the rise of organized labour, growing regulation of industry by governments and the leadership of a few pioneering progressive companies to produce the conditions that prevail today. Hopefully, the process of improvement in countries like Mexico or China can be worked through in a shorter time-frame, but this depends at least as much on the policies and actions of national governments and intergovernmental agencies as on those of corporations.

Her central thesis is that as more people discover the brand name secrets of 'the global logo web' their outrage will fuel the next big political movement, 'a vast wave of opposition squarely targeting transnational corporations, particularly those with very high brand name recognition'. Her prime target is those companies with strong international brands and which, as she sees it, produce brands rather than products. Yet she weakens her case by lumping together all large international companies with strong brands, ignoring the fact that there are hundreds of companies such as Mercedes, Du Pont or GE that are heavily engaged in manufacturing both in their home countries and overseas. She is quite wrong in stating that brands were first developed as a means of enabling consumers to differentiate between mass-produced products that were virtually indistinguishable from each other. The brands I remember from childhood represented goods and products that were quite distinctive in their quality, and value for money. Names such as Cadbury's, Mars, Lux toilet soap, Ovaltine, Singer and Hoover were bywords for quality and better than a written guarantee. She also ignores the key role played in a manufacturing process by product development and design. Her description of what goes on is confined to two activities – making the product and marketing it. But before a product can be made – whether it be a computer chip, a running shoe or an automobile – it has to be designed and developed and it is in the quality of that design and the extent to which it meets consumer expectations that the true value of the associated brand lies.

It is naïve in the extreme to believe that strong brands can be built on the basis of advertising and image building alone, although it is true to say that to associate a product with a particular lifestyle or set of aspirations can be an effective marketing tool. In focusing as she does on Nike she has picked a soft target. In this case it may be justifiable to say that the brand is the product. People don't buy trainers, they buy Nike and all the associations of sporting excellence that have been built up around that brand. The contrast between the wealth of Nike shareholders and managers and, not least, the sport stars who sponsor the product on the one hand and the young persons who work in the many factories in the developing countries on the other understandably makes people like Klein angry.

The process of building an image of a particular lifestyle or ideal around a product for marketing purposes is not, however, a new one. Why, when we have reason to celebrate, do we order Champagne instead of sparkling Chardonnay? It is because clever marketing over many years has led us to associate the brand name 'champagne' with success and happiness. When we drink to the health of the happy couple at a wedding reception from bottles costing up to 10 times the cost of a good sparkling wine, how many of us stop to think about the hourly wage of the grape pickers on the estates of the great chateaux? Brand symbols – logos – not only act as a means of instant recognition to the prospective purchaser, but also act as a badge of status once purchased.

Running right through Klein's book is an underlying assumption that on balance global companies do more harm than good. I would strongly dispute this. To take just a few examples, the cure for river blindness provided by Merck (see Chapter 7), the bringing of cheap computing power into millions of homes by companies like Dell, and the joy on a young child's face on entering Disneyworld are each, in different ways, benefits that would not be possible without large-scale business.

WHAT BUSINESS ARE WE IN?

Western free market capitalism is evidently under attack. If it is to survive it is vitally important that business organizations, including the financial institutions, should come to terms with these pressures for the adoption of a wider set of goals beyond shareholder value and that they should produce a balanced response to the expectations that the various groups of stakeholders, and the public generally, have of the business.

An important consideration is that a financially sound, prosperous and growing business is more able to afford to respond to these pressures and adopt an inclusive approach than one that is struggling to survive. In this important sense, therefore, a company's first responsibility to society is to be financially viable; to use the resources, material and human, that it takes from society so as to create wealth, rather than destroy it. Nor should it be overlooked that the goods and services supplied by a company, together with the employment it creates, constitute its major contribution to society as well as being the source of its profits. This focus on the importance of business success and the social as well as economic role of wealth creation and the means of sustaining it is fundamental to the inclusive approach.

Given, however, that society increasingly and rightly expects much more from the business enterprise than shareholder value, value for customers, jobs and fair dealing with suppliers, the practical problem for managers is how to meet these additional demands and yet remain competitive in a world of intensifying competition.

The expectations they have to meet fall into two broad categories.

Firstly there are those which relate to the various groups with which the company enjoys direct relationships. These are usually referred to as the 'stakeholders' or 'business partners' and in most cases comprise the shareholders and other investors, employees, customers, suppliers and local communities in places where the company has operations. The second category is the more diffuse area of responsibilities to society in general, including to future generations. Issues such as global warming, human rights or the exercise of political power by global corporations lie in this latter category.

In today's business environment the list of requirements under these various headings is formidable. Faced with such an array of demands the harassed company director might ask, 'What business are we in? Are we here to make a profit and thereby create value for our shareholders or are we now part of the social services?' He or she might point out that were the business to attempt to meet all these expectations fully the consequence might well be to go out of business. Nevertheless, the fact remains that these issues are more and more becoming subject to legal sanctions with the result that there is no option but to meet them. The regulations on such matters as health and safety of consumers and employees, waste disposal, discrimination on ethnic or gender grounds, the selling of insurance policies and other financial instruments are growing all the time. During the period of the first New Labour administration in the UK (1997–2001), additional regulations affecting business included the adoption of European Union directives on working time, data protection and pollution, minimum wage legislation, the introduction of stakeholder pensions, the Disability Discrimination Act, the Part-time Workers Directive and others. The arguments for self-regulation are strongly made by business spokespersons, but in the absence of a really effective and concerted response in favour of effective self-regulation by the great majority of companies the trend to increased legislation will continue.

One issue that has to be faced squarely by all the stakeholder groups is that meeting these rising expectations will in many instances significantly increase the cost to customers of the goods and services they consume. To manufacture a less polluting internal combustion engine takes huge resources in research, development and tooling. The result is cleaner air but more expensive motor cars. To filter the gases emitted by a chemical plant involves huge capital expenditure that increases the price of the chemicals being produced. In adopting a less polluting process a company might incur a cost increase in the immediate future in order to save a much greater cost later. However, those judging a company's financial performance take account only of the fact that current costs are increasing.

Trade-offs have to be made between quality of life considerations and short-term economic ones. A particular problem arises in the context of international trade when an industry in one country, seeking to behave responsibly, incurs higher costs and hence charges higher prices compared with the same industry in another country that does nothing to avoid pollution or protect its workers from toxic processes.

Even in cases where there is the will to translate the fine words about the inclusive approach into action there are some formidable practical difficulties. Until relatively recently the task of management was less complex. The clear aim was to make a profit; this was achieved by the exercise of commercial judgement, organizing ability and what used to be called 'man-management' skills. In making decisions the manager had to observe a few simple rules of the game. Today it is not just that the rules of the game have become much more complex, it is a whole new game demanding different skills, particularly leadership skills, and such a range of issues to be taken into consideration that, increasingly, the 'stoppages' take up more time and energy than the 'play'. The decision maker is faced with a whole series of regulations and a wide range of representations from consumer groups, pressure groups to do with the environment, media attention, government agencies etc. The decision-making process involves genuine dilemmas where it is far from clear where the best course of action lies. This was famously so in the case of Shell and the problem of the disposal of the Brent Spar oil platform.

As AT&T points out on its Web site, the need for simplicity can lead people to confuse ideas with solutions. 'The triple bottom line is an idea, a guide... not a plug and play sustainability solution in a box. Ideas can help you think about a complex world, but they can't do the thinking for you.

Aligning economic, environmental, and social interests sometimes presents few difficulties. For example, teleworking reduces pollution and greenhouse gas emissions, improves quality of life for erstwhile commuters and helps build a sense of community. Businesses get happier, more productive, more loyal employees, and need less office space. All the triple bottom line indicators are positive. But easy examples are the exception. It's hard to know what is best for "the environment", because the environment is extraordinarily complex and diverse and seen from different perspectives by people from different cultures. This leads to social issues, where determining what is equitable and fair is often impossible to do to the satisfaction of all parties.

In many instances there are complex trade-offs between the three aspects of the triple bottom line. Consider the protection of old-growth rain forests. Companies could switch to paper made from nonwood fibre, and boycott wood and paper products from the region in question and thus gain a reputation for being 'green'. Economically, the companies may be relatively unaffected, at least in the long term, and the easiest path is to avoid controversy by agreeing to the demands of pressure groups concerned with protecting the rain forests. Environmentally, the decisions are much more difficult, as there is significant evidence that manufacturing paper from nonwood fibre may well be worse – not better – for the environment. Socially, the decisions are even harder: boycotting an entire region may cause significant hardship… destroying jobs, disrupting communities, damaging families, and hurting individuals.

The triple bottom line is an excellent guide to examining complex situations, but only if the limitations and conflicts are recognized and understood. It can help all concerned – firms, NGOs, communities and governments – behave in more rational and desirable ways. But it cannot make the complexities of the world simple or provide a formula for achieving a reputation for responsibility and integrity. Our responsibilities for performing in a socially, environmentally, and economically responsible manner cannot be reduced to superficial slogans.'

THE KEY ROLE OF LEADERSHIP

To meet the changing expectations of society will call for radical changes in attitudes and behaviour on the part of Boards of Directors of businesses large and small and the investment community. This is particularly true in respect of people's expectations in respect of sustainable development. Companies will need the cooperation of all their stakeholders in this process. The changes that will be involved will affect people in their various roles as consumers, savers and investors, employees and citizens. If significant progress is to be made in such areas as climate change and the conservation of non-renewable resources the scale of change will be huge. Such massive changes can only come about as a result of large-scale movements initiated by visionary leadership of the same quality that changed the political climate of South Africa or brought down the Berlin Wall. We shall need hundreds, even thousands, of leaders at all levels of society to articulate the case for sustainability and to demonstrate by their own actions what it is possible to achieve; leaders such as those whose contributions are described later in this book, including Ray Anderson of Interface, John Neill of Unipart, Andy Law of St Luke's and Lord Browne of BP.

Leaders like these are already to be seen at work in industry, in NGOs, in consumer groups, and among the pioneers of socially responsible investment. Where they seem to be conspicuously lacking is at the highest political levels.

> *Politicians rarely yet have the vision, let alone the courage, to steer their governments, parties and electorates in this new direction. As a result it is inevitable that a growing portion of the sustainability agenda will land, by default, in the lap of business and of what is increasingly called 'civil society'; all the institutions and public activities which create the context within which markets evolve and business is done.*
>
> (John Elkington)

Business leadership today

The current position taken by business leadership can be illustrated by analysing the content of the Reith Lecture given in 2000 by Lord Browne of BP. His argument, summarized by Mark Goyder (Goyder, 2000) is set out on the left of Table 6.1. It reflects the attitudes and values of an increasing number of visionary leaders in major corporations, but it does not represent the position of something called 'business'. The relevant decisions are taken by the leaders of individual businesses and many of the most progressive among them are now working together in the context of associations such as the World Business Council for Sustainable Development (WBCSD). On the right of the table are statements that, in my opinion, describe the attitudes and positions held by those – possibly still the majority – with less vision.

The point of this comparison is to emphasize that decisions and actions are not taken by abstract entities called, collectively, business. Boards of Directors take them. In many cases, too, one forceful chairman or chief executive dominates these Boards. The consequence

Table 6.1 *The attitude of business leaders*

Browne's statements	An alternative view
Business is not in opposition to sustainable development; it is in fact essential for delivering it.	Many business leaders are apathetic about sustainable development or believe their only responsibility is for shareholder value.
Few businesses are short-term; they want to do business again and again, over decades.	Many business leaders look for short-term gains in shareholder value to create a reputation for themselves and then move on for a bigger job at a bigger salary.
Business needs a sustainable planet and society for its own survival.	Many business leaders believe they will be retired or even dead before real catastrophies occur, if at all. They feel no responsibility to future generations.
Business is the driver of innovation; new technologies can deliver the means for genuine progress.	Some business leaders cut the Research and Development budget on taking office.
If you want problems solved quickly and effectively come to business.	Many business leaders will only allocate resources to solving environmental or social problems when forced to do so by legislation.
What keeps business honest is the combined influence of employees, shareholders, the public and government. People who work in business care about the planet.	How effective were these pressures in cases such as Mirror Group Newspapers, Guinness etc? Many business leaders think that those who care about the planet are idealists and cranks.
Civil society can also influence business and this will happen through a process of transparency.	Many business leaders strongly oppose full disclosure.

is that a company that has followed policies of contributing to sustainable development for years can change its policies overnight following a change of chairman or chief executive. In other words, not all top executives of multinational companies think like Lord Browne.

A MORI poll conducted in 1998 put the statement 'Industry and Commerce do not pay enough attention to their social responsibilities' to a range of respondents. Less than 40 per cent of 'captains of industry' agreed with this statement compared with nearly 70 per cent of the general public. The degree of complacency shown by business leaders may have diminished since 1998, but clearly there is a huge perception gap to be closed.

Even in cases where the CEO has the vision to see where things are heading there is no guarantee that his or her successor will take the same line. BP may well be genuinely trying to contribute to sustainable development under Lord Browne's guidance, but there can be no guarantee that his policies will be continued by his successor. It is vitally important, therefore, that the education and training of our future business leaders should ensure that they are fully aware of sustainable development issues and that personal values and understanding of the social context of business should be treated as more important than the exercise of so-called leadership skills. There is some evidence that this is beginning to happen, as we shall see in Chapter 12.

Business leaders like Browne who are genuinely trying to resolve the real dilemmas involved in working towards sustainability sometimes feel aggrieved at being personally attacked by activists and feel that their attackers fail to make any distinction between those business leaders who are really concerned about these important issues and those who are not. There is some justification for these feelings.

Social institutions are vulnerable. They can easily fall under the control of people whose motives include greed, lust for power, racial or religious bigotry, or who are simply incompetent. Thus we have children abused within families, elderly patients abused within hospitals, 'institutionalized racism' within police forces, corrupt governments, prisons which are places of torture and dehumanization, schools which conspicuously fail their pupils and so on. Business organizations are no exception. There are many examples of sharp practice on the part of corporations, in some cases resulting in loss of life or large-scale pollution.

But just as not all families are havens for child molesters, not all caring institutions fail in their duty of care, not all prisons are human sinks, so not all business organizations engage in practices which are damaging to the society or the environment. Nor is there anything specific about being large or global in reach which makes it more likely that a company will rightly be judged as unethical. Indeed, I have always been puzzled by the widespread acceptance of the concept that 'small is beautiful', since in my experience both as employee and employer the worst offenders against society are often to be found among small firms which try to evade minimum wage legislation, neglect the health and safety of employees or dump their waste illegally. Moreover, the very size and visibility of multinational firms makes it less possible for them to engage in dubious activities without incurring rapid exposure and consequential condemnation.

By and large, the people who emerge as directors of these huge corporations are respectable, honest and upright citizens who are trying to achieve some combination of growth and profitability for their companies by means which are not only within the law but are also morally acceptable. Where they fail it is more likely to be on grounds of incompetence or ignorance of the wider consequences of their decisions rather than malevolence.

The importance of leadership was highlighted in the report of a joint research project, *Leading and Managing in the New Economy* (2001) by The Centre for Tomorrow's Company and the consultancy GPL. The researchers found that the firms they studied fell into three categories – *Defenders*, *Developers* and *Creators*.

In the Defender companies the new economy in its various manifestations was seen as something to be kept at arm's length and to be viewed with some suspicion. Leadership was often seen as coming from a single figurehead individual.

In the Developer companies there was both more effective and imaginative use of new technology and the beginnings of measurement of issues relating to stakeholder needs and expectations. Leadership was seen as important but as something restricted to the top few managers.

In the Creator companies new technology was being used to interact with stakeholders, and there was visibly a real attempt to include and measure stakeholder issues and a focus on long-term value added. Leadership was founded on trust, common values and respect for diversity. It could be seen at every level of the organization.

In a world of change and ambiguity, holistic leadership offers a path to greater business success. At its core is the need to grasp the paradoxes inherent in the New Economy and to master the competencies required by the business environment now being created. Holistic leadership relies on the leader acting as an inspirational force working with others – whether staff, partners, customers, experts, enemies or friends – to develop the best.

THE ROLE OF MEASUREMENT

It is natural that business leaders should look to some systematic framework for decision making in this area by developing an appropriate set of measures and attempting to apply to social and environmental issues techniques of measurement and evaluation more usually associated with financial performance. Indeed, as will be explored in Chapter 9, a growing number of companies now publish social and environmental reports or sponsor an independent social 'audit' of their performance in the social responsibility field. This is praiseworthy, but it is important to point out that the true end products of inclusive behaviour are not all capable of precise measurement. They include such things as social justice, enhanced human dignity and improvements in the overall quality of life. No matter how many figures are put into a social audit, the key issues are the breadth of vision and the values of company leadership and the way these are translated into decisions and actions.

CONCLUSION

It is important to put the whole question of industry's responsibility to society into perspective. It can be seen as part of the wider question of the values of a society and the shared vision of that society's future. Certainly people have a right to expect industry to behave responsibly. It cannot exercise this right with conviction, however, if it does not simultaneously demand the same standards of its other institutions – its political parties, agencies of government, the media, as well as of its individual citizens in their roles as employees, consumers, shareholders and parents. Society increasingly demands a socially responsible industry. At the same time, a socially responsible industry cannot exist without socially responsible stakeholders – employees, customers, suppliers and investors – together with a government that treats economic growth and quality of life considerations in a balanced way.

The issues at stake are clearly quite complex; they cannot be unravelled quickly, they involve genuine dilemmas. They cannot be solved by demonstrations, whether peaceful or violent. What are needed are joint programmes of change with clear objectives on the part of governments, supranational bodies, NGOs and Corporations. There is also a need for a much more informed debate on such issues as globalization and world poverty. The business community needs to be much more articulate in communicating the benefits of its activities and what it is doing to make good the harm that has been caused in the past and, indeed, is still being caused today. The next few chapters give an account of some of the most significant achievements in the past five or so years.

7

Purpose and values

Tomorrow's company is clear about its distinctive purpose and values...
it defines its purpose in a way that inspires whole-hearted commitment
to achieving goals which are shared by all those who are important to the
company's success. Tomorrow's company communicates its purpose and
values in a consistent manner and acts in a manner consistent with its
statements.

(RSA Inquiry, 1995)

THE END OF SHAREHOLDER VALUE?

Alan Kennedy's book *The End of Shareholder Value* (2000) chronicles the
rise of the idea that the purpose of business is the maximization of
shareholder value. According to Kennedy, shareholder value had its
origins in the observations of a number of academic accountants
who saw that they could better predict stock market price levels
by discounting future cash flow streams rather than looking at
traditional measures of performance such as earnings per share. US
investment bankers took up this idea in the late 1970s and early 1980s.
The insights given by the new methodology were used to buy

companies whose stocks appeared to be undervalued. These companies, once acquired, were then 'restructured' to release hidden
reserves of value before being sold on to new owners.

This created a need for a defence against corporate raiding of this
kind and Boards began to pay closer attention to shareholder value.
Companies began to realign executive compensation to place more
emphasis on stock options. Driven by these incentives, directors of
companies set about restructuring their companies to cut out under-
performing divisions, cutting costs, closing older plants, moving
production to emerging economies and outsourcing much non-core
activity. The results were seen in significant increases in company
performance and a related surge in stock market prices.

In Kennedy's view, things then started to go wrong. The means to
an end became an end in itself. By the end of the 1990s shareholder
value was becoming counterproductive. Directors saw that they could
become seriously rich just by pushing their company's stock to new
heights. The result was extreme short-termism. The interests of stakeholders other than investors were 'trampled'. Long-serving
employees were laid off or forced into early retirement, suppliers were
squeezed until they went out of business, and customers' needs were
neglected. Now, he argues, stakeholders are forming into pressure
groups such as consumer associations and associations of pension
funds and beginning to fight back. Thus the title of his book, which
implies that the era of obsessive concern with shareholder value is
now coming to an end. The evidence he produces in support of this
argument is somewhat weak and most experts would feel that the
obituary notice is premature.

Kennedy charts the growth of the obsession with shareholder value
in the United States, starting with GE under Jack Welch. He concludes
that the companies that have followed Welch's example have mort-
gaged their futures in return for a higher stock market price in the
present.

Kennedy concludes: 'In the UK and the rest of Europe, there is still
time for companies and managers to extract the best from shareholder
value – especially the notion that performance really counts and
managers ought to be held accountable for it – while avoiding the
downside so many of their US counterparts now face'. For this to
come about would involve Boards of Directors looking upon shareholder value as an outcome rather than a purpose.

*There is accumulating evidence that corporations fail because the
prevailing thinking and language of management are too narrowly based*

on the prevailing thinking and language of economics. To put it another way, companies die because their managers focus on the economic activity of producing goods and services, and they forget that their organization's true nature is that of a community of humans. The legal establishment, business educators and the financial community all join them in this mistake.

(Arie de Geus, 1997)

John Plender (1997) points out that in the stakeholder or inclusive model of corporate governance managers are seen as trustees of the wealth inherited from the past, with an obligation to preserve and enhance that wealth in the long-term interest of the company, so as to ensure its sustainability. He points out that the so-called Anglo-Saxon model of corporate governance seeks to maximize returns to the shareholder rather than maximizing the company's wealth. One result of this is the tendency to maintain or improve dividend levels almost regardless of the company's performance with the result that income on equity shares has become increasingly fixed rather than residual. Thus investors are having it both ways – the benefit of a low-risk fixed return as well as enjoying the lion's share of profit growth. Pender implies that this results in more pressure during economic downturns to cut spending on such things as research and development, investment and training and is a major factor in the popularity of downsizing.

The most compelling argument for putting shareholders' interests first is that they are the business's owners, and as such are free to do with it as they wish provided they stay within the law. At one time this may have been so, but today, in the case of the vast majority of firms of significant size, the 'owners', both individuals and institutions, are better described as 'investors'. They are free to move their capital to where it will achieve the greatest short-term gain. By no stretch of imagination do they see themselves as owners.

Purpose is something independent of shareholder value thinking or stakeholder thinking. It comes first. Once a purpose has been chosen, it then has implications for each stakeholder. If there are shareholders, their returns will be affected by the purpose chosen. In my experience many companies have a weak purpose. By default they find themselves focusing on making money for their shareholders.

(Andrew Campbell, Ashridge Strategic Management Centre)

WHY PURPOSE AND VALUES MATTER

The point is often made that if a company declares the creation of shareholder value as its purpose then this is hardly likely to be inspiring and motivational for the shop floor or graduate entrants. Even a statement of purpose that is about meeting the needs of all the stakeholders is unlikely to call forth exceptional commitment and effort. For this to happen the purpose needs to be inspiring or challenging, seen as worthwhile, as serving society in some higher way than the material interests of the stakeholders. It also needs to be capable of being clearly articulated in very few words and sufficiently tangible and quantifiable that the extent of its achievement is capable of verification by measurement.

> *I want to discuss why a company exists in the first place... I think many people assume, wrongly, that a company exists simply to make money. While this is an important result of a company's existence, we have to go deeper and find the real reasons for our being... We inevitably come to the conclusion that a group of people get together and exist as an institution that we call a company so that they are able to accomplish something collectively that they could not accomplish separately – they make a contribution to society.*
>
> (Dave Packard, Hewlett-Packard)

In 1983, when Colin Marshall became chief executive of British Airways, at a time when it was loss making, unloved by the travelling public and suffering from low staff morale, the objective which he set and which he was able to share with the employees was to become the 'world's favourite airline'. Given the state of the company's reputation at the time, this was indeed challenging. It was brief, clear, capable of measurement, and made no reference to shareholders or profits. The equally brief but powerful value statement, 'Putting people first' supported it. The goal was both tangible and verifiable in that there are various annual surveys that indicate the popularity of the world's major airlines. The result was one of the most remarkable turn-arounds, both in profitability and in reputation, in the history of UK industry.

By the autumn of 1985 BA was able to tell its staff that it had been named airline of the year for the second year running by the magazine *Executive Travel*. At the time Marshall said: 'A corporate mission is much more than good intentions and fine ideas. It represents the framework for the entire business, the values that drive the company and the belief that the company has in itself and what it can achieve'.

LEADERSHIP, PURPOSE AND VALUES

The authors of *When Good Companies do Bad Things* (Schwartz and Gibb, 1999) point out that 'Much of the work being done by corporations in terms of social responsibility is not being driven by codes, agreements or legislation. It is being driven by the operational interests and needs of thoughtful, moral executives themselves who are given encouragement to act responsibly when faced with difficult decisions.'

Some companies remain true to the ideas about purpose and values first set out by a visionary leader from the past – usually the company's founder. One such example is Ove Arup. The company that bears his name states its objectives as follows:

> *Our objective is to help our clients meet their business needs by adding value through technical excellence, efficient organization and personal service.*
>
> *The breadth and depth of our technical skills are applied to projects throughout the world, large and small, simple and complex. We seek to continuously improve our products and services and, by these measures, we add value to our clients' projects and achieve quality that they can rely upon.*

In 1970, Ove Arup spoke to a meeting of his partners from around the world. The talk that he gave has become known as the Key Speech and in it he stated the aims and the principles that guide the company:

▌ 'We must strive for quality in what we do.

▌ We should act honourably in our dealings with our own and other people.

▌ We must aim for prosperity for all our members.'

From time to time members of Arup have asked whether what Ove said in 1970 remains valid. On each occasion they have found that it does.

The example of Vagelos

An outstanding example of a leader translating values into action is the case cited by Ciulla (1999), of P Roy Vagelos, one-time CEO of Merck. In 1979, when he was director of the company's research laboratories, he was approached by a researcher who had developed a theory that an anti-parasite drug called Invermectin might prove to be an effective treatment for river blindness, a disease leading to loss of eyesight in the developing countries. He asked for permission to pursue the research. Despite the fact that the market for this drug would be confined to the world's poorest countries and was, therefore, commercially unattractive, Vagelos gave his assent.

The research led to the production of a drug called Mectizan, which was approved for use in 1987, by which time Vagelos had moved to be CEO of the company. He employed Dr Henry Kissinger to try to raise funding for the drug's distribution from sources such as the World Health Organization, but this was unsuccessful. The company was left facing the prospect of having a drug that the intended beneficiaries would not be able to afford to buy. Vagelos consulted his directors and then announced that Merck would give the drug away. By 1996 Mectizan had reached 19 million people, at a cost to Merck of US $200 million. This decision was in line with Merck's core value, that 'medicine is for the patients, not for profits'.

George C Merck, son of the company's founder, had asserted this from the early days of the business. Merck's statement of purpose and values defines its purpose as 'to provide society with superior products and services. We are in the business of preserving and improving human life. All of our actions must be measured by our success in achieving this goal. We expect profits from work that satisfies customer needs and that benefits humanity.'

> *I've always believed that the greatest contribution a business could make to society was its own success, which is a fountainhead of jobs, taxes and spending in the community. I still believe that – but I don't think that is enough any more. And I don't believe that even generous philanthropy on top of that prosperity is enough. In these times, companies cannot remain aloof and prosperous while surrounding communities decline and decay.*

(Jack Welch, Chairman, General Electric)

VALUES AND FREE MARKET CAPITALISM

The basic value underlying free enterprise or capitalism is the most precious one of freedom. In the commercial sphere this means freedom to trade, to risk one's capital, to engage in competition. This freedom interacts with freedoms in the society at large, where people are free to decide how to spend their money, what kind of lifestyle to follow, what kind of food to eat, as well as what political party to vote for. These freedoms are highly cherished even if taken for granted; the freedom of movement which comes with car ownership is among the most prized of all; policies designed to cut car usage significantly are therefore facing a very strong headwind.

In a democracy freedom is limited by the constraints required if the enjoyment of freedom by one class of citizens is not to destroy the possibility of other classes doing so. Over the years we have seen extreme forms of laissez faire abandoned as legislation has progressively limited freedom in the interests of the most vulnerable members of society. Hence we now have laws to prevent child labour, to protect the rights of ethnic and religious minorities, to ensure safe and healthy working conditions and so on. Capitalism today is certainly not 'unfettered'. It is highly regulated by law, although there is clearly room for improvement in law enforcement. Over and above what the law requires there are further constraints on commercial freedom resulting from the pressure of public opinion. Nevertheless, there is and always will be a price to pay for freedom. For example, the freedom to use our cars results in thousands of deaths each year from road accidents. The political spectrum is split between those who feel the price of freedom is worth paying on the one hand and those on the other hand who would prefer much more control over the way we live in the interests of such goals as greater social justice or enabling people to live healthier lives.

I find it surprising that some of the apologists for capitalism – and apologists is the right word since they always seem to be on the back foot – while citing in its defence the fact that it is more efficient in creating wealth than the alternative of communism do not always argue strongly the case that freedom and free enterprise are inescapably linked. Those who attack market capitalism have either forgotten the fate of political dissidents under Eastern European communist regimes and the suppression of basic human rights or are perhaps too young to have lived through such times.

As for the concept of a third way, the much-derided idea of a political and economic position midway between the two, there is no need for such a concept. Today's capitalism is very different from that of the 19th century or of the middle years of the 20th century. It is steadily acquiring a more 'human face' as a result of changing attitudes and increasing regulation. I agree with Adair Turner (2001) that 'the potential for a "capitalism with a human face" remains largely undimmed by the emergence of a global economy, and that we should be confident of our ability to combine the dynamism of the market economy with the needs of an inclusive society and improved physical environment'. The free market system is finding its own middle path. The task of all those who would like to see a more just society and a better quality of life for its people is to keep pushing in the right direction.

For those who choose to spend their lives in the economic sphere, as distinct, say, from public service, the church or the media, there are other important values besides freedom. These include enterprise, initiative, self-reliance and innovation as well as the attractions of material reward. These values and their acting out in people's behaviour make a vital contribution to the quality of life in society as well as to its material prosperity.

> *The corporation is a creation of society whose purpose is the production of needed goods and services, to the profit of society and itself. As an institution of society, a corporation must reflect that society's shared values – social, moral, political and legal as well as economic. It must change as society changes. However, as a dynamic institution, it can also seek to influence the ultimate form and expression of those changes.*
>
> (Ian Wilson, 2000)

CHANGING VALUES

In the developed societies of the West and increasingly in other cultures such as Japan, the closing decades of the 20th century witnessed massive shifts in human values. Among the most obvious examples are those to do with race, sexuality – particularly the decriminalization of homosexuality in a number of countries, considerable strides towards the acceptance of female equality and, not least, the collapse of belief in Marxist doctrine. The early advocates of such changes were not only regarded as deviant; they were in many cases quite literally treated as criminals. Today, radical protesters against the misuse of the power of global corporations are in a similar position – they are either branded as anarchists or dismissed as cranks and idealists. Yet in many cases the values they espouse are ones which will become mainstream in the future. The elimination of gross differences in the quality of life, the conservation of species, the acceptance of obligations to future generations and the goal of sustainable development will in the end become fully accepted and embedded as parts of our values systems. Far-sighted industrialists can see this and at the very least are swimming with the tide. A very few, such as Ray Anderson, whose visionary leadership is described later in this chapter, are ahead of the game.

Classifying social values

Francis Kinsman, in his book *Millennium* (1989), discussed three principal groups of values in late 20th century society – 'sustenance driven', 'outer directed' and 'inner directed', drawing upon an analysis first introduced by the Research Institute of Social Change (RISC) in 1981.

People in the 'sustenance driven' group struggle to meet their basic needs. They are mostly poor, underprivileged and excluded from mainstream societal decision making. Their immediate priority is to maintain, or better still, improve their standard of living. Over half the world's population would be classed as 'sustenance driven'.

'Outer directed' people have all their basic needs met and are motivated by their perceived, relative societal status. In Western society this means they not only have access to the materialistic benefits afforded by modern technology but they take great pleasure in them. In fact, in their eyes, status in society is directly measured in terms of the external signs of economic affluence.

'Inner directed' people are much more values driven, demonstrating a considered inner sense of purpose. They are generally sensitive to ethical concerns and tolerant of alternative cultures. Their purchasing patterns and lifestyles reflect their more compassionate nature.

The analysis is often further refined into a larger number of groupings, namely:

▌ Sustenance driven: Aimless and survivors.
  – The aimless are either old, purposeless and apathetic or young, hostile to authority and often violent.

- The survivors are traditionalists, often hard working, cheerful and community minded.

▌ Outer directed: Belongers and conspicuous consumers.
- The belongers are also traditional in outlook, conventional, security seeking and strongly change resistant.
- Acquisition, competition and status motivate the conspicuous consumer group.

▌ Inner directed: Experimentalists, social resisters and self-explorers.
- Experimentalists include the more sophisticated big spenders; they are gadget fiends and try new ideas like meditation or new age therapies.
- Social resisters include the older idealists, usually with egalitarian views and younger people active in various social or political causes.
- The self-explorers are concerned with self-expression and self-actualization. 'Of all the social value groups, self explorers have the broadest horizons, the highest tolerances and the greatest propensity to tackle problems on a global scale… What they think today much of the rest of the world tends to think tomorrow.'

Since the 1970s, market researchers have polled the general public to measure the percentage distribution between the three main social values groups. Table 7.1 shows the results of a series of surveys carried out since 1981.

Table 7.1 *Changes in social values*

Date	Country	Source	Sustenance Driven	Outer Directed	Inner Directed
1981	United States	RISC	11%	68%	21%
1981	UK	RISC	40%	30%	30%
1987	UK	Applied Futures	29%	35%	36%
1998	UK	Synergy Consulting	55%	20%	25%
2020	UK	Kinsman forecast	15–25%	30–35%	40–50%

The implications of this analysis for the achievement of sustainable development are self-evident. Some of the sets of values are conducive to taking a longer-term view, of being willing to forgo material consumption in favour of an ideal or a cause, and behaving altruistically. Others are clearly not.

The 'sustenance driven' are essentially people whose lives are taken up with the struggle for the basic needs of survival. They are unlikely to be engaged by the arguments for sustainable development, and even if they were would probably not see ways in which they could make any contribution towards achieving it.

The populations of very poor countries are likely to lie almost exclusively in the 'sustenance driven' category. For them, concern for future generations will focus on securing for them such basic goods as housing, security of food supplies, clean water, sewage and communication infrastructures. At the other extreme, 'inner directed' people are likely to be much more in tune with the concepts and goals of sustainable development. As such, they will welcome, adopt and support moves towards its achievement. This will be reflected not only through their purchasing decisions, but also through the ballot box and their changing lifestyles. It is of some concern, therefore, that there has been an apparent decline in the proportion in this group in the UK and that Kinsman's forecast is turning out to be optimistic.

Applying the social values analysis to companies

An article on the BT Web site applies the foregoing analysis to the classification of types of business organization.

A 'sustenance driven' company would be one that is struggling to maintain its corporate head above the financial waters. Difficulties in making a profit and keeping cash flows positive mean that it will be difficult to apply resources towards community development and related issues.

An 'outer directed' company would be exclusively driven by the profit motive and the creation of shareholder value. It would consider itself to have no wider responsibility to society than to contribute to economic development.

An 'inner directed' company would be far more values driven. This is not to say that it would not be strongly competitive, striving to deliver a sound financial performance in recognition of its shareholders as legitimate stakeholders in the business, but that it would do so in the context of an inclusive approach. Such a company would be much more in tune with, and support the principles of, sustainable development.

COMPANIES' VALUES

In recent years more and more companies have fitted the 'inner directed' model and have questioned and reformulated the basic values and beliefs that underlie their business strategies. In many cases this process has been carried out in consultation with external stakeholder groups such as customers, suppliers and community representatives and NGOs as well as employees. The well-nigh universal outcome of this process is the acceptance that the company has obligations beyond the creation of value for shareholders. Some examples are given below.

Levi Strauss

Levi Strauss & Co. has been recognized worldwide for its firm commitment to core values and for a mission that specifically references the company's responsibilities to the larger society. In addition to formal mission and vision statements, the company has an 'Aspiration Statement' that addresses such issues as trust, teamwork, diversity, ethics and empowerment. Each of the company's statements serves as part of a roadmap, guiding managers and employees in their day-to-day business operations and long-term planning. As part of the company's corporate culture, values are considered a living element and the foundation of all business decisions. The company regularly involves employees in a values exploration process in which people assess what they personally feel is important and examine ways to integrate those values into business decisions.

South African Breweries (SAB plc)

This international company sets out its values in eight statements:

1. We conduct our business with integrity, respecting all applicable laws.

2. We are straightforward and honest in the commitments we make, seeking mutually beneficial and enduring relationships; and being open and accurate in our communication.

3. We respect the rights and dignity of individuals. We value cultural diversity and promote inclusivity through employee participation and empowerment.

4. We optimize the creation of wealth to provide fair reward, and recognition, for the contributions of all our stakeholders.

5. We create and sustain a safe and healthy working environment that, in addition, provides job satisfaction and the development of each employee's potential.

6. We provide products and services of uncompromising quality to meet the needs of our customers.

7. We are a responsible corporate citizen and fulfil our responsibilities as an integral member of society. In our business decisions, while asserting our right to trade freely, we give appropriate consideration to social and environmental impacts.

8. We expect these company values to be upheld by all employees and by the third parties we engage to act on our behalf, such as our suppliers, contractors and other agents. In joint ventures, we seek to ensure that our business partners apply these values.

Bovis Lend Lease

Bovis Lend Lease is a UK company that has set out its core values very clearly and published them on its Web site. The values include:

▍ Integrity. Maintaining the highest ethical standards and upholding the reputation of the company.

▍ Respect for people and cultures. Embracing diversity and providing an environment that allows employees to achieve the right work and life balance.

▍ Client satisfaction. Focusing on building sustained relationships, and on meeting and exceeding expectations.

▌ Teamwork. Creating value through partnerships.

▌ Corporate citizenship. Taking responsibility for the environments in which the company operates, focusing on safety and corporate responsibility in all areas of operations.

▌ Safety. Being committed to providing employees, stakeholders and the surrounding community with the safest possible working environment.

Land Securities

This UK company has a very comprehensive statement of business ethics and values. In the preamble to this it stresses the importance of retaining a set of core values and approaches to the process of doing business.

The Group recognizes its obligations to all those with whom it has dealings – shareholders, stockholders, employees, customers, suppliers, competitors and the wider community. It sees the reputation of the Group and the trust and confidence of those with whom it deals as one of its most vital resources. The Group asserts that it demands and maintains the highest ethical standards in carrying out its business activities, and that practices of any sort which are incompatible with the Group's policy will not be tolerated. Ethical performance is regularly monitored.

The company's ethical principles are set out under the following headings:

▌ Dealings with customers/tenants. 'Personal contact, helpful and responsive action are features of the service we provide to develop long-term relations with our customers/tenants.'

▌ Relations with shareholders and other investors. 'It is the Group's aim to provide shareholders with long-term sustainable growth in the form of a secure increasing income together with capital appreciation.'

▌ Relations with employees. Under this heading the company espouses equal opportunities, health and safety, fair and just remuneration and protection from harassment.

▊ Relations with suppliers, advisers and agents. The aim is to develop relationships based on mutual trust.

▊ Relations with the government and the community. 'The Group will seek to serve and support the community in which it operates by providing services efficiently and profitably, and by providing good employment opportunities and conditions... The Group is concerned with the conservation of the environment in its broadest sense, and recognizes that certain resources are finite and must be used responsibly.'

▊ Relations with competitors. 'The Group will compete vigorously, but honestly.'

▊ Behaviour in relation to mergers and take-overs. 'The Group undertakes to follow the guidelines set out in the City Code on Take-overs and Mergers and other rulings of the Panel on Take-overs and Mergers'.

▊ Ethical issues concerning directors and managers. 'As a publicly quoted UK Company it will conform to the major guidelines of good corporate governance.'

▊ Compliance and verification. 'The Group aims to create the climate and opportunities for employees to voice genuinely held concerns about behaviour or decisions that they perceive to be unethical.'

Case: Interface

An example of a company with an inspiring and challenging purpose is the carpet manufacturer Interface. Interface is the world's largest manufacturer of commercial floor coverings and, as a company, has a long-standing commitment to not only becoming fully sustainable but also to becoming a 'restorative' company, ie one which enhances the environment rather than depletes it.

Headquartered in Atlanta, Interface celebrated its 25th anniversary in 1998. In December 1997, and again in December 1998, Interface, Inc was named one of the Top 100 Companies to Work for in the United States by *Fortune* Magazine.

Interface Flooring Systems, Inc, began in 1973 when Ray Anderson, currently chairman of the board and chief executive officer, recognized the need for flexible floor coverings for the modern office environment. He led a joint venture between Carpets International Plc, a British company, and a group of US investors to produce and market modular soft-surfaced floor coverings. Anderson established operations in LaGrange, GA, and Interface Flooring Systems, Inc, began manufacturing and distributing modular carpet tiles in 1974. The company quickly grew to its current status as the world's leading producer of soft-surfaced modular floor coverings, and has expanded over the past 25 years through internal growth and strategic acquisitions.

Interface is now a global company, producing in 33 manufacturing sites located in the United States, Canada, the United Kingdom, the Netherlands, Northern Ireland, Australia and Thailand; and selling these products in more than 110 countries. It produces commercial broadloom carpet, textiles, chemicals, architectural products, access-flooring systems, and manufactures and sells more than 40 per cent of the entire amount of carpet tile used in commercial buildings today.

> Worldwide, all of us at Interface have a common goal: create zero waste. For the last five years, we've been working hard to get there. We call our effort QUEST. It's an acronym that stands for Quality Utilizing Employee Suggestions and Teamwork. Through QUEST teams around the world, we're re-examining our sources of waste and creating ways to reduce and finally eliminate them. We're redesigning and rethinking products so that we can deliver more with less. We're re-engineering production processes to reduce resource consumption. If part of a process or product doesn't add value, we eliminate it. And that philosophy goes beyond manufacturing. Our aim is zero waste in every discipline, from accounting to sales to human resources. We've come a long way already, eliminating more than $90 million in waste since 1994.

Ray Anderson sees his mission – his company's mission – as leading 'the second industrial revolution'. Until the mid-nineties the company was content to comply with environmental legislation. But then customers and distributors began asking what Interface was doing about the environment. This was 1994, two years after the historic Rio Earth Summit. Interface's experience was not unique. Most companies and their customers were paying more attention to the environmental impact of their actions.

But Anderson, at one time Co-chair of President Clinton's Council on Sustainable Development, had had an epiphany, and his response was like few others. In an address to a taskforce convened by Interface employees, he challenged them to make Interface a sustainable, even restorative company. 'Take nothing more than we can give back. Close the loop and create no waste. That's the vision.' With that, Interface and its 7,500 employees began what Anderson calls 'the climb'.

In 1995, Interface spent $802 million on raw materials, roughly 1.2 billion pounds of natural capital. One-third was in the form of abundant and benign resources. Two-thirds were petroleum derived, of which two-thirds was burnt. Interface calculated that it took 1.59 pounds of inputs, 'what we call stuff', to derive a dollar of sales. To Anderson, this was 'simply not sustainable'.

So they developed a metric: pounds of 'stuff' to produce a dollar of sales.

Between 1994 and 1998, Interface improved its performance to 0.94 pounds per dollar of sales. This translates into US $23 million in 'sustainable' sales. So far, Interface has eliminated 46 per cent of its waste stream, saving US $87 million in the process.

'Business today is a take, make, waste proposition,' argued Anderson. 'So we're building the prototypical business of the twenty-first century.' What would that business be like? Anderson presented a seven-point plan:

▓ Eliminate waste, with zero waste as a goal.

▓ Benign emissions to both the biosphere and lithosphere.

▓ Renewable energy (Interface just recently inaugurated a plant that uses only solar energy).

▓ Close the loop on waste, with less energy used to recycle and reuse than to extract the resource.

▓ Resource-efficient transportation.

▓ Sensitivity hook-up: get suppliers, employers, and all the links moving in the same direction.

▓ Cradle-to-cradle responsibility, what we know as upstream and downstream supply chain management.

One of Interface's ways of approaching new business thinking is the innovative Greenlease scheme for commercial customers. Greenlease recognizes that no customer actually wants to buy a heap of nylon fibres and glue; what they really want are the benefits provided by the carpet's warmth, appearance and texture, not the carpet itself. Customers would also welcome an alternative to a carpet that gradually wears out and then has to be disposed of (at a substantial environmental cost) and then replaced at a significant capital outlay.

The way Greenlease works is that a company leases carpet services from Interface, getting the benefit of new carpet tiles which are regularly inspected by Interface and automatically replaced when they become worn, effectively creating a carpet which consistently provides a high standard of presentation and function. Interface continue to own the carpet and any recovered worn carpet is rejuvenated or recycled into new carpet without the need to call upon virgin resources. It is in the interests of Interface to make the carpet go round in cycles as many times as possible, re-engineering and reformulating the production process to aid recyclability. From the customers' viewpoint, initial capital outlay, and its resultant effect on cash flow, is removed and the cost of providing a constant standard of carpeting to the business is truly reflected in their accounts.

The success of this simple but innovative idea has led to other carpet manufacturers following suit, notably Milliken Carpets, whose 'earth square' product range is based on a very similar concept.

Following a period of solid growth in sales and profits, Interface met with some serious difficulties. In the second quarter of 1998 its shares went into a decline that lasted a year and a half and from peak to trough lost 87 per cent of their value. Inevitably this called into question not only the company's credibility but also that of the sustainability movement as a whole.

The decline in fortunes reflected several factors. There was at that time a general decline in Interface's business sector as sentiment favoured 'New Economy' companies. The main reasons, however, were self-inflicted. In Anderson's words, 'Interface shot itself in the foot not once, but three times' (2001). The acquisition of some 29 dealer-contractors brought huge problems of assimilation. The distribution systems were neglected while IT staff concentrated on 'millennium bug' problems. An acquisition in Europe also went sour.

Anderson realized that behind all these problems lay insensitive and autocratic management of people. 'The critical missing factor was a corresponding, genuine focus on people, ie social sustainability. In times of greatest stress, rather than patiently and empathetically involving people in the decisions that would affect their livelihoods, our managers, more often than not, resorted to edict.' Interface, in other words, had started to reverse direction in its journey towards inclusiveness.

'Did Interface's commitment to environmental sustainability cause the earnings and share price decline? No, for sure, not! The decline would have been far worse but for business won through customer goodwill created in response to that commitment, and the cost savings and the unique products springing from the new mindset of sustainability. The cause of the decline was largely an incomplete commitment to sustainability in all its dimensions.'

CONCLUSION

In the past, the purpose of business was taken for granted and seldom debated. In the 1960s the Chairman of Unilever was asked to address members of a senior executive development course on the subject of Unilever's objectives. He stood up and said: 'Unilever's objective is to make profits. Are there any questions?' Few chairpersons of major companies would be so blunt today, but many would cite the creation of shareholder value as the sole purpose of the enterprise. The choice of a purpose reflects the organization's values and an exclusive focus on the bottom line reflects materialistic and economic values. By contrast, the adoption of a wider purpose, one that embraces benefits to mankind and obligations to stakeholders, reflects a set of humanitarian values and a desire to be of service to the community. Such a purpose both gives greater legitimacy to the corporation in the eyes of the public and makes it more attractive to potential employees who would like to feel they are making a contribution to society over and above making the shareholders richer.

8

Engaging with stakeholders

Tomorrow's company expects its relationships to overlap and seeks to reinforce the commonality of interest between them.

(RSA Inquiry, 1995)

INTRODUCTION

Relationships with stakeholders comprise only one aspect of the inclusive approach to sustainable business success. Nevertheless, it is the stakeholder issue that has grabbed the headlines and it is around so-called 'stakeholder theory' that a fierce debate has flourished. In particular, a clear division of opinion has emerged between those who advocate an exclusive focus on shareholder value as a corporate goal and those who argue for the stakeholder approach. There are practical business leaders, consultants, investment experts and economists on both sides.

THE STAKEHOLDER CONCEPT

Being a stakeholder means having a stake in something that may be put at risk. The risk could be the risk of losing one's investment, one's job, one's contract as a supplier, of being exposed to health or safety risks or of not getting value for money as a customer. These risks vary greatly in scale.

There are two broad groups of stakeholders – those with whom the company has a direct relationship – shareholders, investors, employees, customers, suppliers and local communities, and those with which there are no direct or transactional relationships such as a whole range of pressure groups and NGOs representing interests that are affected in one way or another by a company's activities.

Some companies list 'society' as a stakeholder; however, a company, no matter how large and powerful it is, has a stake in society which is much more critical for its survival than the stake society has in it in return. If Vodafone or AT&T, for example, were to fail to survive, the impact on society would be relatively slight. On the other hand a breakdown in the social fabric could well destroy either company.

Critics of the stakeholder approach argue that the occasional purchase of a Mars bar does not make one a stakeholder in the Mars company; this is arguable, although if eating a Mars bar were to result in severe food poisoning the case would be difficult to defend. There are, however, differences in the extent to which stakeholders are affected by company activities.

The long-term investor who commits his or her life savings to a single company as a shareholder is a stakeholder in a big way. The short-term holder of speculative shares in a company as part of a widely spread portfolio is not a stakeholder to anything like the same degree.

An employee aged 53 with over 30 years' service has a great deal to lose if made redundant. He or she is a stakeholder in a very real sense, whereas the young person who signs on with a company for a year in order to save up for a trip round the world is not.

The supplier whose whole output is taken by Marks and Spencer is seriously at risk and is a major stakeholder.

The customer who buys a house from a speculative builder and thus makes the most important buying decision of a lifetime is clearly an important stakeholder, whereas buying a newspaper from WH Smith does not make one a significant stakeholder.

Who the stakeholders are also depends on the nature and purpose of the organization. Most companies have four 'active' or transactional stakeholders because they operate in the three marketplaces (for capital, labour, and goods and services) and enjoy services supplied by the local community. But many privately owned companies have no investor stakeholders, and regulated companies might regard the Regulator as a stakeholder.

The balance of power in stakeholder relationships is rarely equal. A private customer buying a car from Ford is relatively powerless compared with, say, the fleet buyer for Shell. Yet for that individual a defective vehicle is more damaging than one faulty vehicle among the many supplied to Shell.

One individual employee would be relatively powerless in his or her relationship with the employer but for the protection offered by Trade Union membership or by the law in relation to such things as minimum wages, unfair dismissal and health and safety.

The inclusive approach to governance implies that organizations will not exploit these power differences to their own advantage; that they will aim to treat each and every customer and supplier as important; that they will treat each individual employee with respect.

Nevertheless, the inclusive approach also means that it is important to take into account the degree of risk at stake. The decision to make redundant an employee of some 30 years' service but who has not yet reached pensionable age calls for more careful consideration than the decision to make redundant a part-time employee aged under 30 with less than two years' service. Similarly, it is one thing for Marks and Spencer to cancel a contract with the company that supplies it with paper clips and quite another for it to cancel a contract with a clothing manufacturer which supplies its whole output to the company and has done so for many years.

Svendsen (1998) points to an important distinction in the way different companies relate to their stakeholders. One approach, which she calls stakeholder management, focuses on managing these relationships, protecting the organization, and is linked to short-term goals; implementation is fragmented and often driven by divisional interests, eg to earn 'brownie points' for the purchasing function.

The more considered approach, which she terms 'stakeholder collaboration', focuses on building relationships, emphasizing win-win opportunities, and is linked to longer-term goals. Implementation is integrated across the company and is driven by the company's mission, values and strategy.

For most companies, the attention of management has been focused on one stakeholder group at a time. Collaborative approaches are often confined to specific parts of an organization. For example, some companies have a participative and democratic approach to employee relations. Others have developed trust-based, highly interdependent relationships with their suppliers and customers. Less common is the company that adopts a comprehensive and strategic approach to relationship building that is governed both by deep social values and by recognition of the importance of the bottom line.

Experience shows that if you work within a set of trusting partnerships then you can get your quality up and your costs down faster than if you proceed by way of arm's length brutal negotiation.

(John Neill, CEO Unipart)

THE 'STRAW MAN' OF STAKEHOLDER THEORY

A number of advocates of shareholder value as the supreme and indeed only goal of corporate endeavour have set up a 'straw man' to knock down in the form of so-called 'stakeholder theory'. There is no such thing as an accepted body of knowledge or theory called 'stakeholder theory'. There are, however, many advocates of the idea that businesses should be managed in the interests of all the stakeholder groups. These include economists, business school academics, business leaders, business journalists and consultants. Some base their advocacy on experience, others on theory; they are not necessarily in agreement with each other, still less is there a commonly accepted body of theory on which they draw.

An early instance of a business leader expressing the idea is a speech given in 1951 by Frank Abrams, chairman of Standard Oil of New Jersey, in which he said: 'The job of management is to maintain an equitable and working balance among the claims of the variously directly interested groups – stockholders, employees, customers and the public at large'.

In the 1960s the Stanford Research Institute in the United States and the Swedish management theorist Eric Rhenman fostered the approach. Enthusiasm for it grew as business leaders saw that the success of the Japanese management system owed much to stakeholder ideas.

One of the strongest critics of the stakeholder approach is Sternberg (1999). She argues that, 'Stakeholder theory is the doctrine that businesses should be run not for the benefit of their owners, but for the benefit of all their stakeholders'. Some advocates may make such an assertion, but there is no generally accepted body of theory in which it can be found, still less is there anything that would justify the term 'doctrine'. The inclusive approach argues rather that companies should be run to create wealth in ways that are sustainable and that to do this means, *inter alia*, taking into account all the relationships of mutual dependence that are involved in its activities.

Sternberg attributes ideas to those who have espoused the stakeholder view to which most of them would probably not lay claim. For example, she states that 'it is an essential principle of stakeholder theory that corporations should be equally accountable to all their stakeholders'. Where is the evidence for this?

She rejects outright the concept of multiple accountability. Yet all Boards of Directors are in law subject to multiple accountability. Their accountability for the health and safety of their employees and customers overrides their accountability to shareholders to make profits; if the company becomes insolvent, their accountability is to creditors, not shareholders; in a growing number of industries they are accountable to a regulator.

Above all, when she says, 'stakeholder theory gives full rein to arrogant and unresponsive management, and to extravagance in respect of salaries, perks and premises. Stakeholder theory licenses resistance to take-over bids that would benefit shareholders, and permits the pursuit of empire-building acquisitions that make little business sense', she is not only making unsubstantiated assertions, she is flying in the face of the research evidence. One wonders if she would care to repeat these allegations in person to the Boards of such successful stakeholder companies as Shell, BP, Hewlett-Packard, Merck or ABB. Even that hero of successful capitalism, Jack Welch, now argues for a stakeholder approach.

Management as the function of balancing multiple goals

Argenti (1996) argues that a company can only operate successfully if it has one clear overriding purpose – ie creating shareholder value. However, he falls into a trap of his own making when he states: 'Companies are there for the shareholders, just as a school is for the children, a hospital for its patients, a trade union for its members and the AA for its motorists'.

What if the school and the hospital are in the private sector? Does a hospital in the NHS exist for its patients, while one in the private sector exists solely for its shareholders? If Argenti, having suffered a heart attack, found himself being carried into a hospital with a banner above the door stating, 'Our sole concern is to create value for our shareholders', his heart condition might take a turn for the worse. And now that Centrica owns the AA, does it suddenly no longer exist for the benefit of motorists? This is not the message contained in its literature.

In the real world, balancing different sets of objectives and meeting different sets of obligations are inescapable challenges. That is what managers are paid to do. Even if the focus is mainly on shareholder value, it is necessary to balance the need of today's shareholders for a high dividend against the needs of future shareholders for free cash flow. If you are running a hospital in the private sector you need also to take account of the extent to which salaries and working conditions are such as to attract and retain the key employees such as consultants and nurses, the needs of suppliers of equipment and medicines to achieve acceptable margins, but above all, for the patients and their families to perceive that they are getting the best possible health care. It is pure ivory tower theory to argue (as Sternberg does) that the most fundamental argument against stakeholder theory is that it provides no guidance as to how the balance between the interests of the different stakeholder groups is to be struck. (She refers to them as 'divergent' interests without justifying the use of this term.) Of course 'stakeholder theory' does not offer such a formula; nor is such a formula needed. The balance to be struck will vary from firm to firm and in each firm from one set of circumstances to another. It is management's job to foster an optimal alignment of stakeholder interests in respect of a particular set of circumstances so as to create a sense of common purpose. Advocates of the stakeholder approach merely remind the manager that to concentrate exclusively on satisfying one party, ie the shareholders, is unlikely to achieve this.

Sternberg's response to this is to argue that although it is indisputable that in practice such balancing problems are routinely solved, the way they are resolved is by using the substantive goal of the organization as the decision criterion. Thus, if the substantive goal of the organization is to maximize long-term shareholder value, the needs of other stakeholder groups will be balanced in terms of this criterion. The key word here is *if*. The main point here, though, is the nature of the imperative used by advocates of shareholder value – 'the management of a business must have one prime focus'. Where does this imperative come from? If a Board of Directors, in the full knowledge of and with the explicit or implied consent of its shareholders, wishes to establish multiple objectives or indeed to choose a prime focus other than to maximize the value of its equity, who is to say this is wrong? It may not accord with classical economic theory, but this would be just one more example of classical economics being at variance with the real world.

In our everyday lives we seldom act in accordance with the pursuit of a single objective. We mostly seek a balance between conflicting goals – between career and home life, for example, or between enjoying food and drink and safeguarding our health. It is no different for companies.

> *You can't create an enduring business by viewing relationships as a bazaar activity – in which I try to get the best of you and you of me – or in which you pass off as much risk as you can to the other guy. Rather we must view relationships as a coming together that allows us to do something no other two parties could do – something that makes the pie bigger and is to your advantage and my advantage.*
>
> (Lord Browne, CEO, BP)

There are countless examples of organizations, including business organizations and, indeed some of the most outstandingly successful ones worldwide, that quite explicitly have either adopted multiple objectives or, indeed, a single objective other than maximizing shareholder value. Merck, for example, sees profits, and hence shareholder returns, as a by-product of its main purpose: that of developing drugs and medicines to fight disease.

Shiv Mathur and Alfred Kenyon (1997) argue that stakeholder theory mistakes the essential nature of a business. A business, they assert, is not a moral agent at all: it is an inanimate object. This is clearly nonsense. An inanimate object cannot be prosecuted for causing a major railway accident as a result of negligence. Inanimate objects do not have a culture, shared values, or a reputation. A company is a set of relationships between people in their different roles, as shareholders, employees, customers and suppliers, bound together by ties of mutual interdependence.

> *Through their decisions business leaders influence the directions their organizations take. Ultimately, organizations are good because they*

emphasize the plural; members belong to something greater than them-selves, which is a source of reassurance and continuity as well as of higher productivity. Business institutions are persons, not just in legal/financial ways, but in moral ways as well. They are expressions of their members' beliefs, rights and obligations. Organizations that focus only on financial results can easily crumble under the weight of indiffer-ence as people retreat into themselves. In this sense, business is an important agent in the great human march toward a civilized society. That is a fundamental argument for building a model organization that helps all stakeholders develop into productive members of a pluralistic community.

(Carl Anderson, 1997)

THE STAKEHOLDER APPROACH AND BUSINESS SUCCESS

Research by Waddock and Graves (1997) looks at the link between stakeholder relations, quality of management and financial perfor-mance. Their analysis of the Fortune 500 Reputation Survey results shows that building positive stakeholder relationships is associated with other positive corporate characteristics. Solid financial perfor-mance goes along with good treatment of stakeholders, such as employees, customers and communities. They also found that compa-nies that treat their stakeholders well are also rated by their peers as having superior management.

Kotter and Heskett (1992) have studied the relationship between valuing stakeholder relationships and corporate long-term perfor-mance and this research is summarized in the Introduction.

Case: Ford Motor Company

The Ford Motor Company has recently taken the step of setting out its policy for stakeholder engagement on its Web site.

Ford defines its key stakeholders as customers, employees, the local commu-nities that host Ford facilities, business partners – such as suppliers and dealers – those who invest in the company and 'society', including governments and non-governmental organizations. The company states its belief that engaging in active dialogue with stakeholders creates value for itself and for society.

Ford lays claim to a long history of building relationships with its stake-holders and states that it has many initiatives in place to communicate and work with them. What is new for Ford is systematically reviewing its stakeholder initiatives in light of its stated goal to be 'a leader in corporate citizenship'. The company recognizes that there is a range of potential engagement with its stakeholders and that much of its engagement at present is through fairly conventional modes of communication, including advertising, lobbying and surveying. As Ford moves forward with its 'corporate citizenship' strategy, it intends to evaluate the quality of its relationships with each stakeholder group. Its intention is also to move towards greater collaboration and a relationship characterized by listening and feedback, respect and partnership.

Through mutual learning, the aim is to reach a better understanding of the shared interests between Ford and its stakeholders and of Ford's interrelated stakeholders' common interests, and to develop strategies that build on these interconnections. There is, however, no mention of any arrangement made for independent verification of the extent to which these policies are carried through into practice and actually do influence business strategies.

Stakeholder dialogue in relation to environmental issues

The key issue for Ford is, of course, the impact of its product on the global environment. John Warburton and Nick Cardoza of the London Business School have discussed the extent to which it is dealing with this via stakeholder dialogue in a prize-winning essay (Warburton and Cardoza, 2001), which is summarized below.

Against the background of growing public concern about the impact on the environment of Sport Utility Vehicles (SUVs) and the strong demand for more and larger cars of this type, 42-year-old William Clayton Ford Jr became Ford Chairman in September 1998. He has strong sympathies with the environmental movement, describing himself as a 'lifelong environmentalist', and his actions since his appointment bear this out to a certain extent. Firstly, the company has invested heavily in R&D to ensure that all its cars and light trucks qualify as 'Low Emission Vehicles' (LEVs), ahead of Federal regulations to do so. Secondly, in December 1999 the company announced its withdrawal from the Global Climate Coalition (GCC), a group of companies that argue there is insufficient scientific evidence to confirm serious warming of the earth due to so-called 'greenhouse' gases. Both of these initiatives indicate a degree of commitment to Ford's stated aim of being the 'world's most environmentally friendly automaker'.

The authors of the essay point out that the emissions decision can, however, be seen as an action that improves Ford's brand position, simplifies its distribution system (as current regulations in some US states already require these standards) and distracts attention from its poor fuel efficiency ratings. The GCC withdrawal can similarly be viewed as an action with a positive impact on the company's political and brand position.

More significant, they believe, is Ford's alliance with Daimler-Benz and Canada's Ballard Power Systems to develop mass-market fuel cell technology. In the long term, this project could radically reduce the consumption of fossil fuels by passenger vehicles. Ford has developed an overall strategy towards the environment which is generally regarded as laudable and which has a positive impact on the company's stock price. It is much more difficult, however, for Ford to align stockholder and broad stakeholder interests in the SUV debate.

Ford's SUV sales totalled 768,743 in 1999. Ford has also expanded its range of SUVs and in 2001 offered six models, up from two in 1990. This significant increase in volume is, however, only a part of the reason why SUVs are so important to Ford. SUVs are also very high margin vehicles with the consequence that their future is clearly central to the prospects for Ford's earnings and its shareholders. Other stakeholders are also affected. Customers appreciate the feeling of safety and utility of the vehicles. Ford's dealer network also has a stake in the success of the high margin SUVs. Employees, many of whom are also shareholders, and suppliers are presumably similarly pleased with the firm's strong performance. Even the communities around Ford's factories, influenced by the economic benefits of the company's success, have a stake in the SUVs' success.

Based on a *narrow* definition of the stakeholder approach, Warburton and Cardoza conclude that Ford has met its social obligations to its stakeholders in relation to SUVs in that it has engaged in dialogue with its shareholders, managers, employees, customers (end users and dealers), suppliers and local communities – the relationships seem to be 'in balance'. Yet Bill Ford acknowledged that SUVs 'pose safety and environmental problems', giving cause for concern to shareholders and dealers in the company's annual shareholders' meeting in Atlanta on May 11 2000.

Ford's admission that SUVs pose environmental and safety concerns is also included in their 'Corporate Citizenship Report', published on their Web site. Effectively they acknowledge four criticisms of SUVs, ie poor fuel efficiency, emissions, safety and inappropriate off-road use. The admission represents an application of Bill Ford's philosophy that the leading socially responsible companies 'lay out the good and the bad and they say how they'll address the bad'.

In the Corporate Citizenship Report Ford outline several steps that the company has taken to mitigate the impact of SUVs in the short term; they also outline a long-term direction for SUVs involving the development and application of new technology. Ford's short-term 'solutions' include:

1. increasing the extent to which new vehicles are recyclable;

2. reducing SUV emissions so that they can be classified as low emission vehicles, introducing a smaller, more fuel-efficient SUV and a hybrid electric version of it that can achieve 40 mpg in 2003;

3. further research into 'vehicle compatibility issues' (ie the danger posed by SUVs to other road users.

These short-term aspirations are significant but limited and do not necessarily place Ford at the forefront of industry developments. Firstly, Ford failed to achieve strong scores for its small and medium SUVs in the annual survey by the American Council for an Energy Efficient Economy of the environmental impact of various models of car and truck, losing out to Japanese marques. Secondly, Ford does not answer the charge that their marketing is irresponsible.

The long-term solution, from Ford's point of view, is to wait for technological improvements that 'will allow significant emissions reductions without loss of function'. They are committing significant resources to developing this technology. While Bill Ford acknowledges that the true social and environmental costs of owning and running an SUV are not reflected in what consumers currently pay, he is reluctant to support government initiatives to try to price these externalities back into the product. He indicates, correctly, that the central problem with trying to educate US consumers to be more fuel efficient is that 'if you pull into a US gas station to buy a litre of bottled water and a litre of gasoline, you pay more for the water' and that Ford would support higher gasoline taxes. He contends, however, that the regulations that force automakers to offer more fuel-efficient vehicles don't work because 'we can't be in the business of dictating what the customer wants to buy'. This reluctance to tackle the SUV issue from the demand side is reflected in Ford's justification for continuing to produce these vehicles, despite acknowledging their environmental problems. He argues that 'if we unilaterally turn our backs on something customers clearly want, then we're going to put ourselves out of business very quickly. And then we won't help the environment at all'.

Ford has taken the lead in aligning the interests of its various stakeholders behind their SUV policy. The interests of consumers and dealers, who seek bigger and better SUVs, have been balanced against those of employees and managers. The admission that SUVs do harm recognizes the ongoing debate. If Ford were basing its ethical stance on a narrow interpretation of stakeholder interest its decisions in relation to SUVs would be consistent.

By comparing its environmental performance with that of other manufacturers Ford is able to use a relative rather than absolute set of measures of its environmental impact. The company is therefore able to develop an ethical stance that does not require it to make the difficult decision to withdraw from the SUV market.

The authors of the essay argue, however, that the approach which defines stakeholders simply as those who interact directly with the firm breaks down where the impact of SUVs on global warming is concerned. The fuel inefficiency promoted by the growth of SUV market share means that tons of extra carbon dioxide are needlessly discharged into the atmosphere. The effects of this go beyond those who interact with Ford's products or who live near

Ford's plants. Given the impact of vehicle use on global warming, and the link between global warming and suffering for numerous people around the globe, it can be argued that Ford needs to broaden its conception of its stakeholders. This would require the company to take the issue of fuel efficiency as seriously as the more obvious issues of emissions and third-party safety risks.

Fuel efficiency strikes at the heart of Ford's success with SUVs, as there is a direct trade-off between weight/size and fuel efficiency. By offering no compromises to the customer but rather committing themselves to delivering what the customer demands, using only their competitors' actions as the benchmark, Ford, they argue, is continuing to behave unethically towards its broader stakeholder community. This is to say that they are not, as Bill Ford himself has said, fighting hard enough in the 'war for the rights of future generations, a war against intergenerational tyranny'.

Warburton and Cardoza, in conclusion, point out that a change in the emphasis of Ford's political lobbying activities towards ones that would result in fuel efficiency becoming a priority on the US government's agenda would be evidence of the company's intentions to pursue an environmentally sustainable policy. A reorientation of the company's marketing position would be a longer-term project but one that could see the company very well positioned to be at the vanguard of developing trends in vehicle fashion and one that would enable them to capitalize on their capabilities in fuel cell technology. This could be reconciled with long-term shareholder interests.

In short, the SUV dilemma is challenging but not intractable for Ford. Within the current paradigm of business ethics, ie that ethical behaviour is in the long-term interests of stockholders, there is more that the company can do to manage their environmental impact. However, really radical change will probably have to wait until the SUV fad is over.

External evidence in favour of Ford's environmental credentials emerged when Ford was a finalist in the Business in the Community's Awards for Excellence, 2000, in the category Business in the Environment. In the view of the judges, Ford's commitment to minimizing the environmental impact of its products is shown through a process of Design for the Environment and Product Life Cycle Assessment. This includes:

▓ work conducted in Ford's European Research Centre;

▓ an industry-leading complete vehicle recycling programme;

▓ marketing of alternative fuel vehicles;

▓ driver information technologies;

▓ eco-driving recommendations to help customers maximize the environmental performance of their vehicles.

Other factors in the citation were the following.

The new Ford Focus was designed with recycling in mind with creative uses for salvaged materials sought wherever feasible. Innovations enabled the Ford Focus to reach 85 per cent recyclability potential by weight and ensured that it was designed for quick and easy dismantling. Staff in the UK, Spain and Germany worked together to make decisions that maximized the environmental credentials of the Ford Focus.

The Ford Environmental System and ISO14000 accreditation sets targets for improving Ford's environmental performance which are met through training, development and individual empowerment.

The company offers a comprehensive employee training and awareness programme for its 20,000 engineers around the world. More than half of Ford's entire scientific research laboratory budget is devoted to environmental matters. Over 2,500 scientists and engineers are working specifically on more than 70 environmental projects in Ford's three research facilities.

In addition, Ford engineers and scientists are investigating how natural, sustainable materials, such as hemp fibre reinforced plastic components, can be used to replace glass-fibre reinforcements, improving recycling and reducing the impact on finite resources.

Ford is actively working to reduce the end-of-life impact of its products. One initiative is a subsidiary company, Environ Automotive, that manages the disposal and recycling of all the prototype and test vehicles used within Product Development. This company, which is tasked with avoiding the landfill of this waste, operates at a profit through its use and reuse of materials. Vehicle exhaust emission testing and design work within Ford's research centres has resulted in today's vehicles emitting 93 per cent less carbon monoxide and 85 per cent fewer hydrocarbons and oxides of nitrogen than those made in the 1970s. One 1976 Ford Fiesta created the same level of emissions as 50 Ka cars – which are also 30 per cent more fuel-efficient.

New technologies also help Ford reduce environmental product impacts and include:

▌ a pilot solar power programme;

▌ water-based ceramic paint (cutting volatile organic compound emissions per vehicle by 80 per cent);

▌ a shredded-tyre recycling system;

▌ catalytic incinerators.

In North America, Ford has more types of vehicle using Alternative Fuel Vehicles (AFVs) than any other manufacturer. Fuels include compressed natural gas and ethanol. Ford has put more than one million alternative fuel vehicles on the road worldwide. In Europe, the company is marketing bi-fuel petrol/compressed natural gas Transits and bi-fuel petrol/liquefied petroleum cars. Ford has formed the first-ever collaboration among automotive, energy and technology companies to develop and demonstrate fuel cell vehicles under 'real world' conditions.

CONCLUSION

It is important to distinguish between 'transactional' stakeholders and other parties or groups whose lives are affected in some way by a company's activities. Few business leaders today would argue against the proposition that, in the interests of the long-term health of the business, it is important to build mutually satisfactory relationships and an atmosphere of trust with employees, customers, suppliers and the community or communities within which the company operates. Not all, however, appreciate that the building of these relationships involves, at the very least, transparency and dialogue, and possibly even involvement in decision making. (The case of Berrett Koehler (Chapter 5) provides an example of a very progressive approach.)

Much more contentious is the question of how companies deal with broader stakeholder issues. As was evidenced by the Ford case, it is possible to envisage a situation in which all the various stakeholders are happy at the expense of large groups of the population. This is clearly the case in respect of the tobacco industry. The shareholders have been doing well in recent years as more and more markets have opened up; the employees generally have well-paid jobs and good conditions; the customers' only complaints are directed against government taxes; the suppliers of leaf depend on the industry for their livelihood. It is the 'passive smokers' in the community who are less than happy; they are stakeholders in a very real sense in that their health is at stake because of the tobacco companies' activities. The pressures that can be brought to bear by such broader stakeholder groups are very limited – for obvious reasons in the tobacco case a sales boycott would not be likely to succeed. Their interests can to some extent be protected by smoking bans imposed by other organizations such as airlines but can only be properly safeguarded by legislation on the part of governments. Given that governments rely heavily on tobacco taxes to balance their budgets, these safeguards are unlikely to be wholly satisfactory.

9

Business success models, measurement and reporting

Tomorrow's company matches performance measurement to its purpose and success model, so that it can assess areas of risk, the health of relationships and the degree of renewal, and can anticipate fully its opportunities... [it] measures what matters most for success. It accepts that competitiveness will be driven by change and will constantly be redefined for the company through an iterative process between itself and its key stakeholders.

(RSA Inquiry, 1995)

THE DRIVERS OF BUSINESS SUCCESS

The drivers of sustainable business success (sometimes referred to as critical success factors) will vary from one business sector to another and even within a single business sector, such as retail, according to such factors as the particular product mix, customer profile, or competitive environment of the enterprise.

For example, for some companies, customer loyalty and hence the level of repeat business may be vital for success. Neely (1998) quotes a study by Reichfield and Sasser that found that for automobile service companies the expected profit from a fourth-year customer is more than three times the expected profit from a first-year customer. For another firm, however, it may be more important to retain key employees. In yet another company, failure to meet delivery schedules may result in critical loss of business, while for some maintaining security of supplies of scarce raw materials may be the determining factor. In some cases there are what Neely calls 'non-negotiable' performance parameters. Examples include safety for an airline, avoidance of contamination for a food manufacturer and security of client account information for a bank.

The inclusive approach calls for each business to investigate and determine the nature of the drivers of success in its own particular business situation. Advocates of the inclusive approach to business success point out that the drivers will include not only such traditionally accepted factors as a company's financial strength, market share, brand strength and growth potential, but also such factors as reputation for ethical behaviour, employee commitment, supplier loyalty, customer loyalty, community involvement and other 'soft' factors.

As well as understanding the relative importance of a wide range of factors in driving business performance, companies must be able to quantify these as far as possible. At the same time, where the nature of a critical success factor is such that it is difficult or even impossible to quantify, this does not mean that it should not be given as much weight as factors than can be expressed in numbers. For example, in the fashion industry the acute sense of what will be next season's most sought-after designs – a flair based on a mix of experience and intuition – is critical to success, but it is hard to imagine this being expressed numerically.

The purpose of measurement is not just to see how well the company has performed in the past – the scorecard approach – but, by examining trends in past and current performance, to be able to predict and influence future performance. For this reason the UK company Reckitt and Colman uses the term 'development measures' rather than performance measures.

For example, if the business success model indicates that retention of key employees is critical to business success and if, despite having taken such measures as introducing share options and performance-related pay, the trend is for staff turnover to be rising, management must find an effective solution to the problem if they are to avoid declining business performance. Similarly, a company can learn more from a measure of its last quarter's orders taken than from a measure of last quarter's sales.

RECENT TRENDS

In recent years, research evidence shows that there has been a rapid increase in the number of companies measuring aspects of performance other than purely financial ones. The companies featured in the year 2000 Fortune list of The World's Most Admired Companies were the subjects of a survey by the Hay Group. The findings showed that compared with their peers the most admired companies are more likely to focus on customer- and employee-based measures of performance. Almost 60 per cent of the admired companies do so, compared with only 38 per cent of their peers. Forty per cent of the admired group measure employee retention, career development and other employee-related indicators – more than three times the percentage among the peer group.

> *In contrast with those of their peer companies, senior executives in The Most Admired Companies believe that many of these performance measures encourage cooperation and collaboration. Many executives reported that such measures help their companies to focus on growth, operational excellence, customer loyalty, human capital development and other critical issues. The top organizations create performance measures that focus on all the drivers of their businesses – financial performance, shareholder value, employees and customers.*
>
> (*Fortune*, 2 October 2000)

This tendency has been both stimulated and exploited by standard models of the factors affecting business performance, such as Norton and Kaplan's Balanced Business Scorecard and the business success model of the European Foundation for Quality Management. Such 'packaged' models, however, have inevitable limitations – like an off-the-peg suit, they can only provide an approximate fit to any particular company circumstances.

The achievement of economic sustainability at the level of the enterprise is not necessarily something that can be guaranteed by even the highest quality of management. New technologies or prolonged and deep recessions can destroy whole industries, let alone individual companies. Nevertheless, investment analysts will want to be assured that a company in which they are considering investing has in place strategies to sustain competitiveness. These will include the provision of adequate financial reserves, adequate investment in modern plant and equipment, for which figures are normally readily available, and in human capital and intellectual capital, where figures are still relatively rare. Other factors to be taken into consideration are the company's reputation with the public at large, the level of satisfaction and loyalty of its customers, the quality and reliability of its suppliers and the robustness of its processes and systems.

It cannot be stressed too strongly that a very weak indicator of economic sustainability is the company's current and recent level of profitability. Mark Goyder, of the Centre for Tomorrow's Company, writing to *The Times*, points out that in an article about Marks and Spencer the company was described as 'having destroyed most shareholder value in the past three years'. He suggests that the real story was that although the price of the company's shares fell heavily during that period, shareholder value was in fact being destroyed in earlier years while the company's profits were still buoyant. 'Creation and destruction of shareholder value are the result of how a company is led, how it innovates, what commercial decisions it makes and how well it listens to and learns from its customers, employees and suppliers.'

Developments in reporting practice

It is one thing to measure a broad range of non-financial aspects of a company's operations; it is another to report these results in an objective and transparent way to all stakeholders and the public at large. A range of approaches to company reporting of performance across a wide range of issues have been developed recently; these have in common the twin aims of providing a broader-based set of performance measures than the traditional financial ones and of creating greater disclosure and transparency in relation to corporate activities. The new methods are variously known as social reporting, triple-bottom-line reporting, social audit, social and ethical accounting or inclusive reporting.

Sometimes these terms are used to mean the same thing, ie a report that covers the economic, environmental and social performance of a company may be called simply a social report; sometimes the various terms are defined more narrowly.

One of the first companies to produce a form of social report was General Motors. In 1971 the company convened a conference with prominent educators and representatives of foundations and investment institutions 'to explain the progress General Motors has made in a number of areas of public concern and to obtain the participants' thoughts as to the Corporation's activities and goals in these areas'.

The topics covered included automobile emissions, industrial pollution, minority opportunities and automotive safety. Following the conference the company published the first in a series of reports covering a wide range of environmental and social issues.

The number of major companies now producing similar reports is growing rapidly. No fewer than 202 examples were considered for the Global Reporting Survey described later in this chapter. One of the latest European businesses to join the trend in 2001 is the Anglo-Dutch company Unilever.

GUIDELINES

Several NGOs and a number of consultancies working in this field offer guidance to companies embarking upon the process of broad-based reporting. The main ones are described in Appendix A. The advice they offer is very similar and it is summarized below:

1. A guiding statement of purpose, vision and values. The starting point should be a clear vision of the path to sustainable development and the goals that will support the achievement of that vision, together with a clear statement of the organization's underlying values. This vision must link closely with the organization's business strategy and not be seen as something apart from it. It is the role of leadership to develop the vision and articulate it. Top management commitment to the process and active engagement in it is essential.

2. An inclusive or holistic approach to the range of issues to be addressed. The report should be inclusive, adopting a systems approach, involving a review of the whole range of the organization's activities and processes, and their economic, environmental and social impacts and the interactions between them.

3. An inclusive approach to stakeholder involvement. Stakeholder dialogue is essential to establish the issues to be reviewed. The process should encompass a wider range of stakeholder groups than those engaged in direct transactions with the company.

4. Adequate scope. This implies a time horizon long enough to respond to the needs of future generations as well as those current

to short-term decision making. The scope of the report should include not only local but also long-distance impacts on people and ecosystems. It should reach back into the supply chain and forward to the ultimate use and disposal of the organization's products. It should also cover joint ventures and other business alliances.

5. Practical focus. The selected indicators and assessment criteria should be clearly linked to the vision and values. A mid-course should be steered between a comprehensive report and the need to be sharply focused on the key issues. Standardized measurements should be used wherever possible to permit comparison and benchmarking. Measurements should be evaluated in relation to targets, reference values, ranges, thresholds, or direction of trends, as appropriate

6. Transparency. The methods and data that are used should be accessible to all. All judgements, assumptions and uncertainties in data and interpretations should be made explicit.

7. Verification. Independent, qualified assessors should verify the accuracy and comprehensiveness of data.

8. Effective reporting and communication. Reports should be designed to address the needs of the audience and set of users. Reports should be designed for simplicity in structure and use of clear and plain language; they should be stimulating and capable of capturing audience attention. The Internet should be used for reporting. Reports should as far as possible be in real time rather than confined to annual reviews. They should be forward looking rather than focused on the past. They should be the basis for dialogue rather than one-way communications.

9. An ongoing process. A capacity for repeated measurement to determine trends should be established. Goals, methods and indicators should be revised as new insights are gained. There should be a clear feedback process leading to performance improvements.

10. Institutional capacity. Continuity of assessing progress toward sustainable development should be assured by clearly assigning

responsibility and providing ongoing support in the decision-making process, and by providing institutional capacity for data collection, maintenance and documentation.

INCLUSIVE REPORTING

In its publication *Sooner, Sharper, Simpler* (1998), The Centre for Tomorrow's Company proposed a scorecard to test the extent to which a company's annual report was inclusive. The main headings in the scorecard were as follows:

▌ Purpose and values. Does the company clearly state its purpose and values?

▌ Success model as a basis for measurement. Does the company make use of a clear model such as the balanced business scorecard to demonstrate linkages between aspects of performance and financial results? Does it include measures of such things as learning, knowledge management, etc?

▌ Progress in key relationships. Does the company give a clear account of the progress it is making in developing its relationships with its stakeholders, including reports of dialogues and other forms of stakeholder engagement?

▌ Licence to operate. Does the company demonstrate that it is adding value to the community, thus enhancing its licence to operate?

▌ The annual report as part of a total communication process. Does it offer the reader opportunities to acquire further information and to engage in a dialogue?

▌ An account of the Board's stewardship over time. Does the report chart progress over time with regard to key indicators? Does it include forward-looking indicators?

▌ Clarity. Does the report use plain English, graphics and layout to good effect?

THE GLOBAL REPORTING SURVEY

A survey of company practice in relation to triple-bottom-line or social reporting in 2000 was carried out by the UK consultancy SustainAbility in association with the United Nations Environment Programme (UNEP). The reports to be evaluated were selected in the following ways. First, 202 reports were identified by nominations from a range of experts or NGOs. From this list 22 were chosen. These were companies that fulfilled at least one of three criteria:

▨ They had received a top score of 20 in the 1997 survey.

▨ They had taken part as test companies in the development of the Global Reporting Initiative (GRI) Guidelines (see Appendix A).

▨ They were recipients of one of a number of awards in this field.

A further 28 companies were chosen by a selection panel comprising representatives of the GRI Steering Committee and the SustainAbility Network, making a total of 50. Scoring was allocated as follows:

Context and commitment: how well the company explains the business context for sustainability		40 points
Management quality: How well the quality of the information given allows for judgements to be made on a company's actions in relation to its stated intentions		28 points
Performance:		
Economic	28 points	
Social	28 points	
Environmental	32 points	
Multidimensional	12 points	
		100 points
Accountability/assurance		28 points
Total possible score		196 points

The 10 top scoring companies were:

1= BAA, Novo Nordisk
3= The Cooperative Bank, BT
5= BP, Shell
7 WMC
8 ESAB
9 Bristol Myers Squibb
10 Volkswagen

Of the 50 companies, 27 were European (average score 88), 13 were from the United States (average score 75), 7 from other OECD countries (average score 83) and 3 non-OECD (average score 81). Of the 27 European companies the majority were UK-based.

External assessment and audit

CSR Europe recently published the results of an assessment of some aspects of the social performance of 46 European companies, focusing on employment. The companies were selected from the FTSE 300 list so as to give a balanced distribution across countries and sectors. The main source of information was the companies themselves, but additional information was obtained from NGOs, the media and trade unions. In some cases it was very difficult or impossible to find people in the selected organizations who were willing to cooperate, and this carried implications for the reliability of the results.

Awareness that the results were to be published resulted in two polarized reactions. In some cases it lessened the degree of collaboration while in others it increased it. Companies were assessed on four factors:

▌ employability, covering such indicators as growth of employment, number of apprentices and offering temporary employment to long-term unemployed;

▌ entrepreneurship, including supporting employees to start their own businesses and professional support for redundant employees;

▌ adaptability, including training expenditure and flexible working;

▌ equal opportunities, employment of women, ethnic minorities and disabled people.

The authors of the report state: 'The analysis has shown a relatively good level of social cohesion in all sectors and in all countries. The aggregated sector-based scores for the four domains are always above 2 in a range of 0 to 5'.

There was a high level of performance in Adaptability. This reflected the fact that virtually all sectors were in the process of restructuring and facing consequent redundancies, coupled with the need to retrain and develop new skills.

EXAMPLES OF INCLUSIVE REPORTING

In 1995, the Body Shop developed the concept of stakeholding by introducing an independently verified audit of its own performance promises on social and environmental issues – The Values Report. The report, three independently verified statements on the company's environmental, animal protection and social/stakeholder performance, was hailed as trailblazing by UNEP (the United Nations Environmental Programme). The subsequent Values Report 1997 was also recognized by UNEP, again winning its award for social and environmental reporting.

The second half of the 1990s saw an explosive growth in social reporting among large blue-chip international companies. Some of the best examples are reviewed below.

BT's social report

BT has for some time reported on aspects of its performance, using both financial and non-financial measures. The 1999 social report built on this track record by assessing more accurately and comprehensively the social impact of the company's activities in the UK.

To produce this social report, BT undertook two parallel exercises – stakeholder consultation and data collection. The process of stakeholder consultation comprised a series of 12 focus group discussions and 18 one-to-one interviews with representatives of some of the organization's key stakeholder groups (employees, customers, institutional investors, private shareholders, opinion leaders, the community and experts in the field of social reporting).

BT says about its report:

This is about the things that we actually do, not about any spin we might put on our aspirations. And we are convinced that it is through this cautious, but determined approach, that we can best build enthusiasm both among our own people, and with others outside the company, whose active support is essential. We take our commitment to this process very seriously indeed. This report is emphatically not an exercise in 'gesture politics' or public relations, nor is it simply an attempt to 'cover off' expectations of appropriate corporate conduct, or to put a tick in the box. What it emphatically is, however, is part of a learning process, a first step down a long road.

The Business and Society Unit at Ashridge Management College has acted as the external verifier to this process of stakeholder consultation. In this role, Ashridge has advised upon:

▌ the approach to the audit process;

▌ the identification and selection of stakeholders;

▌ the scope of the focus group discussions and interviews;

▌ the analysis and reporting of the results.

The process of stakeholder consultation was largely carried out by the independent research organization, MORI. Throughout, the primary goal was to identify those factors that are considered by stakeholders to be the significant social impacts and effects of BT. The process of data collection was conducted internally by BT people. Ashridge made no attempt to verify either the data collection systems or the information generated by them.

On the basis of its involvement, Ashridge reported its satisfaction that the information presented in the report met two key requirements: 1) the reported data reflected the concerns, issues and expectations raised in the stakeholder dialogue; 2) the reported data presented a far-reaching picture of the way in which BT activities impact upon UK society.

However, Ashridge pointed to a number of areas in which the process of social reporting could be improved:

▌ It would be desirable to widen the scope of the consultation exercise – talking to more people who are stakeholders in the company.

▌ The information gathered from this process of consultation should be more clearly articulated in the social report. The hard measures of social performance should be complemented with some of the more reflective views expressed by stakeholders.

▌ The company would benefit from developing the formal management procedures used to collate and compile the information presented in the social report.

▌ In addition, there should be a transparent audit trail that would allow the external verifier to comment upon the veracity of the data and data sources.

▌ The process of reporting would be strengthened by a commitment to verifiable key performance indicators and targets across a greater range of the organization's activities.

▌ Finally, it is important to recognize that the social report mainly covers data for BT in the UK only.

Ashridge concluded that, overall, BT should be commended 'for taking this brave and innovative step in reporting, in a frank and honest manner, on its social impact. This move towards greater openness and accountability is driven not through statutory requirement or external pressure, but by a genuine desire to build a more meaningful relation with the organization's stakeholders'.

Royal Dutch Shell

The Shell Report online reports on the actions Shell has taken to meet its economic, environmental and social responsibilities. This information is kept as up to date as possible throughout the year.

The contents of the report include:

▌ An overview of Shell, including pages on the Shell Group structure, strategy, history, managing directors and Shell's core businesses.

▌ A statement of the company's values, including the Shell General Business Principles, guides to managers to support these principles and the systems and standards in use to manage the business.

▌ A section on 'Issues and Dilemmas' which addresses the many issues the Shell Group faces, from climate change to fuel prices.

▌ 'Impact and Performance' provides information on Shell's economic, environmental and social performance, including case studies from around the world and HSE data. The performance data are audited and verified by KPMG and Pricewater-houseCoopers.

▌ 'Tell-Shell' includes links to the Shell forums, e-mail and independent views.

▌ 'Energy Zone' is an area of general interest providing information on chemicals, fossil fuels, power generation and renewable resources.

Shell invites visitors to the Web site to make use of forums and e-mail.

The Cooperative Bank

The Cooperative Bank has developed one of the most comprehensive social audits yet seen. As early as 1997 the bank set itself some 68 targets, under three headings:

▌ *Delivering Value* covers such targets as profitability cost control, customer and employee satisfaction and supplier relationships.

▌ *Social Responsibility* includes ethical policy implementation, charitable support and community involvement.

▌ *Ecological Sustainability* focuses on such things as waste control, energy consumption, use of water and recycling.

To review its performance in these areas the bank consults with representatives of its various business partners:

▌ shareholders;

▌ customers;

▌ staff and their families;

▌ local communities;

▌ society at large;

▌ past and future generations.

The conclusion was that the bank had achieved 45 of its targets, 10 had been partially achieved and that much more work was needed in regard to the remaining 13.

These findings were audited by a specialist consultant – ethics etc.

In addition, three 'expert witnesses' were invited to examine and comment on the results achieved in the three areas. Mark Goyder of the Centre for Tomorrow's Company commented on Delivering Value. Richard Evans of the NGO ethics etc reviewed the achievements in the field of Social Responsibility, and David Cook of The Natural Step UK assessed the work under the heading of Ecological Sustainability.

South African Breweries (SAB plc)

This company's mission statement reflects its inclusive approach:

> *SAB is an international company committed to achieving sustained commercial success, principally in beer and other beverages, but also with strategic investments in hotels and gaming. We achieve this by meeting the aspirations of our customers through quality products and services and by sharing fairly among all stakeholders the wealth and opportunities generated. Thereby, we fulfil our goals of business growth and maximized long-term shareholder value, while behaving in a socially responsible and progressive manner.*

SAB's 2002 Corporate Citizenship Report covers its economic, social and environmental achievements. It is externally verified by the London-based consultancy Corporate Citizenship Ltd.

Among the highlights of its performance are:

▌ investing in employee skills;

▌ achieving efficient usage levels of water and electricity in clear beer production;

▌ responding to consumer demand for new and innovative products;

▌ setting and meeting high ethical standards against bribery and in its dealings with business partners and governments;

▌ contributing to local communities through corporate social investment.

In the opinion of the consultants, 'the accountability framework which took effect from June 2001 – essentially the internal process by which continued progress will be managed – offers a model for best international practice. It has at its disposal broadly comprehensive data about non-financial performance for the directly managed companies and partial data for those where significant influence is exercised'.

The review also highlighted some areas where substantive performance can be improved – accident rates, diversity in management grades, extending the Business Principles to joint ventures and key suppliers, and addressing a broader range of environmental impacts including recycling in the consumer market place.

RELATING INCLUSIVE PERFORMANCE TO EXECUTIVE COMPENSATION

It can be argued that setting targets for the achievement of non-financial objectives is unlikely to have a major impact on a company's behaviour unless the achievement of such targets is linked to executive compensation. In some cases this is now being done, as the examples below indicate.

Kodak

Eastman Kodak Co adopted a unique performance plan – the Management Performance Commitment Process (MPCP) – in 1995 to measure the performance of about 800 management employees with respect to shareholder satisfaction, customer satisfaction and employee satisfaction/public responsibility. The manager's MPCP score plays a significant role in determining base salary, stock option grant and annual bonus. In 1997, Eastman Kodak's board declined to award any bonus to its CEO because of poor company results, including company performance that was below target in all three key areas noted above. In 1996, the board cut its CEO's bonus by 13 per cent, in part because customer satisfaction was 'below expectations'. Another key component of Eastman Kodak's management appraisal process is the Touchstone Review, which measures how well managers evidence six corporate values: respect for the dignity of the individual, integrity, trust, credibility, continuous improvement/ personal renewal and reward and recognition. To measure these values, the company annually distributes a questionnaire to each manager's supervisor and a selection of the manager's peers and subordinates.

Du Pont

E I Du Pont de Nemours and Co bases executive compensation in part on environmental stewardship. Compensation for Du Pont's executive officers consists of salary, variable compensation, stock options and, in limited circumstances, restricted stock. Du Pont's Variable Compensation Plan provides approximately 8,600 Du Pont employees, including executive officers, with total annual compensation that varies up or down based on the performance of the company, the performance of their business unit and their individual contribution. In addition to financial criteria, variable compensation by business unit may be differentiated on a subjective assessment of performance in such areas as environmental stewardship, workplace environment, treatment and development of people, strategic staffing and safety. In 1999, payments among businesses ranged from 43 to 158 per cent of the average payment level as a result of the majority of business units receiving adjustments based on the above factors.

Intel

Intel's general compensation philosophy, as outlined in its 2000 proxy statement, is that 'total cash compensation should vary with the performance of the company in attaining financial and non-financial objectives and that any long-term incentive compensation should be closely aligned with the interests of the stockholders'. Intel's 1999 Employee Bonus Program (EBP) formula included financial and non-financial goals such as sales, customer satisfaction, productivity measures, cost reduction and employee training. Also for the 1999 performance period, the compensation committee on Intel's board of directors chose to base bonuses for executive officers on the EBP, rather than Intel's Executive Officer Bonus Plan. As a result, bonuses paid to the executive officers were dependent in part on achievement of the 1999 business objectives cited above.

Procter & Gamble

Procter & Gamble made headlines in 1993 when it released a summary of its executive compensation philosophy. In 1992, P&G had received a shareholder resolution on this issue that was supported by 17.2 per cent of the shares voted. The company's summary reviewed P&G's executive compensation principles and outlined its evaluation process. Among other criteria, the company identifies developing organizational capacity, which includes the advancement of women and minorities, as a key performance area. The company has established five-year diversity goals, noting in 1998 that minorities were being promoted at a rate greater than their overall representation in its management workforce. In addition, each business sector regularly develops business plans that include environmental strategies. A manager's performance assessment and, in turn, compensation are based on delivering results according to these strategies and plans.

Texaco

Texaco has placed considerable emphasis on enhancing its diversity programmes since the resolution of one of the most highly publicized and costly race discrimination cases in the United States in November 1996. (See Chapter 10.) Beginning in 1997, the compensation committee of Texaco's board began including the ability to recruit, retain and develop a diverse workforce as one of the performance criteria upon which it determines bonuses for officers and key employees. In a November 2000 speech, Texaco's Vice President and General Counsel noted that, 'For us, this is as important in executive compensation as profits, workplace safety and the environment'. In 1998, the company withheld a portion of bonus compensation when it narrowly missed one of its diversity goals

CONCLUSION
Systems thinking and the triple bottom line

The concept of the 'triple bottom line', referred to in Chapter 2, is appealing in its simplicity, but it can lead to oversimplification of the problem. Profits or investments made in the last financial year clearly come under the heading 'economic'; a community-based programme to provide clubs for young people is clearly 'social' and a reduction in the amount of emissions is clearly 'environmental'. In practice, however, these categories often overlap and become inseparable. For example, a 20 per cent cost reduction, leading to increased profits, would seem to be reportable under the economic heading. But if it is in fact the result of adopting strategies for recycling and waste control, should it not be classified as environmental?

Zadek (2001) makes a similar point:

> *Social, environmental and economic gains and losses arising from particular business processes cannot simply be added up. We do not know, for example, whether an additional four weeks of employee training, minus a dozen or so trees, plus a ton of profit, add up to more or less sustainable development... In fact we do not and probably cannot know enough about the system to understand in this sense the relationship between the activities of one organization and the whole system.*

However, the important thing about any reporting process, financial or otherwise, is not what it tells you about past achievements, but what it conveys about future potential. Sustainability is clearly about the future and, looking ahead, the categories of economic, social and environmental merge into each other. Take, for example, the decision to build a new company 'university' – as many companies are now doing. It will increase the company's skill base and hence make it more competitive in economic terms. It offers people opportunities for personal growth and development and so has a strong social dimension, and if it is designed to operate with minimum energy consumption and its curriculum includes training in environmental issues, then the environmental element of the triple bottom line is also covered. Where, then, does it feature in the triple-bottom-line accounting process?

What is needed, therefore, is not so much a triple bottom line that says, 'Look at what we have done to contribute to society and to conserve the environment as well as create long-term shareholder value'. It is rather a report which says, 'These are the things we are doing now that will help ensure the economic sustainability of our company and that will, at the same time, contribute to the sustainability of society and of our world'.

Also, the use of the term 'bottom line' conjures up the image of tasks completed, lines being drawn, scores totalled up, whereas the reporting process should ideally be a continuous one, looking forward as much as drawing up some kind of balance sheet representing past performance. For these reasons the term 'Inclusive report' may be preferred. Use of this term would also remove the problem that some companies use the term 'Social report' to describe a document which reports on economic and environmental issues as well as social ones.

As John Elkington (1997) has pointed out, 'Systems thinking tells us that sustainability cannot be defined for a single corporation. Instead, it must be defined for a complete economic–social–ecological system, and not for its component parts'. In the same way, the corporation itself is a complete economic–social–environmental system.

10

A licence to operate

Tomorrow's company recognizes that its long term future is enhanced by a supportive operating environment and acts, with others where necessary, to strengthen its licence to operate.

(RSA Inquiry, 1995)

FORMAL AND INFORMAL LICENCES

All organizations have licences to operate. Not in the formal sense of pieces of paper or certificates, although these are issued in certain cases (such as the airline industry or the operator of the National Lottery), but in the informal sense of whether people are willing to accept and deal with the organization. Anyone who chooses to deal with an organization is, in effect, implicitly granting that organization a licence to operate, just as anyone who elects not to deal with a particular organization is denying that organization's licence to operate, At a practical level this means that all organizations are granted licences to operate by several different parties (regulators, employees, customers, suppliers), and that each of these parties can seek to revoke the organization's licence to operate at any time.

(Neely, 1998)

In the past, there was a more tolerant attitude to corporate behaviour, or at least there were lower expectations that companies would or should behave ethically. As long as companies made the products people wanted and provided jobs, people were prepared to overlook their shortcomings. This is no longer the case. Better educated, more affluent, better informed citizens are much more concerned that corporate excesses should be checked and indeed punished.

The fact that increasing numbers of people have access to the Internet makes companies more vulnerable if their actions do not meet public expectations. Large global companies have attracted around them a whole array of Web sites devoted to exposing every failing. Investigative journalism and TV programmes like the BBC's *Watchdog* add to the flow of exposure of cases of wrongdoing or sharp practice.

Svendsen (1998) argues that companies are starting to recognize that in a networked world their reputations depend on communicating openly, behaving ethically, and developing credible relationships with their stakeholders and particularly with the communities in which they operate.

Charles Handy (1997) argues that a corporation is a society in miniature. It cannot divorce itself from the wider society in which it operates, or from the implications of what it is to be a civic community in this age.

Following an international trend towards privatization, many public service activities are now operated and delivered by private sector corporations. In the UK these include the utilities, public transport, telecommunications, television broadcasting, the National Lottery and some prisons and schools. In these areas a formal grant of a licence to operate from government is needed as well as an informal one from the public. Proponents of privatization welcome it largely on the grounds that improved efficiency and better service will result. Opponents argue that shareholder value will get priority over quality of service.

In these instances the task of the Regulator or the equivalent appointed authority is to monitor the standards of service in the public interest and to revoke or fail to renew licences if standards are inadequate.

In relation to issues of corporate responsibility, organizations of this kind are particularly exposed to public scrutiny. Dissatisfaction with the standards of public service, which was once aimed at government, is now aimed at the private sector companies who have taken on these responsibilities. At the same time this trend has been a factor in the steady rise in the number of companies embracing the stakeholder approach to governance. It is difficult for a business charged with the duty of providing an essential public service such as education to claim that it exists exclusively to create shareholder value.

As an indication of the growing importance of perceptions of corporate social responsibility as a shaper of reputations, a recent survey of 26,000 consumers conducted by Harris Interactive Inc included 'social responsibility' as one of six main categories used to gauge the reputations of well-known companies. An article in the *Wall Street Journal* (7 February 2001) reported on the survey and noted that Daimler-Chrysler, Home Depot and Johnson & Johnson ranked highest in perceived social responsibility.

The survey report pointed out that if companies were to behave more like responsible citizens they would avoid the embarrassment of running an expensive advertisement at the same time as receiving some adverse publicity due to some irresponsible act. Advertising

Volvo spent years building a reputation for making safe cars; not fast cars or sexy cars – but cars that gave their owners a feeling of security for themselves and their families. Yet in May 2001 the company suffered a great deal of negative publicity and the threat of prosecution for manslaughter, having been accused of failing to disclose a potential fault in nearly 20,000 cars that could cause partial brake failure. It was alleged that two children were killed by one car as the driver frantically stamped on a brake pedal that failed to respond. Documents obtained as a result of a raid on a Volvo dealership showed that the company became aware of the fault in 1997, alerted dealers, but did not recall the vehicles that potentially had the problem, merely recommending that rectification be carried out during routine servicing. The company admitted that the problem was unlikely to have been rectified on every car and that failure to disclose it may have been a 'misjudgement'.

This is an example of how a company's reputation ties in with its business success model. Volvo's share of the passenger car market rests largely on its niche position as the manufacturer that puts safety first. Anything that damages the company's reputation on safety issues strikes directly at the basis of its market share and ability to command a premium price.

people call this 'combined inactivity', the paid-for publicity being cancelled out by the negative impact of the company's actions.

Research by Columbia University indicates that about one-third of shareholder value in many sectors of industry is accounted for by company reputation. A study by Ernst and Young estimates that the intangible assets of skills, knowledge, relationships and reputation account for two-thirds of market valuation for companies focused on knowledge creation.

A company's reputation is an important factor in enabling it to recruit and retain highly talented people. *Fortune* magazine has established that the single most reliable predictor of overall excellence in a company is its ability to attract and retain talented employees.

LANDMARK CASES

Shell

The most well-known case in recent years is that of Shell. The reputation of this highly respected Anglo-Dutch company took a bad knock in the mid-1990s over two issues – the scrapping of the Brent Spar oil platform and its involvement with the military regime in Nigeria. The latter incident was the more serious and echoes of it still exist today. In 1995 Ken Saro-Wiwa, a writer and opponent of the regime in power, together with eight colleagues, was tried and executed. They were accused of conspiring to murder several people killed in political disturbances in Ogonland in the previous year. These disturbances involved clashes between minority groups and the government and between the groups and Shell over alleged environmental despoliation of their region and over the distribution of government oil revenues. The convictions were the outcome of a trial that independent observers considered unfair. In spite of appeals from other countries, including UK Prime Minister John Major and Nelson Mandela, the executions went ahead. Protests against Shell broke out all over the world. In the short term the impact on Shell's business was relatively slight, in that at the end of the year its share price and profits stood at record levels. Nevertheless, the impact was profound. The image of the company had been tarnished. Individual senior executives felt branded. The company's confidence in its scenario planning techniques was badly dented – it had failed to anticipate or deal adequately with the situation. The lessons were quickly learnt and Shell produced its first Social Report in 1998. This was despite the fact that in 1997, John Jennings, the retiring chairman, had stated that the Board could not accept the demands of activists that the company should produce one.

Predictably, reactions to the report varied from seeing it as a public relations exercise to welcoming it as a first step on the road to transparency. The company now stated that, 'Shell companies will no longer form joint ventures where partners decline to adopt business principles compatible with ours'. This does not remove the dilemma of what to do about existing relationships. Shell remains in Nigeria, where it has been involved since colonial days. Oil companies face particular problems in that they have to operate in parts of the world where oil is to be found. Once they decide to go to a particular country they have to make a long-term commitment because of the nature of the exploration and extraction business and, over time, democratic regimes may be displaced by other kinds.

Meanwhile, in April 2001, the US Supreme Court announced that it will allow a civil action to proceed in which Saro-Wiwa's relatives will claim that Shell aided and abetted the writer's torture and death.

Texaco

A reputational issue of a quite different kind hit another oil company – Texaco – at about the same time. In 1994 six black employees filed a race discrimination lawsuit against the company. This was the outcome of a meeting between one Bari-Ellen Roberts and the head of the Human Resources Department. She alleged that in the course of this meeting the executive reacted angrily to a number of proposals to improve diversity that she and a colleague had prepared in response to a management request to do so. In 1996 their lawyers released to the New York Times a tape of Texaco executives allegedly making racist remarks and conspiring to conceal company documents. This aroused huge media interest and generated a public outcry. The company's new CEO, Peter Bjur, wisely chose not to go into denial, but instead announced that the company would derive benefit from the affair by making the achievement of diversity a competitive advantage. He negotiated a settlement of the lawsuit for $115 million, a one-off salary increase and an investment of $30 million in programmes to improve the company's racial climate. He also sought the advice of Afro-American community leaders, following which he decided to produce a long-term plan to ensure that commitment to diversity became embedded in the company's policies and practices. In the end the company came out well, largely due to Bjur's open style and personal involvement.

Nike

The third high-profile case in the 1990s was that of Nike. In 1996 there were demonstrations by activists at the opening of the company's San Francisco store on the grounds that the company's products were produced under sweatshop conditions. At first the company's response was defensive. It argued that a poorly paying job was better than no job; that the issue of low wages in developing countries was not something any one company could do anything about and that protests should be directed to the UN; and that in any case Nike was dealing with the problem.

Nike was to some extent responsible for drawing the fire of activists to itself because of the high profile the company had built for itself and its brand. (It spent $280 million on advertising in 1994.) Its promotional expenditure, involving millions of dollars in fees to sports stars to wear its products, contrasted sharply with the miserly wages paid to its employees and those of its contractors. The company was accused of ruthlessly moving contracts from country to country in search of lower labour costs.

Following worldwide concern over its activities, the Nike Board changed its approach. First, it stopped the use of the hazardous chemical toluene. Also, it began supporting research initiatives and conferences on international manufacturing practices and instituted some independent monitoring of its production sites. The Nike case led to the setting up of an independent monitoring service, the Apparel Industry Partnership and the Apparel, Footwear and Retailing Working Group of the NGO Business and Social Responsibility.

By 2001, Nike's products were being manufactured in 700 subcontractors' factories worldwide. No person under the age of 16 is allowed to work in any factories making apparel and none under 18 in factories making footwear. As well as internal teams that regularly visit these factories there are audits by PricewaterhouseCoopers. The factory sites and the results of the external audits are posted on the company's Web site. Nike has joined the Global Alliance for Workers and Communities that was set up in 1999. This group identifies workplace issues, highlights compliance problems and provides guidance for the funding of education programmes, health clinics and community programmes.

The company's Community, Environmental and Labour Affairs Department employed 90 people, with two Vice presidents of Corporate Responsibility – one to manage the team and one for external outreach and strategy. Hannah Jones of Nike (Jones, 2001) states that 'Nike believes that the integration of ethical behaviour and sustainable development into every aspect of society and business is fundamental and essential to the long term health of the world and to our business'.

She goes on to say that 'that's an easy, blithe statement to make, when the reality is complex, multi-faceted, and there are no easy, one stop answers available to put consumers' concerns to rest'.

Naomi Klein remains strongly critical of Nike, as we saw in Chapter 6. Nevertheless, it is undeniable that the company is making efforts to improve its record in relation to labour conditions.

The lessons

Meanwhile, such problems still exist. At the time of writing, we are being asked to boycott chocolate because of the use of forced children's labour in the cocoa plantations of West Africa. The question immediately arises as to how far respected chocolate manufacturing firms in the developed countries were aware of these conditions and what they were doing about them. We can expect some sharp questioning at future AGMs.

When major issues of this kind arise, company responses fall into the following broad categories:

1. Denial. These companies treat the issue as a matter for the public relations function to handle, comforting themselves with the belief that sooner or later media attention will switch to other issues and other companies. Top management keeps a low profile and refuses requests to meet the media.

2. Defence. These companies take the issue seriously but attempt to defend and justify the company's position. Top management becomes involved. Lawsuits are defended.

3. Initial defence followed by acceptance of the need to change. In such cases it becomes clear to top management in the course of

conducting a defence that the weight of public opinion is over-whelmingly strong. Also, it is sometimes the case that as top managers are briefed they come to appreciate the full extent of the impact of the company's activities.

4. Openness, dialogue and jointly developed action programmes. In these cases top management gives clear leadership. Once rare, this response is becoming more common and will one day become the norm. More and more companies, before responding to an issue, take advice not from the traditional PR agency, but from one of the many specialist consultancy firms which have sprung up in the field of social responsibility.

Ideally, of course, companies should not be in the position of being taken by surprise when an issue surfaces in the public domain. The strategic planning process should involve scanning the horizon for such potential problems, asking such questions as 'What could happen that could seriously damage our reputation?' or 'What could happen that could put us out of business?' Even more important, 'What could happen that could implicate this company and its officers in the death and serious injury of human beings?'

Winning with Integrity

A comprehensive set of guidelines designed to help large and small businesses become more socially responsible has been produced by a UK taskforce established by Business in the Community. The guide, Winning with Integrity, outlines various ways for businesses to measure and report on their impact on society. UK companies are being asked to sign up to use the guidelines and report their progress on a connected Web site.

The taskforce describes the document as 'a first attempt in the UK to refine corporate social responsibility to its essential core'. It gives details of how companies can begin to tackle such matters as human rights, workplace conditions, the environment, and outlines various performance indicators that could help measure progress on social responsibility matters.

Nine companies quickly signed up to measure and report their impact on society against the criteria outlined in the document. These were Carillion, The Cooperative Insurance Society, Hasbro, Jaguar, J Sainsbury, Prudential, Severn Trent, Thames Water and Zurich Financial Services.

NGOs, GRANTERS OF LICENCES?

The number of NGOs operating in the field of corporate social responsibility is vast and their concerns and targets are diverse. Some focus on the whole range of issues – social, economic and environmental, others on a broad area such as the environment, others still on narrower issues such as the fur trade. Increasingly they are as global in their scope of concern and their structures as the global corporations whose activities they monitor.

A frequently quoted model of how attitudes to such bodies have changed is Greenpeace. Seen as extremists and left wing activists 30 years ago, when they launched their first dramatic challenges to governments and corporations, many of their objectives have now become incorporated into legislation and corporate codes of conduct.

NGOs generally have been moving along a continuum starting with protests and demonstrations, moving to dialogue with companies and from there to partnership in problem solving and monitoring performance. This trend has created tensions within the NGO movement, some supporters seeing partnership with corporations as the equivalent of sleeping with the enemy.

The challenge for NGOs is to justify their presence in the Boardroom. From where do they get their legitimacy? Clearly it derives ultimately from the strength of their public support which provides them with much more than funding. Public support in turn rests on established reputations for integrity and consistency as in the case of institutions like the Red Cross/Red Crescent Societies and Oxfam, the quality of their research, and the reliability of the information they provide. It is the strength of their public support that puts them, in effect, in the position of granting licences to operate.

COMMUNITY PROGRAMMES

One way in which companies are attempting to build a reputation for social responsibility and hence maintain their licence to operate is by means of active involvement in local community betterment programmes.

For example, BT's Community Partnership Programme is the largest of its kind in the UK. Its policy on community investment is to focus on the importance of communications, both in human terms and through the use of technology. The emphasis is on helping create the skills that will be needed for the knowledge-based economy, to the benefit of the UK and its people and, in turn, to the benefit of businesses, including BT.

All the UK's telethons (Comic Relief, Children in Need etc) have depended from the outset on special network services from BT so that they can accept telephone donations. In 1997 BT worked with Comic Relief to enable people to give money online. This was the first time that the Internet had been used in the UK for such an appeal and this has subsequently prompted other telethons and charities. Support for the voluntary sector also extends to using technology to provide information on social issues. For example, BT supports One World Online. This Internet site provides links to hundreds of voluntary organizations as well as information on major international ethical and social issues.

Some of BT's support for voluntary organizations aims to make an impact on a particular social issue. For example, funding for a new national 24-hour helpline has enabled Shelter to triple the number of people they help. BT has also supported ChildLine, the confidential counselling service for children worried about sexual abuse, bullying and family disputes.

Xansa (formerly FI Group) is another company that engages in important ways with local communities. Its community programme is focused specifically on support for the young unemployed homeless and education. Priority is given to supporting programmes that will help young people lead successful working lives, particularly through the medium of information technology. The programme receives widespread support from employees and endorsement from Xansa's community partners.

Xansa concentrates its resources on promoting and encouraging employee volunteering rather than on providing cash donations or sponsorship. All its offices and several customer-based teams have established programmes of support for local homeless organizations or schools.

By considering the needs of all stakeholders the company ensures that the programme meets its own business objectives and achieves real and measurable impact on the community. Seventy per cent of Xansa's Group Board Executive Directors are currently involved in the programme, either as representatives of Xansa on national or regional leadership teams or, in a personal capacity, as volunteers in Xansa's regional activities.

Business in the Community's Awards for Excellence

The Awards for Excellence follow a rigorous assessment process. Criteria are based on the Business Excellence Model. Entries are independently assessed by experts within specific fields and overseen by The British Quality Foundation. Finalists of the Programme Impact Awards are entitled to use the Impact Endorsement Mark. The Mark shows that a community programme has reached a standard of excellence set by Business in the Community, recommended by The British Quality Foundation and endorsed by the Department of Trade and Industry. The Impact Endorsement Mark provides an effective way of communicating that a company's programme is meeting real need in an appropriate way.

Business in the Community is a movement of companies across the UK committed to continually improving their positive impact on society, with a core membership of 650 companies, including 75 per cent of the FTSE 100.

The awards are in a number of relevant areas, including:

Enterprising Communities
Power in Partnership
Investing in Young People
Focused Action
Cause Related Marketing
Community Investment
Business in the Environment
Diversity Award Innovation
Impact on Society Award

The three finalists in this latter category in 2000 were BAA, United Utilities and Camelot.

The Ron Brown Award for Leadership

To be eligible for this US award top management must demonstrate commitment to corporate citizenship and corporate citizenship must be a shared value of the company, visible at all levels. In addition, corporate citizenship must be integrated into a successful business strategy.

Programmes that are eligible must:

▌ be at the 'best practice' level – distinctive, innovative and effective;

▌ have a significant, measurable impact on the people they are designed to serve;

▌ offer broad potential for social and economic benefits for US society;

▌ be sustainable and feasible within a business environment and mission;

▌ be adaptable to other businesses and communities.

Some examples of awards are given below.

Hewlett-Packard was recognized for its *Diversity in Education Initiative*, designed to improve people's economic potential by better preparing K-12 students to enter college and by increasing the retention, graduation and employment rates for under-represented engineering students.

In 1997, HP and the HP Company Foundation committed approximately $5 million over five years to the *Diversity in Education Initiative*. The programme supports four urban university and K-12 school partnerships (Boston; El Paso, TX; and Los Angeles and San Jose, CA) that initiate or expand effective programmes serving African-American, Hispanic, Native American and female students. In addition, 80 HP Scholars have been awarded four-year scholarships of $3,000 per year and as they enter their freshmen year of engineering or computer science, the promise of three paid summer internships. HP employees also volunteer as mentors and/or hire and manage HP Scholars. Via the HP Scholar E-mail Mentoring Project, during the school year students correspond with an HP employee who encourages the student and offers advice on resume writing and interviewing. The *Diversity in Education Initiative* fosters diversity in the workplace by maximizing the potential of not only HP Scholars, but also the mentors and hiring teams who welcome them at HP and support them during their internship.

IBM was recognized for its $40 million *Reinventing Education* grant programme. As the centrepiece of IBM's commitment to fundamental school reform since 1994, *Reinventing Education* enables IBM to work with schools across the United States and abroad to create and implement innovative technology solutions that are raising student achievement. Each project under the programme works to overcome a specific barrier to school reform, and collectively the projects address nearly every aspect of education reform: from connecting parents to teachers to data management and analysis, classroom instruction, teacher training and student assessment. US partners include 21 school systems in states such as Vermont and West Virginia, and in major cities. *Reinventing Education* is also in action in Brazil, Ireland, Italy, the United Kingdom, Singapore and Vietnam. Evaluative reports on the programme have demonstrated significant gains in both reading and mathematics achievement, and the Harvard Business School has called *Reinventing Education* a paradigm for business/education partnerships.

The 12th Annual Business Ethics Awards for the 100 Best Corporate Citizens

This US award nominates those companies that excel at serving multiple stakeholders well. It looks at corporate service to four key stakeholder groups (stockholders, employees, customers and community).

IBM (No. 1 on the list) was virtually alone in serving three groups well: stockholders, community and employees. More typically, Hewlett-Packard (No. 2) excelled in serving two: community and employees. No company excelled in serving all four, although the top 25 performed at least average in serving all stakeholders.

The data were based on research by Kinder, Lydenberg, Domini & Company (KLD), a social research firm in Boston, which ranks service to stakeholders on a scale ranging from 1, a 'major concern'; through 3, 'neutral'; to 5, a 'major strength'.

What KLD looks at in each area will vary by company. There is no set formula. But the following gives some idea of the range of materials examined:

▍ Under the heading of environment are programmes in place such as pollution reduction, recycling and energy-saving measures; as well as negative measures such as level of pollutants, EPA citations, fines, lawsuits and other measures.

▍ In the field of community relations lie philanthropy, any foundation the company has, community service projects, educational outreach, scholarships, employee volunteerism, and so forth.

▌ Employee relations matters are to do with wages relative to the industry, benefits paid, family-friendly policies, parental leave; team management, employee empowerment, and so forth.

▌ Diversity scores are added to other employee scores. This looks at the percentage of minorities and women among employees, managers, and board members; any Equal Opportunity Commission complaints; diversity programmes in place; lawsuits, and so forth.

▌ Customer relations might include quality management programmes, quality awards won, customer satisfaction measures, lawsuits, and so forth.

These are among the factors KLD will look at in assigning a score. There is no strict formula for how a company is evaluated. All available measures, news articles, lawsuits, annual reports, etc are compiled for each company – including input from the company itself – and a researcher then assigns a rating.

For example, in measuring community service, the company ranking second highest is *Polaroid*, with a score of 4.83. One thing innovative at this company is that employees make the decisions on charitable contributions. The Polaroid Foundation, which serves primarily Boston and New Bedford, Mass., has two committees – one for each community – staffed by employees who are overseen by professional staff. Donna Eidson, executive director of the foundation, has one vote like all other members. The foundation's focus is increasing self-sufficiency among the disadvantaged by building their skills.

EQUITY AND EXECUTIVE PAY

The compensation gap between top managers and rank and file employees has been growing rapidly in recent years – most noticeably in the United States, but also in the UK and other European countries. The term 'fat cats' has come into popular use to refer to this phenomenon.

In the United States, from 1965 to 1980 the indices of pay growth for CEOs and rank and file workers grew at about the same rate, thus maintaining a pay differential which had existed since the end of World War II. The gap then started widening and then explosively so. A sense of outrage has been growing and epithets such as 'obscene' or 'shameful' are frequently heard. A company can make the case for the level of compensation it provides for its CEO, citing the levels paid in comparable companies and the need to be competitive to retain top executive talent. But such arguments count for little when the public and employees make the comparison that matters to them – comparing the CEO's salary with their own. The sense that something is wrong has been aggravated by evidence that there is a lack of correlation between high levels of pay and company performance. Institutional investors on both sides of the Atlantic are using their clout to press for reform.

At the other extreme there have been cases of companies setting an example of moderation. Few would go along with the formula adopted at one time by Ben and Jerry's ratio of five to one between the highest and lowest paid workers. Peter Drucker has suggested twenty to one, an approach adopted by companies such as Herman Miller. In companies like Intel, Monsanto or BP it is more like several hundred to one, once options and bonuses are taken into account.

There is now considerable investor pressure for greater moderation in the allocation of executive options and for stronger links between remuneration and performance. Companies are urged to establish their own ratio of CEO pay to shop-floor pay, to explain the rationale for it to shareholders and to justify further any drift from this ratio subsequently.

There is pressure of a different kind for the extension of share options to all employees. In the United States the National Center for Employee Ownership estimates that 15,000 US companies now have broad employee share ownership. Participants in ESOPs (employee stock ownership plans) cover over 9 million employees and control, on average, between 10 and 15 per cent of the stock in their companies.

REPUTATION AND GLOBAL EMPLOYMENT CONDITIONS

The growth of international competition in a whole range of markets has seen the wholesale shifting of much manufacturing activity from countries with high labour costs to countries where costs are very much lower. This trend has created a number of challenges for the companies involved.

The social issues raised by such actions are twofold: on the one hand the destruction of jobs and related community sources of livelihood in the countries from which jobs are being exported and on the other hand the apparent exploitation of cheap labour in the host countries – a problem exacerbated when child labour or forced labour is involved.

Among the most publicized cases involving allegations of exploitation and abuse have been those involving Adidas and the Nike case discussed earlier in this chapter. Adidas was accused of using the labour of political prisoners in Chinese prisons to sew footballs for the 1998 World Cup.

Companies argue that they are in a competitive market and cannot afford to pay more than the going wage. Put another way, however, this merely states that the company fails to pay a living wage, just like every other company in the same labour market.

The SA 8000 code of conduct deals with wages and working conditions in global supply chains. The relevant standard calls for wages paid for a standard working week to meet at least legal or minimum industry standards 'and shall always be sufficient to meet basic needs of personnel and to provide some discretionary income'.

The SA8000 standard was developed by a process of extensive consultation with the business community, NGOs, trades unions and intergovernmental bodies, including major UN agencies. It has been endorsed by the international trade union movement and the International Textiles and Garments Workers Union (ITGWU) in particular. It has, however, been criticized for not reflecting the views of NGOs in developing countries.

Simon Zadek (2001) describes how two organizations with high reputations for social responsibility saw these reputations tarnished through failure to keep faith with their traditional values. In 1997 leading US apparel and footwear manufacturers including Nike, Reebok, Sarah Lee and Liz Claiborne formed the Apparel Industry Partnership (AIP), later called the Fair Labour Association (FLA), with a view to developing an agreed code of conduct and a process of monitoring and external auditing.

Levi-Strauss declined to join on the grounds that the adoption of externally imposed standards was not consistent with its own policy and approach to such matters. In 1999 the company closed a number of its US and European factories, ending a long-standing tradition of protecting its workers' livelihoods in difficult times. The company came under attack on the grounds that it had broken a long-standing commitment not to produce in China because of that country's human rights record. In fact the commitment had been not to expand its production in China but nevertheless its reputation was becoming tarnished. In mid-1999 it joined the FLA and the UK's Ethical Trading Initiative (ETI), thus accepting the need for external verification.

The ETI was launched in the UK in 1998 with government support and a group of leading retail industry companies as its founding members, working with NGOs in the field of human rights and the international trade union movement. Marks and Spencer (M&S) declined to join, citing its historic tradition of forming long-term relationships with its supply chain. At that time its reputation for fair dealing was such that it was unaffected by the growth of pressure on companies to become more transparent. The first major attack on its reputation came in the form of a Granada TV documentary programme revealing the presence of child labour in the M&S supply chain. Shortly afterwards it became clear that the company was suffering a serious drop in sales and profits. In an effort to reduce its losses it cancelled at short notice supply contracts it had held with UK suppliers for decades and subsequently caused outrage in continental Europe by trying to close its European operations without prior consultation. Although it reversed its previous decision and joined the ETI it had largely destroyed the reputational capital that had been built up by previous generations of leaders over many years.

REPUTATION, IMAGE AND BRAND

In July 2000, BP spent £135 million in a complete corporate rebranding operation. Out went the shield logo that had symbolized the company for over 70 years and in its place came a yellow, green and white sunburst with the slogan 'Beyond Petroleum'. According to an article in the *Independent* (19 April 2001), this has met with a mixed reaction. At first it was welcomed by environmental NGOs who interpreted it to mean that BP, looking to the future and concerned about climate change, was envisaging its own future in leading the development of alternative forms of energy. BP did not actually state this at the time, but nor did it go out of its way to refute it. Moreover, the reputation of its CEO Lord Browne as a person deeply concerned for the environment gave credence to this interpretation. In the intervening months

BP has pursued its oil exploration programme as vigorously as ever, however, and, according to the *Independent*, the BP Press Office now says that the words 'beyond petroleum' mean only supplying natural gas as well as oil and putting groceries in petrol station shops.

This illustrates the dangers in this field of creating an impression of a gap between corporate statements of policy and intent and what actually happens. BP is today the target of much hostile comment from activists and it is probable that the strength of their attacks has been heightened by the fact that false hopes have been raised.

One piece of negative publicity can undo years of building a reputation for fairness and integrity. Shell lists integrity among its core values, yet a report in the *Sunday Times* (15 April 2001) of a survey by the Petrol Retailers' Organization cast doubt on the extent to which this was reflected in the company's business practices.

Shell's critics have had their expectations of the company's behaviour raised in a succession of social reports since 1998. As a result, any scepticism remaining about the genuine nature of the company's statements will have been given fresh life by the results of this survey. Managers of petrol outlets were asked to rate their relationship with the oil company they worked for. While 76 per cent of Jet-owned stations said their relationship was good, only 23 per cent of Shell managers said the same. On a specific question on integrity Jet had 74 per cent saying 'good' but the equivalent percentage for Shell was only 17 per cent. (Texaco scored 45 per cent, BP 36 per cent and Esso 30 per cent.) This result sits discordantly alongside Shell's statement of values.

> *Having unshakeable moral values and sound business principles means we take pride in what we do. It gives us clarity when making decisions, it unifies and motivates staff, and it allows society to measure our performance beyond the generation of wealth. Since our earliest days, we have been guided by a passionate commitment to honesty, integrity and respect for people. We believe in the promotion of trust, openness, teamwork and professionalism.*

This report was drawn to the attention of the company and the following comment was received:

> *We acknowledge that we do not always get everything right. In the past few years we've invested considerable time and resources in improving our relationships with those people who run our filling stations. It is*

very important for companies to respond to situations where they are not delivering what some people would like. Shell is a customer-focused company, committed to providing the best products and services to all its customers. When things are not right, we always respond to make improvements.

The lesson is that if such a fine-sounding statement is made it must be lived and followed at every level in the business; it must be incorporated into laid-down policies and processes; not least in importance, it must be incorporated into the remuneration system.

Case: Camelot

At the time of writing, Camelot is the current operator of The National Lottery. The National Lottery Commission initially rejected its bid to run the lottery for a further period of time – a decision that the company successfully challenged. For self-evident reasons Camelot is a company which has been to considerable lengths to earn a licence to operate both in the formal sense and, informally, in the light of public opinion.

To this end Camelot produced its first Social Report covering the reporting period January to December 1999. It aimed to measure Camelot's performance as a corporate citizen against its values and objectives as a business and the expectations of its stakeholders. The company's aspiration is 'to live by our values in all our business relationships. We aim to be *FITTER* by achieving our success model as a company and in meeting the expectations of our stakeholders'.

FITTER is an acronym standing for:

▌ 'We believe in Fair Play for our people;

▌ We behave with Integrity;

▌ We can be Trusted to deliver on our commitments;

▌ We work together as a Team;

▌ We strive for Excellence in everything we do; and

▌ We discharge our Responsibilities to all our stakeholders.'

The social accounts explore Camelot's practice as a corporate citizen. They are not an audit of The National Lottery as a whole. However, Camelot is the most public face of The National Lottery – in the public mind Camelot is The

National Lottery. Some of the issues the stakeholders raised are issues that concern The National Lottery as a whole and are not within the jurisdiction of the operator to resolve.

The Social Report was designed to make transparent what issues rightly belong to Camelot as the National Lottery operator to resolve and what issues Camelot does not have the authority or jurisdiction to resolve because they rightly belong to other partners within The National Lottery. All the issues identified during the audit process as 'belonging' to another partner have been referred to that partner.

As a result of the audited Social Report, Camelot aimed to:

▌ 'Measure how well we live by our values and meet our success model;

▌ Indicate issues that we and stakeholders have identified as areas where we still need to improve upon performance to reach our success model;

▌ Outline strategies we are either in the process of implementing or intend to implement as part of continuous performance improvement.'

This first report did not include environment in social and ethical performance. Camelot did not see itself as having a major environmental impact. However, Camelot has developed a formal company environment policy and management infrastructure.

The company consulted, on a one-to-one basis, with 479 individuals, in 174 organizations, and an additional 5,469 individuals via other research methods. The social accounts and report were independently audited by New Economics Limited. In addition, Camelot set up an independent Advisory Panel on Social Responsibility to oversee the process. The members of the Panel volunteered their services to help and received no payment for their contribution. They are professionals whose experience broadly equates to that of the stakeholder groups. Individuals on the Panel took responsibility for a stakeholder group, examined the consistency of stakeholder consultation and reviewed and recommended acceptance of the social reporting methodology.

The members of the Panel who recommended acceptance of the process are: Louise Botting: Chair, Clive Morton (then of Anglian Water), Rodney Garrood (BP/Amoco), Anna Bradley (National Consumer Council), Stuart Etherington (National Council for Voluntary Organizations), David Bryan (Association of Community Trusts and Foundations – now Office For Public Management), Mark Goyder (The Centre for Tomorrow's Company) and Roger Clarke (National Federation of Retail Newsagents).

To own and embed learning from the reporting process Camelot appointed a Director, Social Responsibility, a small team dedicated to work on the Social and Ethical Audit and a development team of senior managers from across the business.

Camelot started with the company values and the intention to measure how closely its policies and practices were built upon them. The first stage of data collection for the social reporting process gathered together all of the company's existing policies relevant to each stakeholder group. Linked to these was an extensive existing range of company measures that were already being collected. Together, these formed the basis of the social accounts. Then, via active stakeholder dialogue, the survey examined:

▌ how well each group thought Camelot's policies reflected its values;

▌ what values and issues mattered to them;

▌ how well existing company measures captured their concerns; and

▌ any gaps in performance and strategies for continuous improvement.

The stakeholders were encouraged to voice their concerns. Gaps in existing information were identified and, where possible, additional survey work was undertaken to enable the social accounts to be compiled. Where this was not possible, a commitment was made in strategies for continuous improvement to undertake further research in the period of the next Social Report.

The company is seeking to embed the learning from this report into its mainstream business processes and procedures through incorporating appropriate indicators into its Key Performance Indicators and strategies for continuous improvement into the appropriate operational staff performance objectives. These will be reviewed as part of annual performance appraisal.

The 2000 report

Because of the delays and problems that arose in relation to the awarding of a second licence, Camelot had, at the time of writing, produced only an interim report for 2000. This report shows the progress made in 2000 on its 'next steps' commitments and records the outcome of dialogue with all its stakeholder groups.

Each stakeholder section of the report is divided into:

▌ progress on next steps contained in the 1999 Social Report;

▌ indicators (including trending data);

▌ outcomes from the stakeholder consultation.

For most stakeholders Camelot only undertook qualitative consultation for this report, therefore some of the indicators normally collected using quantitative research are not available. Where possible, headline indicators were updated and alternative indicators offered where this was not possible. Owing to the extraordinary circumstances of the year, the company did not achieve target for all of its indicators.

The report was produced in accordance with the AA1000 standard covering consultation, verification and reporting. This enables Camelot to demonstrate that it is tying social and ethical issues into the organization's strategic management and operations. As one of the commitments of the 1999 social report, environment is now included within the list of stakeholders.

The verifier for this Interim Social Report 2000 was Adrian Henriques, now an independent consultant, previously Head of Accountability for the New Economics Foundation and the lead verifier for the 1999 report. The membership of the Advisory Panel for Social Responsibility remained unchanged:

> During the course of our 1999 Social Report a number of issues emerged that had been raised by more than one group of stakeholders. As a result Camelot took some of the issues concerning the potential for excessive play to a cross-stakeholder group in early 2000. During the stakeholder consultation for this interim report it became clear that there are many issues that could benefit from such an approach. We believe that a greater degree of cross-stakeholder thinking will help the business to approach issues in a more holistic manner. We also believe it will aid greater maturity of understanding and appreciation of different interests and the potential for conflicting stakeholder viewpoints and hence conflicting demands upon us as a company. The company has undertaken some initial mapping work on the issues that would benefit from cross stakeholder dialogue and will use this as a driver to planning consultation over the next year.

In February 2000 a cross-stakeholder seminar was held to discuss strategies for prevention of under-age sales. Representatives from youth, family, gambling research and support organizations, National Lottery retailers and trading standards organizations joined Camelot senior managers from sales, marketing, retailer training and services, security and social responsibility. As a result of this meeting a comprehensive 'Tackling Under-age Sales' action plan was drawn up. This was discussed with the National Lottery Commission and an internal group was set up to implement the plan.

> As a company, separately from the generation of good cause monies, we also want to contribute funding, skills and knowledge to find innovative solutions to combat social disadvantage in partnership with the community. We want our community investment to be the embodiment of our values across our four policy priorities: Developing Skills; Opening up Opportunities; Supporting Communities; and Social Responsibility in our Industry.

For example, under the heading 'Developing Skills', 100 reading clubs have been set up in the UK in secondary schools to tackle the loss of reading skills that some children experience in the transfer from primary to secondary education. To date, 3,350 pupils have been involved in the clubs with an average of

2,320 pupils attending each week. Early indications have shown that reading ages have already increased considerably.

CONCLUSION

The term 'licence to operate' implies that various stakeholder groups – investors, consumers, communities – have the ability to take actions that result in offending companies suffering severe damage to their commercial interests. Setting aside those industries that are regulated by governmental licences, how far is this the case? The main weapons available are consumer boycotts and screening by managers of funds based on social responsibility or sustainability criteria. It is fair to say that, thus far, even in high-profile cases such as Exxon, Shell and Nike, companies do not appear to have suffered greatly, either in profits or in the price of their shares. Nevertheless, the pressures are increasing and can exercise a powerful influence on Board policy – hence, for example, the rapid rise in social reporting. Companies are more concerned than in the past to avoid the kind of publicity that might damage reputation. They need to be fully aware, however, that once they claim the moral high ground they will be more vulnerable to criticism than ever before.

Part III

Inclusive leadership and organization

11

Inclusive leadership

In Tomorrow's Company senior executives lead the way in:

▌ Articulating a clear and inspiring vision

▌ Creating a culture and an organizational infrastructure that enables people to achieve

▌ Maintaining the coherence of the vision, values and standards which guide the company

▌ Ensuring that the company supports, reviews and measures key aspects of the vision, such as learning.

(RSA Inquiry, 1995)

INTRODUCTION

This chapter is about the kind of inclusive leadership that will inspire and enable tomorrow's company to compete successfully in tomorrow's world. Its purpose is to offer some ideas to those responsible for leading companies as they face tomorrow's social, technological, environmental and economic conditions.

As will be argued in Chapter 13, there are clear early warning signals that the organizations of the early decades of the 21st century are likely to depart quite radically from the traditional hierarchical and bureaucratic structures with which we are familiar. Traditional, top-down leadership provided by people in positions of formal authority is increasingly irrelevant as new forms of organization are developed.

Despite these evident trends, much of the writing about leadership in recent years, on the part of both academics and practitioners, still reflects the underlying assumptions that leadership is essentially something to do with innate qualities of individuals and that leaders are charismatic, Moses-like figures who, from the tops of organizations, lead everyone else to the promised land of world-class performance.

This viewpoint is strongly challenged here and the ideas of some of the more progressive thinkers in this field are briefly summarized.

LEADERSHIP DEFINED

Leadership as an element in social interaction is a complex activity, involving:

- a process of influence;

- actors who are both leaders and followers;

- a range of possible outcomes – most obviously the achievement of goals, but also the commitment of individuals to such goals, the enhancement of group cohesion and the reinforcement or change of organizational culture.

From this it follows that the study of leadership cannot be validly carried on from the perspective of individual psychology and theories of personality. It is a social process and its study must embrace the study of decision-making processes and the functioning of organizations. Much leadership research in the past has taken the form of trying to identify the differentiating qualities of great leaders. The researchers interview people identified as outstanding leaders and try to tease out the qualities of personality, character and temperament that have led to their success. This is a highly subjective process and, taken to extremes, can become a form of hero worship. The profiles that emerge from the various studies are so different as to cancel each other out. Also, some of the 'outstanding' leaders featured in such studies turn out, as time passes, not to have been capable of sustaining their success.

The leader's personal qualities are undoubtedly relevant but they are only one factor in a complex process of interaction, and to understand what is taking place it is important to take into account the attitudes, beliefs and values of all the players as well as the organizational cultures in which the interaction takes place.

Leadership and management

Table 11.1 sets out the main difference between leadership and management.

Table 11.1   *The manager's world and the leader's world*

The Manager's World	The Leader's World
Exploiting financial, material and human resources (capital, plant and equipment, premises and labour)	Empowering people. Building commitment and alignment with the organization's purpose
Relationships with employees, customers, suppliers are contractual	Relationships with stakeholders based on mutual trust
Key tasks are planning, organizing, directing and controlling	Key tasks are defining purpose, creating shared vision and values
Legitimacy is conferred by virtue of the office held and the authority vested in it	Legitimacy resides in trust based on perceived competence and integrity

The 'profession' of management is very much a 20th-century invention – as ownership of the means of production became separated from control and a new professional managerial class emerged. Managerial authority is legitimized – at least in theory – by the role of the manager as agent of the owners of the business.

The legitimacy of leadership as a source of influence, however, does not stem from holding any particular office. Leadership derives its legitimacy from a number of factors. We accept leadership or not on the basis of judgements we make about the people offering leadership and such things as the trust we are willing to place in them, what we perceive as their integrity, their possession of relevant knowledge and skill, the extent to which their behaviour sets an example we are willing to follow and the extent to which we feel that what they propose fits the needs of the situation. These qualities and behaviours, it must be emphasized, are the ones we perceive; our perception of them is based on a range of observations filtered by our own preferences and values. Being human, however, we also have stereotypes and our judgement can be swayed by superficial characteristics such as gender, ethnic origin, age, accent or even style of dress. Our stereotypes may be more like Russell Crowe in the film *Gladiator* than a real-life leader such as Nelson Mandela.

The qualities we look for will be strongly influenced not only by our values but also by the culture of the organization. Workers on a building site will expect and will look for a different style and approach from those sought by senior civil servants, scientists in a research laboratory or the members of an artists' commune.

Kotter (1990) puts forward the thesis that whereas management brings order and consistency to complex organizations and involves planning and budgeting, leadership is about setting a direction, developing a vision of the future and strategies for achieving the vision. The visionary aspect of leadership is well exemplified by the farsighted way in which Ray Anderson of Interface set his company on course to become the world's first restorative company (see Chapter 7).

The key role of vision

Charles Handy (1992) associates effective leader behaviour with the ability to develop a vision. He sets out five conditions which, in his view, need to be met if visionary leadership is to be effective:

▌ First, the vision has to be different. 'A vision has to reframe the known scene, to reconceptualize the obvious, connect the previously unconnected, dream a dream.'

▌ Secondly, the vision must make sense to others. It should be seen as challenging, but capable of achievement.

▌ Thirdly, it must be understandable and capable of sticking in people's minds.

▓ Fourthly, the leader must exemplify the vision by his or her own behaviour and evident commitment.

▓ Finally, the leader must remember that if the vision is to be implemented it must be one that is shared.

In the UK, the Eden Project – the creation of two vast biodomes in a disused china clay quarry – provides a superb example of vision translated into action. In the words of the project's initiator, Tim Smit, 'Eden isn't so much a destination as a place in the heart. It is not just a marvellous piece of science-related architecture, it is also a statement of our passionate belief in an optimistic future for mankind'. The achievement of Smit's vision called for it to be shared by a large team of specialists in areas of expertise ranging from drainage systems to long-term finance; it required an act of faith and the will to overcome seemingly insurmountable obstacles; it involved a set of shared values summed up in one word – stewardship.

> *We are also here to show that environmental awareness is about the quality of life at all levels. The environment is shorthand for issues that impact on us in a thousand ways every day, from the food that we eat and the clothes that we wear to the weather we enjoy or suffer. Most of all we wanted Eden to be a symbol of what is possible when people put their mind to the challenge of regeneration and restoration.*

Kotter (1988) asserts that what matters about a vision is not its originality but how well it meets the needs of the key stakeholders – customers, employees and shareholders – and how easily it can be turned into a strategy which improves the organization's competitiveness.

TRANSFORMATIONAL LEADERSHIP

In recent years much attention has been focused on the processes of organizational change, particularly radical change of the kind that can be called transformational, and on the leadership qualities and behaviours involved in facilitating it.

Tichy and Devanna (1986), having observed a number of transformational leaders in action, drew the conclusion that they shared a number of common characteristics:

▌ They clearly see themselves as change agents. They set out to make a difference and to transform the organization for which they are responsible.

▌ They are courageous. They can deal with resistance, take a stand, take risks and confront reality.

▌ They believe in people. They have well-developed beliefs about motivation, trust and empowerment.

▌ They are driven by a strong set of values.

▌ They are lifelong learners. They view mistakes – their own as well as other people's – as learning opportunities.

▌ They can cope with complexity, uncertainty and ambiguity.

▌ They are visionaries.

Charismatic leadership

Some leadership 'gurus' argue that successful transformational leaders possess exceptional personal qualities of the kind that can be summed up in one word – 'charisma'.

Bernard Bass (1989) quotes Max Weber's view of charisma, which has five elements:

▌ a person with extraordinary gifts;

▌ a crisis;

▌ a radical solution to the crisis;

▌ followers attracted to the exceptional person believing that they are linked through him [sic] to transcendental powers;

▌ validation of the person's gifts and transcendence in repeated experiences of success.

Bass has studied charismatic leadership, using a questionnaire instrument, the Multi-factor Leadership Questionnaire (MLQ). He reports that charisma emerged as the most important element in quantitative studies carried out by himself and his colleagues since 1985 in educational institutions, the armed forces, business, industry, hospitals and other non-profit organizations.

In the MLQ surveys the following findings emerged:

▌ Charismatic leadership was found at all levels in organizations but most often at the top.

▌ Many followers described their leaders in terms that indicated charismatic characteristics. Some of these had complete faith in their leaders and were proud to be associated with them.

▌ Subordinates who described their immediate superiors as charismatic also rated their units as more productive.

▌ Charismatic leaders were seen to be more dynamic. Those working under them had higher levels of self-assurance and saw more meaning in their work.

▌ Those working under charismatic leaders worked longer hours.

▌ They revealed higher levels of trust in the leader.

▌ High correlations were found between ratings of the charisma of leaders and measures of group effectiveness.

All the above approaches have in common an assumption, explicit or implicit, that leadership is something that takes place mainly at the apex of the organization and is a process observable only in the case of a very few exceptionally gifted people. This view is being increasingly challenged.

Critics of the charismatic transformational leader concept

Nicoll (1986) argues that the 'hero' or 'saviour' leader is largely mythical. The myth rests on our wish for leaders to be 'higher, stronger and better than we ourselves are: our saviours'. This desire, he points out, places huge burdens on the leaders. The myth also implies a passive followership role for the rest of us. It causes us to underestimate the importance of the interactive aspects of leader–follower relations. Nicoll suggests that direction and goals are 'not dreamed up and delivered to us by a leader'. These messages are 'created within and through our interaction with a leader'.

In Nicoll's view, leaders need to begin thinking about their responsibilities and roles 'in startlingly new ways' if they are to be effective in the emerging business environment. They need to see themselves as part of an 'action dialogue' or 'shared trusteeship' – as part of a mutual, interactive process. They need to remove some implicit prejudices from their thinking – the polarization of leader and follower roles, the hierarchic bias, the concept of the follower as passive.

Nicoll's views are echoed by Warren Bennis (1997), who argues that 'our contemporary views of leadership are entwined with notions of heroism, so much so that the distinction between "leader" and "hero" often becomes blurred. In our society leadership is too often seen as an inherently individual phenomenon.'

Collins and Porras (1995), in their major research project which looked at the factors associated with long-term sustained business success, concluded that 'a high profile, charismatic style is absolutely not required to successfully shape a visionary company'. They cite William McKnight who served 3M successively as general manager (15 years), CEO (20 years) and chairman (17 years) – a soft spoken, gentle, man; humble, modest and unobtrusive. Others lacking obvious charismatic qualities included Bill Hewlett of Hewlett-Packard, Bill Allen of Boeing, and George W Merck.

Peter Drucker (1992) argues forcibly that effective leadership has little to do with charisma. He quotes Eisenhower, George Marshall, Harry Truman, Konrad Adenauer and Abraham Lincoln as examples of leaders who, while highly effective, possessed 'no more charisma than a dead mackerel'. Moreover, while John F Kennedy was possibly the most charismatic president in US history, few presidents got as little done.

In Drucker's view, leadership is about work and about performance, beginning with thinking through the organization's mission and articulating it, setting goals and standards. 'The leader's first task is to be the trumpet that sounds a clear sound.' The effective leader, he asserts, is also one who sees leadership as responsibility rather than as rank or privilege. The third requirement, according to Drucker, is the ability to earn people's trust, which is a function of the leader's integrity and consistency.

Level 5 leadership

Jim Collins of Stanford University led a research project (2001) in which the starting point was a search for companies that were truly transformed from being average performers into outstanding ones. He and his team began with 1,435 companies that appeared in the Fortune 500 list from 1965 to 1995. They looked for a particular pattern of stock market returns – 15 years at or below the average, then a transition point, followed by returns at least three times above the market average for the next 15 years. Only 11 companies matched the criteria. These averaged returns 6.9 times the market average for the 15 years after the transition point. This can be compared with the return of 2.8 times achieved by GE under Jack Welch between 1986 and 2000.

For each of the 11 companies the researchers picked a comparator based on similarity of business, size, age and performance in the period leading to the transition. Six other companies were identified as 'unsustained' comparators – companies that showed only temporary improvement.

No fewer than 22 research associates worked on the project and they sifted through mountains of articles and company documents, conducted 87 interviews with executives and analysed masses of statistics. They then drew their conclusions, identifying the drivers of lasting transformation of performance.

Among these, what Collins calls 'level 5 leadership' was critical to success. Level 5 leaders are characterized by a seemingly paradoxical combination of humility and shyness on the one hand (Ying) and wilfulness and fearlessness on the other (Yang).

Among the 'Ying' characteristics are shunning publicity, acting with quiet, calm determination, ambitious for the company rather than self, accepting full responsibility for failures, giving credit to others for success, developing successors. The 'Yang' qualities include unwavering resolve regardless of difficulties, and unwillingness to settle for anything but the best.

(The idea of five levels of leadership was developed during the research and is built on the assumption that level 5 is a high level of leadership effectiveness that is founded on four other capabilities, starting with being a highly capable individual, then a contributing team member, then a competent manager, then an effective leader short of creating enduring greatness.)

Further evidence of a relationship between effective leadership and a degree of humility comes from a research project by The Industrial

Society (1999). This involved asking some 3,000 observers to rate the performance of leaders on 38 competencies. Each leader was ask to complete a self-rating and then four ratings were obtained anonymously from their immediate reports or from members of other teams in the same organization.

The top 100 leaders in the sample were rated at 6.3 or above on a 7-point scale on all 38 items in the questionnaire. Their own self-ratings were, however, much more modest, scoring in most cases between 4.6 and 5.8. The bottom 100 leaders, by contrast, showed no such self-criticism. Their self-rating scores showed that they had an inflated sense of their own abilities relative to the opinions of the observers.

INCLUSIVE LEADERSHIP

Hooper and Potter (1997) point out that the key issue facing future leaders is: 'Unlocking the enormous human potential by winning people's emotional support… our leaders of the future will have to be more competent, more articulate, more creative, more inspirational and more credible if they are going to win the hearts and minds of their followers'. In the following part of this chapter some relatively recent concepts of leadership which have in common a focus on releasing human potential will be examined

The learning leader concept

Although its title says nothing about leadership, Senge's work – *The Fifth Discipline – The Art and Practice of the Learning Organization* (1993) – is in fact a very pertinent guide for the leaders of today and tomorrow. It is about leadership as the process of nurturing people's commitment to, and capacity for, learning at all levels of the organization.

The first of Senge's five disciplines is *Personal Mastery*, which involves a commitment to lifelong learning and is about 'clarifying the things that really matter to us… living our lives in the service of our highest aspirations'.

Next comes *Mental Models*. This discipline is about learning to become conscious of our own mental models and subjecting them to rigorous scrutiny so as to get closer to reality.

The third discipline is *Building a Shared Vision*. Senge stresses the value of a genuine vision, as distinct from a vision statement. The leader's role is 'to unearth a picture of an attainable future' that is capable of fostering real commitment. To try to dictate a vision is usually counterproductive, but to offer one for consideration and debate can start a very powerful process.

Team Learning is discipline number four. It is vital since teams rather than individuals are the 'fundamental learning unit in modern organizations... Unless teams learn the organization cannot learn'.

Systems Thinking is the fifth discipline. It is essential if we are to see the interactions between things that make up the whole and if we are to be able to manage change effectively.

In the learning organization, the leader has three functions. He or she is *designer*, *steward* and *teacher*.

The design work of leaders is about creating an organization's policies, strategies and systems and making them work. It is about integrating parts into a cohesive whole. The leader's first task lies in the field of vision, mission and values.

Stewardship is to do with the long-term survival of the organization and with its contribution to the wider society. It provides an ethical foundation to the leader's role.

The leader as teacher is continually helping people to see 'the big picture' – how the different parts of the organization interact, how apparently different situations have things in common, and the wider implications of today's decisions.

Leadership and creativity

For creativity to flourish in an organization it is not enough for executives to be able to come up with original thoughts and ideas. It is equally important that they should recognize, value and champion those of others. Indeed, it can sometimes be dangerous when a chief executive has a rich flow of new ideas since he or she may not be entirely objective when evaluating them. Executives who use their position of power to champion their own ideas run two risks. One is that the idea is not, in fact, as good as they think. The other is that although the idea is good it will meet with resistance if members of the organization, whose efforts will be required to implement it, do not feel a sense of ownership.

Fostering creativity in others, however, calls for some special leadership skills. Most people have learnt from experience to be cautious in

Learning leadership in action
JOHN NEILL, CEO OF UNIPART

Unipart was created in 1987 by a management buyout of the parts division of the former state-owned British Leyland (now Rover, formerly a BMW subsidiary).

In an interview published in *Strategy*, the newsletter of the Strategic Planning Society (1997), Neill tells how he turned round a company with a third-rate manufacturing operation, struggling to meet quality and delivery requirements. 'We knew that if we were to succeed in manufacturing, we needed to learn from the best in the world.' The turning point came when the company won a contract with Honda because of the learning that Honda was willing to share with its new supplier. He sent a team of six people to study with Honda's fuel tank supplier in Japan and the result of this learning was a complete change in both management and production methods at the company's main factory. Engineers and supervisors roles were changed and they were incorporated within autonomous teams, each with its own leaders and team bonuses supplementing monthly salaries. All the operatives now wore spotless white overalls as a visible symbol of quality.

In 1993 Unipart U – the Company University – was established. It now offers 180 different courses that have been developed and are taught by Unipart staff. The courses are designed to be practical, so that attendees 'train for work' and can apply 'this morning's learning to this afternoon's job'. Within the 'University' is 'The Leading Edge' – a state of the art technology showroom and training centre where all employees can drop in at any time of the day to work out new ways in which technology can help them unlock their creative potential. There is also the 'Learning Curve', a learning resource centre that acts as a lending library for books, periodicals, provides access to online information, and even supplies laptop computers which employees can use at home.

Unipart is a company which is led and managed on inclusive principles and is a Foundation Member of the Centre for Tomorrow's Company. Its 1996 annual review stated: 'We see the future of our company to be linked inextricably with the futures of our five stakeholder groups – our customers, our employees, our investors, our suppliers and the communities in which we do business.'

putting forward an idea that is at all radical. Conforming to the expected mould is far more comfortable and risk-free. The cartoon showing a company boss sitting at a conference with his direct reports and saying, 'I want your frank and honest ideas; don't hold back, even if it costs you your job' strikes home with all of us.

The stewardship concept

Block (1993) argues the case for replacing our traditional concepts of leadership with a new concept – 'stewardship'.

Most of our theories about making changes, he asserts, are clustered around the idea of leadership and the role of the leader in achieving the transformation of organizational performance. In his view, this pervasive and almost religious belief in leaders actually slows the process of genuine transformation.

Stewardship is about 'the willingness to be accountable for some larger body than ourselves – an organization, a community'. It is to do with 'our choice for service over self-interest', with being 'willing to be deeply accountable without choosing to control the world around us'.

Block draws a basic distinction between 'good parenting' as an approach to the governance of organizations and 'partnership'. The former is based on the belief that those at the top are responsible for the success of the organization and the wellbeing of its members. Partnership is based on the principle of placing control close to where the work is done.

Another distinction is between dependency and empowerment. The former rests on the belief that the people in power know what is best and that it is their job to create a safe and predictable environment for the rest of us. Empowerment reflects the belief that the ability to get things right lies within each person and is our willingness to commit ourselves to making the organization work well, with or without the sponsorship of those above us.

The most fundamental distinction and choice, however, is between service and self-interest. Today our doubts about our leaders are not so much about their talents as about their integrity and trustworthiness. For Block, the 'antidote' to the seductive, but ultimately destructive, force of self-interest is to commit and adopt a cause – the cause being the purpose and vision of the organization.

He sees strong leadership as incapable of creating the fundamental changes that are needed in our organizations if they are to survive and prosper well into this century. 'It is not the fault of the people in these positions, it is the fault of the way we have framed the role.' The search for strong leadership reflects the desire we have that others should assume the ownership and responsibility for our organization. The result is to concentrate 'power, purpose and privilege' in the one we call leader.

In Block's view, we pay a price for our tendency to attribute to leaders the ability to transform organizations. He makes the subtle point that 'the leaders we are looking for have more effect in the news than in our lives'. The illusion of the great leader reinforces the idea that things are only achieved as a result of the actions of individuals so that we give credit to individuals for results that have in fact been produced by teams. We become over-dependent on sponsorship from the top as a means of winning support for our initiatives. The danger for the people at the top, of course, is that they begin to believe their own press cuttings.

The relevance of the stewardship concept to the achievement of sustainability is self-evident.

A business leader who exemplifies the stewardship concept is Dennis Bakke, co-founder of AES Corporation. AES is an international power company founded in 1981 that now has a turnover of over $3 billion and operates over 140 power plants in some 46 countries. Bakke argues that 'the purpose of business and the purpose of AES is stewarding resources in order to meet a need in society'. Bakke believes that 'the stewardship of the earth and its resources for the benefit of all is a primary responsibility of mankind' (Manz and Sims, 2001).

The concept of the servant-leader

The term 'servant-leader' was first used by Robert Greenleaf in 1970 in an essay entitled *The Servant as Leader* (Greenleaf, 1982), the first of a dozen essays or books on leadership which have sold more than half a million copies worldwide. Greenleaf spent the major part of his career with AT&T in the management education role, and went on to work as a consultant to several major institutions in the world of education. In 1964 he founded the Center for Applied Ethics, now known as the Robert K Greenleaf Center.

Greenleaf was greatly influenced in his thinking by the novel *Journey to the East* by Hermane. This is an account of a journey undertaken by a group of people, members of a religious order, on some kind of spiritual quest. The central figure of the story is Leo, the party's servant who accompanies the group and, through his sustaining influence, helps them overcome difficulties. One day, however, Leo disappears. The group rapidly disintegrates and the quest is abandoned. The narrator decides to try to find Leo and after many years' searching, finds him, and discovers that he was, in fact, the head and guiding spirit of the Order, recognized as a wise and great leader.

Greenleaf saw this parable as conveying the central idea of his own approach to leadership – that great leaders are those who serve others. Larry Spears, in his introduction to a book of essays in recognition of Greenleaf's work (1995), identifies the following 10 characteristics of the servant-leader from his study of Greenleaf's work:

1. *Listening*: Servant-leaders make a deep commitment to listening intently to the views of others. They also listen to their own 'inner voice', seeking to understand the messages that their own bodies, minds and spirits are telling them. They spend time in reflection.

2. *Empathy*: Striving to understand others; not rejecting them as people while not accepting their behaviour or performance.

3. *Healing*: In the sense of helping people cope with emotional pain and suffering.

4. *Awareness*: Sensitivity to what is going on, including self-awareness.

5. *Persuasion*: Seeking to convince others of the rightness of a course of action rather than achieving compliance through coercion.

6. *Conceptualization*: The ability to think in conceptual terms, to stretch the mind beyond day-to-day considerations.

7. *Foresight*: The ability to understand the lessons from the past, the realities of the present and the likely future consequences of decisions.

8. *Stewardship*: Seeing one's role in terms of holding in trust the wealth and resources of the organization for the benefit of society.

9. *Commitment to the growth of people*: Valuing people beyond their contributions as employees and showing concern for their personal, professional and spiritual growth.

10. *Building community*: Creating a true sense of community among those who work in an organization.

Spears points to a number of ways in which the servant-leadership model has been influential in institutional life, such as its adoption by leadership education programmes in both the profit and non-profit sectors. One company CEO who is a strong advocate of servant leadership is C William Pollard, chairman of the ServiceMaster company, which employs some 200,000 people worldwide, has doubled its revenues every three and a half years for the past 20 years and is now turning over in excess of $4 billion. ServiceMaster Inc has been nominated the best service company in the Fortune 500 by *Fortune* magazine for the past 10 years.

LEADERSHIP FOR SUSTAINABILITY – AN INCLUSIVE APPROACH

From the various studies which have been reviewed thus far a picture begins to emerge of the kind of leadership style and approach which, in the years ahead, will make a good fit with the inclusive approach to business success. It is an approach that combines the following elements:

▍ the inspirational and visionary qualities of transformational leadership (but without the need to have a charismatic personality);

▍ the willingness to learn, and to facilitate the learning of others, of the learning leader;

▍ the idea of stewardship – of acting as custodian of the organization's reputation, resources and future;

▍ the perception of leadership as service – to the community at large as well as to the organization;

▍ the willingness to share the leadership role with others.

An outstanding account of the concept of inclusive leadership can be found in the work of Ronald A Heifitz, Director of the Leadership Education project at the John F Kennedy School of Government, Harvard University. In one of the most challenging books on leadership of recent times (Heifitz, 1994), he offers five principles to guide leaders:

▮ Identify the problem and the need for change; make clear to all the stakeholders the issues and values involved.

▮ Recognize that change results in stress and that without stress it is unlikely that real change can take place. The leader's task is to contain the stress and keep it within tolerable limits.

▮ Leaders should concentrate on the key issues and not be distracted by such things as personal attacks. They should not accept attempts to deny the problem exists.

▮ They should give people responsibility at the rate they can stand and should put pressure on the people with the problem to contribute to its solution.

▮ Protect those who contribute leadership even though they have no formal authority. People who raise tough questions and by so doing create stress should not be silenced – they can often provoke the rethinking of issues in ways which leaders with formal authority cannot.

These principles are extremely apposite in the case of those top-level business leaders, such as Bill Ford of the Ford motor Company or Lord Browne of BP, who are wrestling with the problems of conflicting interests in the short term as they seek a path to a sustainable future for the stakeholders to whom they hold themselves accountable.

For Heifitz, strategy begins with asking which stakeholders have to adjust their ways in order to make progress in solving this problem. How can the leader strengthen the bonds that link the stakeholders, focusing on their community of interests, so that they can stand the stress of problem solving?

Facing up to conflict and to the realities of the situation is critical to leadership. In the Ford case, as we saw in Chapter 8, the stakeholders who will have to adjust their ways are first and foremost the company's customers – particularly in the United States. But these adjustments cannot be made without corresponding adjustments by stockholders, employees, dealers and local communities.

Heifitz's ideas tie in with the concept of the learning organization and the need to expose underlying problems rather than treating immediate symptoms. Exercising leadership from a position of authority in change situations involves 'going against the grain' in that instead of meeting people's expectations that the leader will supply the answers, the leader asks pertinent questions.

Rather than shielding people from external threats, the leader lets people feel the threat so as to stimulate a thirst for change. Rather than suppressing conflict, the leader generates it; instead of maintaining and defending the status quo, the leader challenges it.

The evolving nature of business conducted by global organizations will also call for a fundamentally different kind of leader. Gone are the days of top-down, hard-nosed direction. Demonstrating flexibility and empathy, while remaining true to the core values of the organization and finding ways to circumvent unpredictable impediments, will be characteristic of tomorrow's leaders. These will be people who are inspirational; technologically savvy but not prone to getting lost in details; entrepreneurial; devoted to service, and inclusive rather than independent or autocratic. Additional key leadership competencies will include: the ability to develop and articulate a value proposition – maintaining it in a dynamic market and energizing others to buy into it; investing in a business model that guides employee decision making at all levels; committing to a culture that values mentorship and learning while aligning individual and corporate goals, and recognizing what it means to develop and manage truly transformational knowledge systems. The common characteristics of these new leaders are all related to issues that are more focused on the intangible aspects of an organization. Over time, those would-be leaders who are unwilling or unable to demonstrate these leadership behaviors will find themselves with few followers.

(Nevins and Stumpf, 1999)

Some inclusive leaders

John Elkington, in *The Chrysalis Economy* (2001), profiles several leaders whom he terms 'citizen CEOs'.

One is Dee Hock, founder of VISA in 1970. His view of the organization of the future was one that 'will be the embodiment of community based on shared purpose calling to the higher aspirations of people'. He invented the term 'chaodic age' to convey the idea of the need to combine chaos and order in a 'self-organizing, self-governing, adaptive, non-linear, complex organism, organization, community or system, whether physical, biological or social, the behaviour of which harmoniously blends characteristics of both chaos and order'. VISA evolved as a striking example, being owned by 22,000 member banks, competing with each other for customers yet cooperating by honouring one another's trans- actions.

Another is the late Dick Dusseldorf of Lend Lease. He described the company goal as ' the improvement of the human condition, not just that of any specific group, be it shareholders, workers, management or others'. Lend Lease, under his leadership, developed a sustainability policy and set up a Sustainability Council.

Elkington also cites Lord Browne of BP, Bill Ford, Ray Anderson of Interface and Carly Fiorina of HP, whose actions and policies have been described elsewhere in this book.

Case: Andy Law

Andy Law read classics at Bristol University. After a spell in the City he began his career in advertising in 1978, joining the now defunct Wasey Campbell Ewald. In the 1980s he became the youngest-ever Board Director of Collett, Dickinson Pearce International. In January 1990 he helped establish a London office for the highly creative American agency Chiat/Day, becoming managing director in 1993.

The turning point in his approach to leadership was his membership of a company taskforce set up by Jay Chiat in 1992 to 'study and construct what the Advertising Agency of the Future might look like'. The members of the taskforce christened themselves the Chrysalis Committee – the aim being to change the company as radically as a caterpillar changes and becomes a butterfly. 'The whole experience changed me and I realized that changing a company was a perpetual process, driven by a high ideal – like a long voyage of discovery, not a one-off plan that could be easily packaged and presented.'

A report with the title 'Something Else is Going On' was produced. It argued that business should be more ethical and play what was termed a Total Role in Society. The group took the view that if companies were to behave more like responsible citizens they would avoid the embarrassment of running an expensive advertisement at the same time as receiving some adverse publicity due to some irresponsible act. As advertising professionals, they knew that this was a frequent occurrence; they called it 'Combined Inactivity', the paid-for publicity being cancelled out by the negative impact of the company's actions. The group debated the stakeholder concept and envisaged Chiat/Day as a company that would make money by doing good, working with companies to assess and review the way they were interacting with society. To the intense disappointment of its members the Chairman/Founder did not welcome the taskforce's report and the group was disbanded.

In 1994 Law was exposed to further stimulating ideas while working, on the Agency's behalf, with the Prince's Youth Trust. He saw business behaving in an enlightened philanthropic way, but wondered whether businesses could change the way they behaved so as to integrate more with society rather than stand on the outside giving donations. He was taken with the concept of Human Capital and felt that it would be possible to unite the whole agency around this idea. He took the whole company of 30 people away for a weekend during which the aim would be to develop a better understanding of each other. They spent a full day doing things that challenged the boundaries of their comfort zones.

The next day Law decided to take the risk of being completely open about himself as a means of creating a high level of trust. He told about his early childhood in a home for 'Waifs and Strays' (literally). He revealed that his father was Indian, his mother English, and that they had been teenage lovers whose relationship had been unacceptable both to the middle-class church-going English community and the Sikh community of his father. Law was adopted at the age of three by a vicar and his wife and grew up in a series of vicarages in southern England. Law believes that from that day on he began to be seen as a managing director people could trust, in a company of people who would work hard to understand each other's strengths and weaknesses.

Another important influence was Anita Roddick and her exemplary company The Body Shop. After a number of meetings Chiat/Day was appointed The Body Shop's Agency for new media and internal communications.

In 1995 Jay Chiat sold his company to the US corporation Omnicom. Law now led a management buy-out, having first checked that the London office's main clients – The Body Shop, Cable and Wireless and The Midland Bank – would continue to support him and his team.

At this point Law took his team on another away-day. The aim was 'to invent the perfect company'. The consensus to emerge was that everyone wanted an open, inclusive, creative company. The answer was found in a rare form of structure known as a Qualifying Employee Share Ownership Trust (QUEST). It was agreed that shares would be distributed equally to all employees, but that because Law had so much extra service and had made such a singular contribution he should have a 10 per cent stake, which he would only be able to realize in 10 years' time.

A year later Law changed this arrangement and gave up the 10 per cent deal. He had learnt that 'unless you are prepared to give up something valuable you will never be able to truly change at all, because you'll be forever in control of the things you can't give up'. The fact that the senior executives of an agency held the same number of shares as the receptionist amazed people in the industry. For Law it was a major factor in the special nature of the company and its difference.

On the day St Luke's was founded, 25 per cent of the trust's shares were distributed equally among the employees. Those who leave must sell their shares back to the trust. But employees need not leave to realize the value of their shares. They may sell part, but not all, of their shares at any time, thus guaranteeing that all employees are always stockholders.

Law gives several reasons for going down the path of shared ownership:

▌ First, to have adopted the conventional model of a plc would have created an us-and-them, bosses and employees, divide that would have run counter to the aim of true cooperative working.

▌ Secondly, it would have been theft of the work of the entire company whose spirited and imaginative serving of the clients caused clients to stay with the agency.

▌ Thirdly, the few with shares would have been left at some future time having to have a sale strategy. But they wanted to create a company that would live beyond them, rather than create something and then destroy it for the sake of personal gain.

So it was decided that every employee would own shares after six months' qualifying service. This decision paid off in loyalty. Staff turnover has virtually disappeared and most departures were due to changes in people's personal circumstance rather than moving to another agency. Equally important has been the increase in client loyalty – a reflection of the improvement in the consistency of service delivered by a stable, committed workforce.

The name chosen for the new enterprise also caused some raised eyebrows. It was chosen because Saint Luke was the patron saint of creative people. To complete the picture of being different the agency eschewed smart West End offices and moved into a former toffee factory near Euston Station.

The organizational model adopted by the new company is based on three principles that are interconnected:

▋ Exploring. 'Our vision – "To Open Minds" – is there before us to remind us what will happen if we stop exploring. We will close down our potential imagination rather than open it up. That would lead to competitive disadvantage.'

▋ Meeting client deadlines with fascinating product.

▋ Being true to ourselves and our personal value systems. This is the responsibility of the six elected trustees of the Qualifying Employees Share Ownership Trust.

The problem of avoiding bureaucratic tendencies while growing has been tackled by what is termed the Citizen Cell Structure. This establishes highly autonomous groups of not more than 35 people. As these in turn grow they must split, amoeba-like, into smaller units.

Another Law initiative was to conduct a Social and Environmental Audit to establish a framework for ethical as well as financial and creative growth. The success of this exciting venture is not in doubt. Having been runner-up in 1996, St Luke's was voted Agency of the Year by *Campaign* magazine in 1997. Among its successful and memorable campaigns have been one for IKEA ('Chuck out the chintz') and one for Eurostar, featuring the former Manchester United star, Eric Cantona.

St Luke's track record is shown in Table 11.2.

Table 11.2   *St. Luke's track record*

	Revenue $m	Profit Before Tax $m	Number of Owners
1996	16.5	.46	35
1997	20.3	1.75	50
1998	18.8	1.06	75
1999	24.0	3.64	90
2000	27.0	4.36	120

CONCLUSION

At the heart of the inclusive approach to leadership is the adoption of a set of values, which places human relationships centre stage and which defines the purpose of the enterprise in other than purely financial or commercial terms. Such a set of values will include respect for the individual, the elevation of service above self-interest, restraint in the use of power and, not least, a concern for sustainable development. It goes without saying that leaders, if they are to be credible, must exemplify such values in their own behaviour.

The mental models which fit closely with such values are such that leaders perceive the organization as a complex network of mutually interdependent relationships, understand the links between the organization and the wider socio-economic environment and in particular see organizational change in the context of social and technological change. Senge's 'fifth discipline' of systems thinking, described earlier, sums up the required mode of thought perfectly. Leaders need to be aware of their mental models or mindsets and of what Schein calls their 'cultural underpinnings'.

It is this deep understanding of the nature of the interdependence that exists between an organization and its dynamic environment that provides the basis for the ability of leaders to contribute to the development of an inspiring yet achievable vision of the organization's future. As Kotter has pointed out, such a vision needs to be one that meets the needs of the key stakeholders and at the same time provides the basis for a strategy to develop and maintain a competitive advantage.

If the vision is to be realized, the cooperation of all the stakeholders must be won. Here the key leadership task is to build strong relationships of mutual trust and respect with all the stakeholders and to strengthen the bonds that link them.

'One plus five'

In the work of the Centre for Tomorrow's Company this task is encapsulated in the phrase 'One plus five'. 'Five' refers to the five key relationships – with employees, customers, investors, suppliers and the community – and 'one' refers to the central role of leadership in providing a vision and a style of leadership which empowers people in the various stakeholder groups and enables them to focus on how to achieve, and share in, sustainable development. This leadership will need to be found not only in the organization's management but also among employees, customers, investors, suppliers and the community.

12

Developing tomorrow's leaders

A society in which there is pacific commerce between its members, in which there is no conflict of any sort, but which has nothing more than that, would have a rather mediocre quality. Society must, in addition, have before it an ideal toward which it reaches... It must go on to new conquests; it is necessary that the teacher prepares the children who are in his trust for these necessary advances. He must be on his guard against transmitting the moral gospel of our elders as a sort of closed book. On the contrary, he must excite in them a desire to add a few lines of their own, and give them the tools to satisfy this legitimate ambition.

(Emile Durkheim)

The fundamental challenge facing business in the 21st century will be meeting the needs of consumers and shareholders... in a way that balances economic, environmental and social requirements... The task for business schools is to engage young leaders and give them a long-term vision of success that includes social responsibility. Companies must behave differently in the next century, and will require new leadership.

(Bill Ford)

CURRENT PRACTICE

First, it is useful to make a distinction between leadership develop-ment programmes and leadership training courses. A course, as the term implies, is a single event that may last anything from a day to several weeks, the purpose of which is to improve the effectiveness in leadership of those attending. A leadership development programme, however, is a series of related events, including courses but also such things as mentoring and coaching, job assignments, attendance at an assessment/development centre, learning sets or various forms of feedback.

In the previous chapter a clear distinction was drawn between two processes – leadership and management. When looking at current practice it is apparent that this distinction is not always made. Some so-called leadership development courses are really about developing managerial skills; some management development programmes include modules on leadership.

In the majority of cases, where leadership development programmes exist, involvement in them is confined to so-called 'high flyers' – young men and women, usually graduates, who are identi-fied as having the potential to attain senior management positions in a hierarchical structure. In only a minority of cases is this kind of devel-opment opportunity open to others such as knowledge professionals or technicians, let alone frontline employees in production or customer service. (One exception to this is the use by companies of outdoor training courses involving activities such as abseiling, orien-teering, canoeing or sailing, where young people drawn from the shop floor or its equivalent are frequently nominated. In most cases, however, such courses are isolated events and not part of a structured development programme.)

A key element in any leadership development programme is the opportunities for learning offered by job assignments. The early assumption of real responsibility is seen as providing particularly useful experience from which many lessons may be learnt, subject to appropriate feedback and coaching.

Kotter (1988) selects the following career experiences as being of crucial importance in the development of leadership skills:

▮ Significant challenge early on. People who are given opportunities to lead and to accept responsibility at a relatively early age learn from their failures and setbacks as well as from their successes.

Leadership roles in interdisciplinary project teams in which individuals do not have formal authority to fall back on are particularly likely to foster the development of leadership competence.

▌ Opportunities at a later career stage to broaden out through such experiences as a lateral move to a different function, secondment to a voluntary organization or assignment to a special project team.

▌ A decentralized organization structure which pushes responsibility outwards from the centre. Johnson and Johnson, 3M, Hewlett-Packard and General Electric are quoted by Kotter as prime examples. In Europe ABB has a similar structure.

▌ Processes which ensure that young employees are visible to top management and have opportunities for interaction with them.

▌ Recognition and rewards for those senior people who successfully develop leaders.

Paul Evans (1992) argues that an important tool for developing leaders is cross-functional mobility – moving people into jobs where they have to get results through people who have more expertise than themselves. He sounds a note of caution, however, pointing out that in many companies assignments are of too short duration, with the result that people start things but don't get to see them through. They then fail to develop good implementation skills.

Mentoring and coaching are being increasingly used as developmental processes. Obviously the effectiveness of mentoring depends critically upon the suitability of the mentor as a role model for a future senior manager and on his or her competence in the mentoring role. Where mentors are drawn from the ranks of existing top managers there is a danger of perpetuating role models that are inappropriate for tomorrow's world.

Self-development

Increasingly, employees are taking charge of their own careers and assuming responsibility for their own development, including their personal development in ways that are relevant to leadership roles. Now that few organizations can offer a 'cradle to the grave' career, people expect their lives to involve working for several organizations rather than one. Given this prospect, they can clearly not just sit around waiting to be developed. Self-development can be seen as a purely individual activity or as something best undertaken on a group basis as a member of a self-managed learning group.

Courses

Courses in leadership effectiveness can be grouped into two broad categories – open courses offered by business schools or training consultants and in-company courses.

Templeton College has developed a course for very senior managers, known as the Oxford Strategic Leadership Programme. The programme includes presentations on different aspects, types and theories of leadership; descriptive case studies of the process of bringing about strategic growth and change in organizations; syndicate discussions and team projects; and feedback, both from peers and tutors, about individual leadership styles and teamwork. This is a prestigious course, involving top-level practitioners as speakers.

Ashridge Management College has pioneered leadership training in the UK and between 1982 and 1998 offered a seven-day course known as the Leadership Development Programme, carried out as a franchise operation licensed by the Center for Creative Leadership, Greensboro, North Carolina. Distinctive features of this programme included:

1. Considerable emphasis on psychometric measurement. Participants are required to complete a battery of tests (taking up some eight hours) before attending the course. These tests cover intelligence, personality, leadership style preferences, vocational interest and aptitude for innovation.

2. Very strong emphasis on personal feedback by highly trained personnel and by peers.

The franchise has now lapsed and in 1999 Ashridge launched its own Leadership Programme, designed in-house.

Ashridge also now offers the Sir Christopher Harding Leadership Programme. Sir Christopher Harding was an outstanding business leader who strongly supported the view that business organizations should face their social and environmental responsibilities. Four companies with which he was closely involved (United Utilities, Consignia, BT and British Nuclear Fuels) have come together to create the Christopher Harding Legacy Project, the purpose of which is to create a special kind of development opportunity for tomorrow's leaders. The programme is designed to provide participants with:

- a tangible vision of values-based leadership;

- the skills to make a real difference to their organization and society;

- a practical opportunity to bring about a positive relationship with organizations seeking to improve the wellbeing of people in local communities.

The participants are drawn from business, the public sector and the voluntary sector. The programme is in three parts. First, during a residential phase of one week, there is a mix of skills development, inputs on the changing roles of government, business and civil society and visits to organizations that benefit from outstanding leadership skills. The second phase involves participants working together in small teams to undertake a 100-hour consultancy assignment for a voluntary sector organization.

Finally, during a further short residential phase participants will share their learning experiences and establish learning networks to secure their ongoing commitment to the goals of the programme. The programme is carried out by Ashridge Management College's Centre for Business and Society.

The Centre for Leadership Studies at the University of Exeter has offered a Postgraduate Diploma/MA in Leadership since 1993. This is a part-time course which embraces a Diploma, consisting of seven one-week modules spread over two years, followed by an optional one-year MA Dissertation. It is designed to help the leadership development of selected individuals, with an age range from late 20s to mid-40s. It includes many of the ingredients of the Templeton College programme, with the focus on the next generation of strategic leaders. Its philosophy is in line with the Inclusive Approach.

In another UK venture, the Leadership Trust Foundation (LTF) and The University of Strathclyde Graduate School of Business (GSB) have together developed a Master of Business Administration degree programme with a specialism in Leadership Studies (MBA/LS). The programme uses a combination of tutor-supported distance (open) learning, formal courses, experiential learning workshops and project work.

The core curriculum of the Strathclyde MBA, which covers the usual business functions, business strategy and strategic thinking, is supplemented by enhancement of participants' self-awareness, self-control and self-confidence through experiential learning in practical leadership and teamwork situations. The development of practical leadership skills takes place at the outdoor leadership development centre of The Leadership Trust, at Ross-on-Wye.

A leadership development programme that focuses specifically on sustainable development is Young Canadian Leaders for a Sustainable Future (YCLSF). This programme is sponsored by the International Institute for Sustainable Development (IISD).

IISD's goal in regard to leadership development is 'to provide young people with the substantive knowledge, communications skills, resources and practical experience necessary to develop international sustainable development policies and to become effective agents of change. This programme will give young Canadian leaders the skills and opportunities to shape their world'.

The programme includes a two-week training session on building sustainable futures in Winnipeg, a six- to eight-month international work placement and a one-week career enhancement session in Winnipeg after completing the placement.

The Foundation for Business and Sustainable Development is a non-profit institution that was set up in 1996 by the World Business Council for Sustainable Development to promote the business understanding of sustainable development and to encourage education and competence building, research and demonstration projects in the field of sustainable development.

The Foundation has, with the help of the University of Cambridge, since 1998 worked on a concept called the 'Virtual University' – a structured distance learning framework built primarily for Internet use. The Foundations' objective is to use this concept for introducing an operational understanding of sustainable development. The courses offered include:

I Corporate Social Responsibility

I Sustainable Business Challenge

I Global Scenario Challenge.

No More Grey Pinstripes: Preparing MBAs for Social and Environmental Stewardship (2001) is a joint report of the World Resources Institute (WRI) and the Initiative for Social Responsibility through Business (ISRB), a programme of the Aspen Institute. As a rapidly growing number of businesses discover sources of competitive advantage in social and environmental stewardship, the report identifies the pioneering US Business Schools and faculty 'dedicated to educating future managers to handle complex social issues and provide stewardship of fragile environmental resources'. The No More Grey Pinstripes survey was sent to the 313 US graduate business schools accredited by the International Association for Management Education (AACSB). Responses were received from 110 schools, with 60 reporting activity on environmental and/or social topics.

One of the top-rated schools was the University of Michigan Business School. All MBA students at Michigan gain basic awareness and knowledge about the importance of healthy social and natural communities for sustainable human development via a compulsory pre-term community citizenship field experience and related seminars, a constant stream of public lectures and panels, assorted modules within required core courses, action-learning projects in the field with non-profit organizations, a required ethics/governance course, and innovative initiatives arising from student organizations. MBAs who wish to acquire deeper/broader insights and skills regarding the management of business, nature and society relations can pursue a broad array of relevant elective courses with the School, co-listed courses offered in other parts of the university, and various Certificate programmes (eg in Industrial Ecology). Finally, students who wish to orient their careers to becoming leaders of organizations dedicated to ecological and social sustainability can seek admittance into highly selective three-year dual degree programmes, such as the Corporate Environment Management Program (CEMP), leading to both an MBA and MS in Natural Resources/Environment. CEMP develops future private and public leaders possessing the requisite mix of scientific literacy, global vision, entrepreneurial creativity and management skills needed to achieve sustainable commerce and governance. CEMP students are trained to deal with complex social, ecological and economic interdependencies via an emphasis on transdisciplinary approaches, systems thinking, public–private partnerships, and experiential learning in the field.

Expedition training

There has been considerable growth in the use of 'expedition' training along the lines pioneered by the Outward Bound Trust. Several UK organizations now offer a similar type of training for junior and middle levels of management – including the Leadership Trust, Endeavour Training and Brathay Hall. The courses offer a variety of physically challenging and adventurous activities such as abseiling, canoeing, rock climbing and orienteering. The underlying assumption is that the lessons learnt in the process of sharing hardships and overcoming stress and fear as a member of a team make participants more effective as leaders. This type of programme, as distinct from those at business schools or company management centres, is more often used for the development of frontline employees.

Best practice

In the UK the findings of research by the National Council for Education in Management and Leadership were published under the title of *Leadership Development* (2001). The researchers looked at leadership development 'best practice' in a number of 'blue chip' companies with a strong UK base. They found that whilst there was no single strategy that would ensure good practice, there were 10 principles that characterized best practice. They grouped these under three headings as follows:

▌ Strategic imperatives
   – Leadership development, to be effective, must be driven from the top with specialist support.
   – It should be designed to support and drive the business.
   – Consideration should be given to the leadership concept (eg 'hero-type' leadership or team leadership), cultural differences and different approaches to development.

▌ Strategic choices
   – An articulated framework for career development.
   – Variable amounts of formal and informal development.
   – 'Grow your own' senior people or hire them in.
   – The use of Business Schools or other external resources.
   – The value of competency frameworks and performance management.
   – Retention and reward strategies.

▌ Evaluation
  – An explicit and shared evaluation process.

Weaknesses of training programmes

Leadership training programmes have some serious flaws. Many of them are more about management skills than they are about leadership, focusing on things like planning or project management. It is too easily assumed that lessons learnt while performing exercises on training courses are transferable to the work situation. Also, employers make the mistake of believing that training programmes will, by themselves, develop leaders.

Nevins and Stumpf (1999) argue that the traditional learning methods most commonly employed in leadership training provide learning experiences that are inadequate in several respects, including:

1. They fail to provide accurate, timely feedback in the areas most critical for success. Feedback enables people to update their expectations regarding the outcomes of their future actions. The timeliness of feedback is important. The value of computer-based learning results, in part, from the way it can provide immediate feedback. The growing use of 360-degree feedback in work organizations provides vitally important information on how others see one's leadership style and effectiveness. Simulations, role-playing and other experiential activities provide opportunities for peers, instructors and observers to provide timely feedback.

2. They should include lifelike situations, including crises, for learning under pressure (similar to state-of-the-art flight simulators for pilots). The invention of complex, behaviourally focused leadership simulations such as war games has helped to reduce this gap in leadership development. Such simulations involve intensive, interactive experiences that recreate organizational life in important decision-making groups. They generate leadership behaviours that are easily recalled by participants and observed by a trained staff, facilitating later review and discussions.

3. They should permit problem solving and issue diagnosis as a central part of the experience. Much of the challenge is in providing a partially defined yet still ambiguous situation for learners to tackle.

4. They should use master–apprentice relationships in the learning process so as to guide an effective ongoing development process:

> *Business educators in formal educational programs are rarely masters of business. Their ability to develop students as apprentices is minimal, and their interest in doing so is often equally low. In contrast with other professions, one might be led to believe that management is something that need not be known in order to be taught. Medicine, dentistry and the performing arts – among other professions – seem to have made a different assumption. A significant degree of personal mastery is necessary for the key skills and concepts to be passed from one person (the master) to another (the apprentice). Formal business education's reliance on books, lectures and instructors who do not practice what they teach is a weakness of many leadership development courses.*

5. They should challenge a participant on the development programme by placing him or her on the firing line to succeed or fail based on decisions and actions (consider survival training for the military or difficult developmental assignments for multinational executives):

> *Significant life events, particularly those that are unexpected and personally threatening, have the ability to create years of learning in only a few moments. Some unexpected events are disasters that start people thinking again about the safety of others and the environment. Other unexpected events are less severe – they may be breaks from ways people have done things in the past, or they may be events that go beyond the responsible parties' ability to forecast.*

Effective professional development in the future will focus less on rote learning of tools and study of cases, and more on experiences that guide the learners to ask such questions as 'What can go wrong?' and 'What might the situation be if we projected the current information out 15 years?'.

A LEADERSHIP DEVELOPMENT PROCESS BASED ON INCLUSIVE PRINCIPLES

A possible process for developing tomorrow's leaders is set out below.

1. The design process of the programme should involve the chief executive and the top team. The first step is to revisit the organization's purpose and values and to consider what kind of leadership style and approach would be best aligned with these and most appropriate to the future needs of the organization. In particular, in the private sector, they need to think through ways in which young people in today's acquisitive, consuming, hedonistic society might be influenced to see leadership as a service to the community rather than simply as a road to share options and high living. They should consult widely while seeking to reach a consensus on these matters, not only with their transactional stakeholders but also with representatives of different ethnic communities and religious groups, the Business Schools and forward-looking NGOs.

   There are many useful models to help in this process and, of course, elements from different models can be combined. Some of the most commonly cited ones have been reviewed in the previous chapter:

   Jim Collins' 'level 5 leadership'
   Block's 'stewardship'
   Greenleaf's 'servant leadership'
   Senge's leader as 'designer, steward and teacher'
   Heifitz's leader as 'educator'

2. The next step is to identify those with the potential to develop the ability to lead. The search for these needs to be cast much wider than the traditional selection of high flyers from an elite group such as graduate management trainees. Tomorrow's organization will need effective leadership of teams of all kinds – in the research laboratory, on the shop floor, in the sales force – indeed in every situation in which people need to be aligned behind a clear vision and sense of purpose. Identifying future potential is, of course, a challenging task and one that inevitably involves a degree of subjective judgement. The degree of subjectivity can, however, be reduced by the deployment of a range of assessment methods, including bio-data, employment track record, psychometric tests and various group exercises which provide an opportunity to display leadership qualities.

   Recent practice has increasingly involved the use of 360-degree assessment of potential by superiors, peers and subordinates – a process that has a high degree of face validity.

BP is one company that uses this approach. Its senior management has defined nine Leadership Competencies required for leadership success. Following some careful professional/technical work, a 45-item questionnaire based on these competencies was designed and piloted. This was then used to provide 360-degree assessments for the top 2,000 managers. There is no reason, however, why similar techniques could not be applied on a much wider basis.

An important factor to be taken into account is the individual's motivation to lead and the values upon which it is based. This should be explored in the context of providing young people with as deep an understanding as possible of what the leadership role entails in terms of acceptance of responsibility, the restrained use of power, service above privilege and the importance of integrity.

3. Those selected to participate in the programme should then be given assignments which will constitute the principal means of developing them. These assignments, according to a research group at the Center for Creative Leadership (McCall *et al*, 1988), should involve five or more of the following challenges:

   ▌ Success and failure should both be possible and evident to others.

   ▌ The situation should involve the leader being left alone to cope without access to higher authority.

   ▌ It should involve working with new people or unusually large numbers of people or people known to be difficult.

   ▌ Working under unusually severe pressure, eg very tight deadlines or very substantial cost at risk.

   ▌ Having to influence people over whom the leader has no authority.

   ▌ Coping with change, uncertainty or ambiguity.

   ▌ Performing while being closely watched by people who have the power to influence future career prospects.

▌ Exercising team leadership in stretching circumstances.

▌ Handling a task with major strategic implications or which is intellectually stretching.

▌ Working with a particularly effective or ineffective boss.

▌ Dealing with a situation in which some key factor is missing, eg adequate resources or vital knowledge.

The researchers suggest no fewer than 88 specific developmental assignments. These are divided into five groups as follows:

▌ small projects and start-ups which mainly emphasize persuasion, learning new things quickly, working under time pressure and with new people;

▌ small scope 'jumps' in responsibility which emphasize team-building, individual responsibility, dealing with the boss and time pressures;

▌ small strategic assignments which emphasize intellectual demands and influencing skills;

▌ course work and coaching assignments that reveal gaps in one's own knowledge or skill;

▌ activities away from work – for example, in community service.

These activities should include, wherever possible, opportunities to meet and interact with the organization's stakeholders and involvement with local communities, voluntary organizations and other bodies external to the organization.

4. Throughout the period of time during which successive developmental assignments are carried out, the participants in the programme should be supported in the following ways:

▌ By being assigned to self-managed action learning groups of four to six persons, meeting perhaps quarterly, to share learning and experience. Each group should have its own learning budget, enabling it to call on outside help if required. If the organization is an international one, these groups should ideally be cross-cultural in composition.

▮ Each participant should be allocated a mentor. Mentors can be drawn from successful leaders within the organization, in which case they should be trained for the role and should be appropriate role models in terms of their own leadership style and behaviour. Alternatively, they can be drawn from specialists in mentoring or appropriate role models from outside the organization.

▮ They should receive prompt and regular feedback on their progress. This feedback should review not only what each individual has achieved but also the manner of the achievement and its consistency with the organization's values. Feedback should be sought from stakeholder groups as well as from peers and line management.

5. External programmes can be used in two ways. One – the most prevalent currently – is for skills development. Participants should be able to practise and develop such skills as public speaking, conducting interviews, chairing meetings alongside strangers so that taking risks, experimenting with different approaches and being prepared to make a fool of oneself can occur without the inhibition of performing in front of one's colleagues.

The other use is potentially more valuable and applies more to open courses where the participants are from different companies or, better still, different sectors of society. This use is to build sustainable networks of future business leaders, linked by having debated their values and developed a common approach to such issues as business's responsibility to society, and the ultimate purpose of economic activity. It is helpful if participants are exposed to real-life situations in which their values can be tested. For example, groups can be asked to take on such tasks as:

▮ Plan and then carry out a day's outing for children with learning disabilities.

▮ Prepare and then deliver a presentation to teenage pupils in an inner city school in a deprived area to explain how industry benefits society.

▌ Design and conduct a survey of the attitudes of young people from ethnic minorities towards job opportunities and discrimination in employment.

CONCLUSION

Leadership development should start at the point of recruitment and should be available to a wide cross-section of employees. Induction programmes, job experiences, career development processes and mentoring should be combined with training to foster leadership potential and encourage the acquisition of the requisite skills and values. The whole culture of business needs to change to become more nourishing in respect of creativity and vision. The Business Schools, too, need to place more emphasis on the social sciences and the humanities.

13

Inclusive organizations

'What makes top performing companies different is their organizational arrangements. Specifically, they are better organized to meet the needs of their people, so that they attract better people than their competitors do and their people are more greatly motivated to do a superior job. They are better organized to meet the needs of their customers so that they are either more innovative in meeting customer needs, more reliable in meeting customer expectations, better able to deliver their product or service more cheaply, or some combination of the above.

(Robert Waterman, 1994)

INTRODUCTION

In the context of tomorrow's business environment, we can expect important changes which will affect the ways in which organizations function, with related changes in structures, processes and, not least, organizational cultures. Among the forces that will influence such changes, the following are already discernible:

▌ the impact of new technology on the external and internal communication processes of organizations;

- the growth in importance of knowledge management and the increasing recognition of the importance of human capital;

- changing societal values, leading to challenges to the power of large corporations;

- the development of strategic alliances or 'co-opetition' and supply chain partnerships, calling for leadership in situations where position power is irrelevant;

- growing awareness of the need for actions aimed at ensuring sustainable development.

Although each company will need to develop its own success model, there are some common issues under these headings that all companies will have to face and to which their organizations will need to adapt if they are to remain competitive.

THE IMPACT OF NEW TECHNOLOGY

As we enter the 21st century and the era of the New Economy there is a rush on the part of business to exploit the new opportunities thrown up by the Internet. Investors scrambled to invest in dotcom companies that had yet to make a profit. Blue-chip companies in what has become known as the old economy reeled as their shares went into relative decline.

Clearly, the revolution in information technology has brought about a whole new field of business activity known as e-commerce, but this may not, in the end, constitute its most important impact on our world. We may find that even greater consequences follow from its impact on the design of organizations and on the way they function.

In traditional organizational hierarchies some of the layers of management were not there to make decisions or supervise operations; their function was rather to act as relays for information, rather like boosters on a telephone cable to collect, amplify, interpret and disseminate information. Modern technology does a better job and tomorrow's technology will do it even better. A new principle, the span of communication, is taking the place of the old span of control. The number of people reporting to an executive is now limited only by the subordinates' willingness to take responsibility for their own communications and relationships. Those subordinates can be located in any part of the world. Being connected replaces being in control.

The key concept in all this is 'connectivity'. People are now more directly and cheaply connected to other people; customers to suppliers; organizations to organizations; networks to networks; educational institutions to students; activist groups to other activist groups; terrorist organizations to other terrorist organizations and so on.

Few people doubt the impact these developments will have on the shape and ways of working of business organizations. The precise nature of the changes is as yet unclear. Organizations, particularly large ones, change slowly; it is often the case that those who make decisions about organization and strategy are less familiar with the potential of the new technologies than younger people at more junior levels. Also, Drucker (1986) makes the point that the organization chart of the information-based company can look perfectly conventional. It behaves, however, quite differently, and requires different behaviour of its members.

One thing at least is clear. The new technology creates the possibility of organization-wide networks and of networks of organizations. It will be a 'joined-up world'. Traditionally, communications in large organizations have been mainly in the vertical dimension, with instructions flowing down and information flowing up; the latter years of the 20th century saw the growth of horizontal communication paths following the supply chain. Today we are seeing the growth of communication links in all directions – diagonal as well as vertical and horizontal. Hierarchies may continue to exist on paper, but the reality of organizational life will be very different. Exercising control from the top will become much more difficult; while at the same time coordination of activities across organizational boundaries, both internal and external, should greatly improve.

Indeed, the boundaries of the modern organization are often far from clear. Joint ventures and strategic alliances and other forms of linking with suppliers, customers and business partners are changing the nature of management as it becomes less and less an internal function and executives become responsible for managing a diverse range of relationships with these external groups. What were once arm's-length transactions are now becoming close and enduring relationships of interdependence. Dell Computers and Cisco Systems are prime examples.

Developments in communications technologies also radically reduce the need for an organization and its members to occupy a fixed space. The traditional concepts of company HQ consisting of a large building in which each manager has an allocated office space are rendered obsolete by connectivity. A new phenomenon, the virtual organization, takes its place. Brown (1999) describes Verifone (since 1997 part of Hewlett-Packard) as 'perhaps the best known virtual company in the world'. Verifone is a world leader in point-of-sale automation systems. The challenge was to develop a virtual organization operating 24 hours a day in over 100 locations. The notion of a head office was abandoned. Responsibilities are distributed locally throughout the global network. The CEO leads by visiting customers, staff and suppliers throughout the world on a regular basis. Talent is recruited where it exists – there is a major IT centre in Bangalore, for example.

All corporate information is available, online, worldwide, for immediate access and e-mail is used to reinforce company philosophy and values.

Brown also cites Oticon, a Danish hearing aid manufacturer, as another company using IT to achieve radical change. In order to achieve a step change in the company's ability to compete with large corporations such as Sony, Philips and Siemens, the CEO set out to create what he called 'a spaghetti organization of rich strands in a chaotic network'. He set out to rethink the organization so that interaction, collaboration and connectivity of people, customers, suppliers and ideas were maximized.

On arrival at work Oticon employees sign in on a PC and their arrival is then broadcast on numerous TV screens located around the open plan building. As visitors arrive in the reception area the first thing they see is a large Perspex tube from which flows a stream of shredded paper. The source of this is the post room where 95 per cent of incoming mail is scanned and shredded. Coffee bars are scattered around the building, with counters for informal meetings standing up. Mobile workstations with limited storage discourage the accumulation of paper. Mobile phones keep staff in contact with each other. Dialogue rooms have circular sofas and small coffee tables.

The ideas behind this approach are important. Traditional departments and job titles are abandoned in favour of project teams. Staff are freed from the traditional ties of office work (fixed hours of work, job descriptions, reports, etc.) and are encouraged to get more interested in stimulating and challenging work than in formal status and titles. The office space is made open and attractive and designed so as to maximize human interaction and a sense of community. Oticon's values include the following central ideas:

▌ Choice. Staff initiate new projects, select teams and can refuse to join a project. Only the best projects pass the process of peer appraisal.

▌ Multiple roles. The project approach leads to a broadening of both expertise and experience.

▌ Transparency. Information is almost totally open. Sharing knowledge is the norm.

▌ Hands-off management. Successful projects emerge from a process that appears totally chaotic. There are no budgets or resource restrictions – just a strong belief in the process by which opportunities are identified and exploited.

Since this approach was adopted Oticon's sales have doubled and its profits have increased 10 times.

Interacting with customers and suppliers

Advances in information technology, coupled with increasing recognition of the role of multidisciplinary teams, make possible greater dispersion of information and decision making. This in turn, argues Day (1999), facilitates the use of interactive strategies in relations with stakeholder groups.

For example, in the case of customer relations, the essence of the interactive approach is the use of information *from* the customer rather than information *about* the customer. While this may be simple and straightforward for companies with very few customers, it is novel in companies dealing with mass markets, such as travel services, publishing or automobiles. Here the traditional approach has been to rely on a combination of mass media and retail and wholesale distribution channels to target broadly defined market segments. To move to a more interactive approach to the market involves organizational change. Partial steps towards interactivity include putting existing promotional materials on the Web and introducing customer retention programmes such as frequent flyer rewards or store loyalty cards. Related structural innovations include:

▦ customer segment managers responsible for designing tailored communications to particular customer groups;

▦ technology support groups to provide in-house capability to develop Web sites or provide technical support to customer retention processes involving intensive use of IT;

▦ outsourcing specialist skills such as usage tracking;

▦ ad hoc multi-functional teams for projects.

Fully interactive strategies require more radical structural change. Day quotes as an example the structure of US joint venture Astra-Merck as compared with a traditional pharmaceutical company. Astra-Merck was created in 1992 as a greenfield-site joint venture start-up. From the beginning the structure was designed with multi-functional teams as the basic building blocks. Thirty-one business unit teams were set up, one for each region of the United States. Each unit included medical information scientists with the depth of knowledge to build relationships with doctors, customer support staff and business managers. These units had the capability of rapidly devising creative solutions for individual customers.

In support of these teams the company invested in company-wide information systems such as ones for accessing product information. Further responsiveness to customer needs was achieved by setting up solutions management teams in each therapeutic area (such as gastroenterinal) to cover licensing, business development, marketing, sales and sourcing processes.

In 1996 Unipart used interactive technology to bring together 6,000 customers from the company's wholesale distribution network at 35 sites around the world to ask them what they thought customers were looking for in an automobile repair centre. Participants were able to vote on strategic issues. Their local knowledge and expertise combined with Unipart's own research and market analysis led to a stronger, more customer-focused agenda for the future.

New technology and the supply chain

For most of the last century, the supply chain of manufacturers, suppliers, distributors and customers was a process bedevilled by vast amounts of paperwork. It often involved questionable inventory forecasts, manufacturing plans that might or might not be met and hypothetical shipping schedules. The Internet has changed all that; it has transformed this archaic process into something closer to an exact science. The Internet-enabled supply chain, with its just-in-time delivery, precise inventory visibility and to-the-minute distribution-tracking capabilities is a strategic weapon that can:

▌ help companies avoid costly disasters;

▌ reap cost-cutting and revenue-producing benefits;

▌ slice the cost of holding too much or struggling with too little inventory.

Automating a supply chain, however, requires careful planning, and must start with an excellent understanding of relationships with partners and customers and a climate of mutual trust.

KNOWLEDGE MANAGEMENT

According to Peter Drucker (1969), 'knowledge is the only meaningful economic resource'. It follows that for organizations the processes by which knowledge is created or acquired, communicated, or applied and used must be effectively managed.

The process of managing knowledge is clearly a fundamental aspect of the concept of the learning organization. It links, also, to the whole question of the management of intangible assets and intellectual capital. Companies are now discovering that they have considerable assets that they have not been exploiting to their full potential; they are also realizing that if they do not invest in the renewal of these assets they will face declining competitiveness in the future. These assets include the knowledge possessed by experienced employees, information which exists in various forms but which is often overlooked, databases, patents, copyrights, brands, licensing opportunities and so on. Many firms now identify the process of knowledge management as a core or key business process. New roles are appearing in organization structures, such as Director of Knowledge Management.

The main activities that make up the process are:

▌ the bringing to light and sharing of existing knowledge so that all employees have access to it and are able to use it in the context of their jobs;

▌ ensuring that people can have easy access to that information, wherever and whenever they need it;

▌ facilitating and resourcing the creation of new knowledge;

▌ supporting and resourcing the acquisition of knowledge from external sources.

The first structural requirement for knowledge management is the designation of a champion at the centre of the company, ideally reporting directly to the chief executive, someone with the power to set up the knowledge architecture, processes and systems and to commit the necessary resources. This person should also possess the leadership qualities needed to influence people to change pre-existing patterns of behaviour, such as guarding rather than sharing knowledge.

The second structural requirement is to establish both physical and virtual networks of people focused on common business goals such as cost reduction or quality improvement. These networks are there not only to pool information and ideas but also to stimulate innovation. It is particularly important to create such groups across organizational and national boundaries.

The processes for knowledge management are, of course, increasingly information technology based. Electronic mail, groupware, the intranet, video conferencing and databases of various kinds constitute a powerful multimedia set of communication processes. Their effectiveness, however, depends primarily on people's attitudes and how they use the systems which have been set up. As ever, the greatest barriers to knowledge management are cultural. The belief that knowledge is power and that to share it is to weaken one's position is a long time dying, as is the attitude summed up in the phrase 'not invented here'.

J A C Brown (1963), an early writer on organizational behaviour, pointed out that in a hierarchical organization there is usually one person, at a senior level, who has the power to make a particular decision, while there is another person, usually much lower in the hierarchy and in status, who has the knowledge on which that decision needs to be based. An important role of knowledge management is to bring those two together into an effective team. This is very difficult in organizations characterized by substantial power distance, which, sadly, remains true of too many large business organizations.

ICL's technological support for knowledge management

Elizabeth Lank (2000) has described how technology has been harnessed to support knowledge management and knowledge sharing in ICL. This company's technology support for knowledge sharing is a global information service called Café VIK. The name was chosen to reflect the fact that a café is where you meet with friends to chat and VIK stands for valuing ICL knowledge. The system was launched in 1996 as a repository of information for employees working at the customer interface, with the objective of 'significantly enhancing speed and quality of service to customers by improving our ability to share knowledge on a global scale'. By 1999 it had established itself as a critical aspect of doing business. Its very success, however, had its downside, in that there was so much information on the system that it became difficult to find what was wanted. The solution was not to attempt to provide all the information people wanted but just enough to enable them to identify the persons with in-depth knowledge. It was also important that people who asked for help should get a rapid response. Café VIK was then redesigned as an interactive support for communities of people rather than a static library of company information. The new form was launched in July 1999. Any group of people in ICL with a common business interest can now create their own space on the system. It then enables them to manage the membership of their 'community', publish and archive their own information, hold electronic discussion groups, poll members on issues, and post the knowledge and experience profiles of each member. Every piece of information on the system has an owner and a review date. The system automatically checks each review date and e-mails the owner to check if the information should be updated or deleted. In the first three months after the relaunch, over 100 knowledge communities were set up. The major lesson from this experience is that it is not technology that makes knowledge sharing happen, it is the communities of people. Knowledge management technology is of value in so far as it results in connecting people.

Managing intellectual capital at Skandia

Edvisson (1997) has described the pioneering work in measuring and exploiting intellectual capital at Skandia. The company's approach is based on the metaphor of a tree – for long-term sustainability it is more important to focus on nourishing the roots than on harvesting the fruit. Taking the view that the company's intangible assets were at least as important as its fixed assets, it was decided to develop an intellectual capital function as well as the existing traditional functions of finance, marketing, etc. In 1991 such a function was set up under a Director of Intellectual Capital. The objective of the function is to grow and develop intellectual capital as a visible, lasting value, complementary to the existing balance sheet. Its activities include developing new measurement tools and ratios, implementing innovative programmes and projects for rapid learning and knowledge transparency, and nurturing profitable knowledge sharing.

In 1992 Skandia started to take stock of its 'hidden values'. The list included such things as trademarks, concessions, customer databases, fund management systems, IT systems, core competencies, key persons, partners and alliances, and about 50 others. They were classified into two broad groups as either human capital or structural capital. This led to Skandia's definition of intellectual capital:

Human capital

+ <u>Structural capital</u>

= Intellectual capital

Structural capital consists of the things that are 'left behind when the staff went home'. They are, for example, the customer database and the IT systems. A key task for the organization is to transform human capital into structural capital.

THE LEARNING ORGANIZATION

The characteristics of a learning organization have been set out by Mayo and Lank (1994) and can be summarized as follows:

1. The word 'learning' is frequently heard and is part of the everyday language.

2. Managers see development of the people they are responsible for as a key element in the job.

3. Documents used in appraisal and development planning make provision for learning plans to be mutually devised by the individual and his/her manager.

4. Giving and receiving feedback is normal practice and people are trained in the process.

5. Managers and others can diagnose their preferred learning styles and go on to select from a variety of learning methods.

6. Individuals are proactive in developing their own learning and supportive of colleagues in theirs.

7. People are interested in analysing incidents and events so as to learn from them. They constantly question the way things are done in the search for improvement.

8. Looking for someone or something to blame when things go wrong is unacceptable behaviour. The emphasis is upon 'what can we learn from this?'

9. People focus on the learning opportunities offered by jobs rather than on the status that goes with them.

10. The 'not invented here' attitude is rejected. Ideas and experience are shared across teams.

11. The organization has an accessible, user-friendly, updated database.

12. The organization continually benchmarks itself against 'best practice'.

13. Spontaneous and informal networks exist and are seen as legitimate.

There are certain conditions that need to be present if the learning organization is to become a reality. These include:

1. Role modelling by top management, by being seen both to be learning themselves and as involved with the learning of others.

2. Effective horizontal and diagonal as well as vertical communication channels.

3. Rewards which reinforce the motivation to learn.

4. Effective systems for scanning the environment.

5. Active involvement in joint ventures, strategic alliances, etc.

6. A culture fostering openness, sharing of information, and egalitarianism. (Pascale (1991) refers to the 'integrity of contention management processes – the surfacing of hard truths and confronting reality'.)

7. Employees are empowered to apply their learning to the way they do their jobs.

The factors that inhibit organizational learning include:

▪ fixation on short-term results and exclusively on 'bottom-line' indicators of performance;

▪ the assumption that experience by itself automatically leads to learning;

▪ a long history of success (as in the classic cases of IBM and Marks and Spencer).

Learning and organizational effectiveness

Mayo and Lank face up to the need to demonstrate the impact of organizational learning on business results. They point out that improved performance may not come about quickly and remind us that few investments pay off in the first year or so. They also make the point that some costs and lost revenues are invisible; for example, it is difficult to assess the value of any contracts lost or the number of new customers the organization has failed to attract because of slow and inadequate learning about what is happening in the marketplace.

They argue the case for regarding people and their skills and knowledge as assets of the corporation just as much as cash, plant and equipment, and buildings. Learning increases the level of knowledge and skill and so enhances the value of these assets. This incremental value, however, does not as yet feature on the balance sheet, despite the fact that other 'intangibles' such as goodwill, the value of a brand and of intellectual property do get taken into account.

It is clear that organizations that aim to sustain their competitiveness as we move forward into the 21st century will need to invest in their intellectual capital and facilities for continuous learning.

MANAGING TALENT

Companies increasingly understand that they must frame their human resources policies in the context of a highly competitive international market for talent. There is a constant flow of talented people from countries with lower living standards and rewards or higher levels of personal taxation to countries where talent can enjoy a higher reward – the so-called brain drain. The competition consists not only in other companies worldwide but also in the attractions, for many talented people, of independence and self-employment.

The twin challenges for business can be summed up quite simply as recruiting and finding talent on the one hand and keeping talent on the other. The distinction between recruiting talent and finding it is important. Sometimes an organization looks outside for new talent when the potential for outstanding performance already exists unrecognized among existing employees.

The recruitment activity itself can be separated into two quite distinct processes. The first is that of attracting people whose exceptional talent has already been established and recognized elsewhere.

This can be called the transplanting type of recruiting – equivalent to digging up a mature tree or shrub in the quest for an instant garden. In such instances companies often make the mistake of assuming that the cash nexus is the most important factor. While it is obviously true that an outstanding performer in any field is unlikely to move from one organization to another if it involves a drop in remuneration, it remains the case that other factors are seldom given enough weight or consideration. For example, in the case of highly talented people, a key influence on the decision whether or not to move jobs is the reputation of the organization in its particular field; is it at the leading edge, does it set the pace for its industry, does it have a reputation for integrity, does the individual feel honoured by being approached? Reputation building, therefore, is a key element in recruiting strategy.

The second process can be termed the seed bed or nursery approach – recruiting young people straight from school or university, nurturing or developing their emerging talent and bringing it to fruition. This is clearly a longer-term approach and one fraught with obvious risks, one of which is the difficulty of predicting ultimate success. The obstacles in the way of successful prediction are many, including:

▮ Different rates of maturing of individuals' abilities. Late developers are often missed.

▮ The relative weakness of psychometric tests when it comes to predicting things like creativity and entrepreneurial ability.

▮ The tendency to give too much weight to academic qualifications.

▮ Failure to value diversity with regard to the work force. A great deal of fine talent is overlooked among ethnic minorities.

▮ The fact that motivation and drive may well be more powerful determinants of performance than sheer ability.

Somewhat less risky is the process of finding talent among existing employees. Assuming they have been in employment for some time, a well-designed appraisal and development procedure can be effective in selecting promising candidates for accelerated development.

Michael Howe, Reader in Human Cognition at Exeter University (1990), is one of the world's leading experts on the subject of talent. He points to the danger of seeing talent in any field as a gift which you either have or have not as the case may be. 'We are easily convinced that the most striking feats must depend on circumstances which, except for certain rare individuals, are entirely unattainable. Some of the most widespread beliefs about exceptional people revolve around the view that certain individuals are not only remarkable but inherently so, while the remainder of us are doomed to ordinariness.' Howe challenges such beliefs and produces compelling evidence of the ability of appropriate training and development to bring about exceptional performance.

Here again, however, the common fault is stereotyping and eliminating some categories of employee from consideration. It is very important for a company to be aware of any cultural bias that may cause it to narrow its search for talent to traditional sources – much as, at one time, the British army tended to restrict membership of the officer corps to ex-public school boys and girls.

When it comes to keeping talent the need for an adequate rewards package goes without saying. What will make the real difference in keeping talented employees loyal is the extent to which the company provides them with a working environment that is favourable to creativity, self-expression and the exercise of initiative. The paradox that faces organizations, particularly very large ones, is that they are hierarchical, bureaucratic and conformist in order to achieve efficiency and uniformity, yet it is just these characteristics that turn highly creative people off.

The term 'skunk works' has entered the language of organizations to describe small, informal, tightly-knit teams who are shielded from standard company practices and rules in order to foster their creative energies. Warren Bennis (1997) gives a graphic description of the very first 'skunk works', set up by Lockheed to develop the first US jet fighter during the Second World War. Lockheed's chief designer selected a team of 23 engineers and 30 support staff. They built makeshift quarters from discarded engine boxes, roofed with a circus tent. They worked in secrecy and did their own cleaning and their own secretarial work. Bennis describes the designer Johnson as 'a visionary on at least two fronts – designing aeroplanes and organizing genius. Johnson seemed to know intuitively what talented people needed to do their best work, how to motivate them, and how to make sure the desired product was created as quickly and cheaply as possible'. His unit was characterized by egalitarian treatment of people, absence of paperwork, informality of dress and open debate.

The culture of an organization is an important factor in its ability to retain talent. The chief characteristics of a culture that can nurture talent are as follows:

▌ Highly cohesive work teams.

▌ Authority resides in expertise and competence rather than rank or status.

▌ Elites are recognized without elitism, in that talented people respect and recognize the contribution of those less gifted colleagues who support them.

▌ Respected leadership. Talented people are critical people. They do not follow blindly and they know when the emperor has no clothes.

▌ Freedom, autonomy, space and flexibility.

▌ Openness and trust.

▌ Encouragement of risk taking.

▌ A taken for granted dedication to excellence – an almost obsessive concern for doing a good job.

In other words, the right approach for organizations anxious to retain their most talented people is not so much to create a skunk works inside the company but to make the company as a whole as much like a skunk works as possible.

INCLUSIVE HUMAN RESOURCE POLICIES

It is also increasingly well understood that employee commitment is an essential ingredient of a strategy for building sustainable competitive advantage.

Pfeffer (1998) argues that the combination of a number of powerful tools and policies of human resource management, acting as a total system, produce the highest levels of employee commitment. He extracted from various studies, related literature, and personal observation and experience, a set of seven dimensions that characterize most if not all of the human resources practices of companies producing profits through people. These are:

▌ *Security of employment*: Pfeffer quotes Lincoln Electric, General Motors' innovative Saturn and Fremont plants and the highly successful Southwest Airlines as examples of companies that offered guaranteed employment and avoided layoffs during recessions.

▌ *Selective hiring*: This first requires a large applicant pool from which to select. In 1994, for example, Southwest Airlines received 125,000 job applications and hired 2,700 people. The second requirement is a sophisticated selection process, which relates the skills and qualities needed in the job to the qualities of the individual. The third is to use this process for all jobs at all levels. Examples of good practice include Subaru-Isuzu in respect of automotive frontline employees, Enterprise Rent-a-car in respect of customer service people, and Hewlett-Packard.

▌ *Self-managed teams*: Pfeffer asserts that 'organizing people into self-managed teams is a critical component of virtually all high performance management systems'. As well as examples from automotive manufacturing such as New United Motor Manufacturing (NUMMI) and Chrysler, where the practice is not uncommon, he cites cases from other industries, such as Bell Telephone, Whole Foods Markets and Ritz Carlton Hotels.

▌ *High compensation contingent upon organizational performance*: 'The level of salaries sends a message to the firm's workforce – they are truly valued or they are not.' It is important, however, that a significant element of compensation should relate to the organization's performance. This element can take a number of different forms such as profit sharing, employee share ownership, or various forms of individual or team incentives. Among the US companies with share ownership schemes are Wal-Mart, Microsoft and Southwest Airlines.

A pioneer in the field of employee share ownership in the UK is Dame Stephanie Shirley. Having arrived in Britain as an unaccompanied child refugee from Germany in 1939, she took an honours degree in

Mathematics at night school and started the FI company on her dining room table with £6 in 1962. In 25 years as Chief Executive of FI Group she developed it into a leading business technology group, pioneering new work practices and improving the position of professional women along the way. She got 24 per cent of the equity into the hands of the workforce at no cost to anyone but herself. She retired in 1993 as honorary Life President. The company floated as F.I. Group Plc in 1996 (now Xansa Plc) and workforce ownership among the 4,000 staff is currently 40 per cent.

Britain's largest employee-owned company is the John Lewis Partnership plc. It has over 50,000 partners, 23 department stores, over 100 Waitrose supermarkets, a turnover of £4 billion and pre-tax profits of over £90 million.

The employees are referred to as partners. Management is tasked with running the company in the interests of all partners 'past, present and future'. Employees receive each year a share of the profits which is paid out as a cash bonus.

John Lewis is highly competitive in both the retail markets in which it operates, aiming to provide good service and value for money. In the department stores it applies its slogan 'Never knowingly undersold' to the point where partners receive a small reward when they point out that a competitor charges less than John Lewis.

The John Lewis Partnership provides good conditions of employment and reward for partners and provides its customers with quality goods at competitive prices combined with excellent service. It is successful and expanding successfully as a result.

Scott Bader holds certificate number 1 under the Common Ownership Act of 1976. Ernest Bader – a visionary of his generation – founded Scott Bader in 1921. Unhappy with the legacy of capital owning labour, he wished to create a new social order whereby labour was the owner of capital. He believed that a business should do more than make a profit. It should be founded on ethical principles, be organized democratically and contribute to the good of the wider community. The structure that was created encourages a high level of employee participation.

A charitable trust, the Scott Bader Commonwealth Ltd, distributes a significant proportion of the company's profits each year by making donations to charities that contribute to the general welfare of society.

Scott Bader has no external shareholders and cannot be acquired. The governance of the company is founded on democratic principles, which encourages a high level of participation. The company has a number of governing bodies, all of which have elected representatives from the working community, and the activities of group companies are reported to company members in General meetings.

The potential value of employee share ownership is illustrated by some recent research. Sustainable Asset Management of Switzerland (SAM) has launched the SAM Employee Ownership Index. This index tracks the performance of the leading European companies in terms of employee ownership.

The SAM Employee Ownership Index (EOI) investable stocks universe is derived from the components of the Dow Jones 600 Index. Each of the 600 companies in the Dow Jones 600 Index is asked to complete a questionnaire and provide additional information about their activities in the area of employee ownership. The selection is primarily made by comparing companies in the same economic sector. The Index comprises 30 components, representing 10 different countries and a wide range of industries. Between June 1998 and June 2000 the EOI increased in value by 88.5 per cent compared with an increase of 11.4 per cent in the Dow Jones STOXX 600.

Pfeffer also lists the following:

▌ *Training*: 'Training is an essential component of high performance work systems because these systems rely on frontline employee skill and initiative to identify and resolve problems, to initiate changes in work methods and to take responsibility for quality.'

▌ *Reduction in status differences*: 'In order to help make all organization members feel important and committed to enhancing organizational operations... most high commitment management systems attempt to reduce the status distinctions that separate individuals and groups and cause some to feel less valued.' This can be accomplished in two ways – symbolically by means of language, job titles, dress, allocation of physical space, car parking privileges and the like and substantively (and much more rarely) through reducing inequality in compensation across the different levels of the company. An example of the latter approach is Whole Foods Markets. Company policy is to limit annual compensation pay to eight times the average full-time salary of all employees. In 1995 the CEO earned $130,000 in salary and a bonus of $20,000. The CEO of Southwest Airlines earns about $500,000 a year, including bonuses. When the company negotiated a wage freeze with its pilots in 1995, in exchange for stock options and unguaranteed profit-related bonuses, he agreed to freeze his own base salary at $395,000 for the next four years.

▌ *Sharing information*: Sharing information, particularly financial information, shows people that they are trusted. Also, if people are to contribute meaningfully to enhancing performance they need to have performance data and to be trained in how to interpret it. The systematic sharing of information as a basis for performance improvement pioneered at Springfield Re-manufacturing in the 1980s and known as 'Open book Management' has been widely adopted in the United States.

Pfeffer goes on to argue that 'the real sources of competitive leverage' are the culture and capabilities of the organization that are derived from the way people are managed. This, he asserts, is a much more important source of sustained success than things like having a large market share or a distinctive brand 'because it is much more difficult to understand capability and systems of management practice than it is to copy strategy, technology or even global presence'.

Ian Wilson (2000) has identified eight elements in what he calls the 'new social contract' between employees and the corporation:

▌ a vision and sense of shared purpose, beyond profit and share-holder value;

▌ inspiring leadership (he quotes Herb Keller of Southwest Airlines);

▌ empowerment of the workforce;

▌ the customization of work – tailoring job content, hours and compensation packages to meet individuals' needs;

▌ a climate of equity, respect and due process;

▌ reduced volatility in employment patterns;

▌ increasing employability;

▌ first-rate on-site amenities and services.

Downsizing

It is stating the obvious to say that building commitment and downsizing do not march well together. Downsizing is sometimes unavoidable in the face of collapsing markets, the obsolescence of products or following a merger or take-over. Nonetheless, even when the necessity can be plainly seen, the damage to morale can be considerable. Pfeffer (1998) gives the following advice in the interests of limiting the damage:

▌ Move quickly once the decision is taken.

▌ Cut once rather than in waves.

▌ Share the performance data and the underlying reasons fully.

▌ Involve staff (and unions where appropriate) in determining the criteria for selection for redundancy.

▌ Communicate discreetly and with sensitivity to those selected.

▌ Provide fair severance terms and first class outplacement services. Help people leave with dignity.

Obviously it is also important to take full advantage of ongoing turnover and early retirement opportunities.

Morale is damaged to a greater extent when the reasons for downsizing are less compelling and convincing – particularly when the promised business benefits fail to appear, as is often the case. Downsizing cannot fix deep-seated problems of product acceptability, quality, service, process design or management style. The damage is compounded when the wrong people start leaving, and too much experience and expertise are lost (corporate Alzheimer's) or when the cut is too deep and those who remain suffer stress due to heavy work loads (corporate anorexia).

In such cases, Pfeffer argues, a downward performance cycle can be triggered. Performance problems lead to downsizing, which in turn leads to employees reducing their efforts, spinning work out to make it last or leaving to find more secure employment. This in turn lowers performance further, leading to yet more redundancies and so the cycle continues.

3M have an interesting safety valve as a means of minimizing the damage that job losses can create. This is known as the 'Unassigned List'. People whose jobs are eliminated are given six months to find another job within the company. During that period they continue to receive full salary and benefits. About 50 per cent do in fact find other jobs within the company. Nearly all the remainder find jobs elsewhere, taking with them a redundancy package of one and a half-week's salary for each year of service.

Other damage limitation strategies include:

▮ short time working;

▮ taking subcontracted work back inside;

▮ building inventory when business recovery can be expected within a reasonable time period;

▮ freezing hiring;

▮ switching people into jobs such as selling and maintenance.

CONCLUSION

As new technology and aspirations for a more egalitarian social milieu gather strength, one result is that choice of structure becomes less and less critical for organizational functioning, while process and culture gain in importance. The traditional concept of organization derives from the historic requirement for a hierarchical structure that could enable the exercise of command and control by a sovereign over his or her subjects or by a commander-in-chief over the foot soldiers. Today's requirement is for a flexible system that connects with customers' needs and establishes a linked set of processes along the value chain from supplier to finished product resulting in customer satisfaction. In this type of organization the key managerial task is the design of these processes; the key leadership task is to create a culture in which creating customer satisfaction is seen as the common objective and in which continuous improvement and standards of excellence are striven for. Unfortunately, hierarchies convey power, privilege and status, so despite their growing redundancy they are unlikely to wither away. Nevertheless, examples like St Luke's in the previous chapter show that they can be dispensed with.

14

Taking stock

What history teaches us is that man does not change arbitrarily; he does not transform himself at will on hearing the voices of inspired prophets. The reason is that all change, in colliding with the inherited institutions of the past, is inevitably hard and laborious; consequently it only takes place in response to the demands of necessity. For change to be brought about it is not enough that it should be seen as desirable; it must be the product of changes within the whole network of diverse casual relationships which determine the situation of man.

(Emile Durkheim)

THE RESEARCH EVIDENCE

Research evidence from a number of studies (Kotter and Heskett, 1992; Collins and Porras, 1995; Pfeffer, 2000; Collins, 2001) shows that companies that are 'built to last' and that are outstandingly successful over long periods of time tend to share some common characteristics. These characteristics can be summed up in the phrase 'the inclusive approach'. Such companies remain competitive in the face of a changing environment for the following reasons:

▌ They have clear purposes which are stated in other than purely financial terms; purposes that are on the one hand inspirational for employees and on the other provide a social as well as economic reason for the company's existence.

▌ These purposes are supported by a set of shared values which are deeply embedded in the company's culture and which have stood the test of time.

▌ They have developed sound corporate governance practices, with effective Boards of Directors and well-regarded reporting practices that are inclusive in the sense that they cover the whole range of a company's activities, including its impact on society and the environment.

▌ They have developed deep knowledge of what it takes to be successful in their particular industries and markets. They have, in consequence, developed a success model which, albeit adapted from time to time to meet the challenge of changes in the marketplace, has formed a consistent foundation for the company's success over many years. The critical success factors have been identified and are systematically tracked by measurements.

▌ They set challenging performance targets and carefully monitor progress towards their achievement. These targets are often ones which take many years to bring to fruition and, if necessary, short-term profits will be treated as of lesser importance than continuing progress towards the longer-term goal.

▌ They deliver excellent value for money to their customers in terms of both quality of product and service and create strong customer loyalty.

▌ They have committed, loyal employees who feel the company is loyal to them in return.

▌ They have developed relationships of mutual trust with carefully selected suppliers. They include in their definition of suppliers all those companies along the supply chain from raw materials up to the level of the component or chemical compound that constitutes their immediate input.

▌ They are well respected in the communities in which they operate, and act as corporate citizens, taking a full part in the affairs of the local communities in which their operations are based.

▌ They have built a reputation for quality and integrity with the public at large. This reputation is often associated with a brand that is, in some cases, the company's most valuable asset.

▌ They are innovative and strive for continuous improvement.

▌ Their organization structures and processes are well aligned with their strategies. In particular they tend to have little in the way of formal hierarchy. Their business processes are designed so as to focus on customer requirements and they put decision making powers as close to the customer interface as possible.

▌ These companies are characterized by a corporate culture in which people and relationships are highly valued and in which integrity and ethical behaviour are important values. Such companies are often ones that have been strongly influenced by the vision and personal values of the founder or founders. These values have in many cases been preserved by a succession of top-level appointments from within; also, such appointees to top jobs have often served for many years in their roles, thus giving the culture plenty of time to take root.

As a consequence of possessing these characteristics they have proved to be sound long-term investments for institutional funds and individual savers alike.

Today, the leaders of such companies, characterized by continuing commercial success on the one hand and an enduring set of values on the other, are foremost in espousing the cause of sustainable development; being accustomed to taking a long-term view they see that without sustainable development for society there can be no sustainable future for the business. They are also sensitive to the tide of public opinion and they can see that in the not too distant future, companies that are seen as failing to fulfil their responsibilities to society and the environment will lose their licence to operate.

They also set an example for other companies to follow. Being highly admired and among the leading companies in their industries, their practices and policies provide models which other companies are following.

THE LIMITS TO CORPORATE ACTION

Nevertheless, there is a limit to what such companies can do. Global competition becomes ever more intense and the margins available for discretionary spending and investment are shrinking. Such companies must look to governments and international trade organizations to grant them a level playing field, so that more ruthless competitors can be restricted in their operations. Obvious areas where demands for greater regulation will grow are emissions, waste disposal, minimum wages, human rights, health and safety of consumers and employees, investment in training and development, employment of those with disabilities and from ethnic minorities, reporting requirements and governance structures.

At the beginning of the 21st century the business community is already more constrained by legislation than at any time in the past. Anti-trust laws in the United States, the UK Monopoly Commission, employment law, health and safety rules, advertising standards, planning regulations, stock market rules and the like have been progressively tightened in the past few decades.

These constraints are expressions of a democratic society's concern that market capitalism should be regulated in the interests of its citizens, in their roles as investors, consumers, employees and members of the community.

Also, compared with any period in the past, considerable numbers of major international business enterprises are going beyond the requirements of the law and, as the evidence presented in this book has demonstrated, are pursuing policies that indicate a genuine ambition to be seen as responsible corporate citizens.

Yet, at the same time, business is under attack to a greater extent than ever before. Books such as David Korten's *When Corporations Rule the World* (Korten, 1996) and Naomi Klein's *No Logo* (Klein, 2000) are worldwide best sellers, while anti-capitalist, anti-globalization demonstrations draw thousands. These demonstrations are, moreover, more widely publicized and supported than ones against extreme human rights abuses by oppressive regimes.

The charge sheet for business is a long one; it includes destruction of the natural environment, exploitation of labour, particularly in the developing countries, discrimination in terms of gender and ethnic origin, neglect of the health and safety of consumers and employees, and so on. The charges stand up; business is indeed guilty on all counts – but to a far less extent than even 20 years ago, let alone a century ago. Yet in the past far more serious crimes against society and the environment were tolerated. Why are lesser offences not tolerated today? Partly the answer lies in changed expectations. Business has become more socially responsible but our expectations in this respect have increased faster. One reason for this lies in the considerable improvement in communications and information. The ordinary citizen's awareness of such issues as global warming or child labour is now much greater than ever before.

Given that it has taken many years for the realization of the urgency of the need to take action on these issues to reach the public consciousness, Boards of Directors that now see the need to alter course and change policies in order to meet the changing expectations of society cannot simply do so overnight. The case of Ford (Chapter 8) illustrates this very well. It is unavoidable in the short term that the pace of corrective action will be gradual – partly because of the expectations and demands of customers who are not prepared to adjust their own lifestyles but also because of the pressures created by the way investment markets are structured and because of fears of employees for their jobs. These problems and others can only be resolved slowly; they involve processes of education and persuasion, as well as steadily growing pressure from NGOs and other groups.

In the context of the debate about such matters as sustainable development and the social responsibility of industry, understanding of the issues is clouded in two ways. First, there is a tendency to refer to the world's major corporations as if they constituted a homogeneous group, acting in the same ways from the same motives. This error is committed both by those who accuse corporations of crimes against humanity and the planet and by the advocates of the virtues of the free market. The assertions 'business does this' or 'business does that' are meaningless. Some corporations exploit their workers, cheat their customers, squeeze their suppliers until they go out of business and blight local communities. Others provide excellent wages and working conditions, have satisfied customers, enjoy good, long-term relationships with their suppliers and are benefactors to local communities. Unless the former enjoy a permanent monopoly position, economic theory, common sense and experience tell us they are unlikely to survive long term.

The second error is to fail to attribute the actions of companies, whether for good or ill, to the people who exercise control over them. Companies do not decide to try to avoid minimum wage legislation. Directors and senior executives decide such things. Companies can come under the control of people who have few moral scruples or who are motivated solely by greed, but so can other kinds of social institutions, including the governments of nations. The business community does not have a monopoly on greed and dishonesty; the voluntary sector has its share of embezzling treasurers; the public service has its share of corruptible officials. As in the case of all kinds of social institutions, people are both the source of the corporation's potential for good and its source of vulnerability.

Causes for optimism

This review of what has happened since the RSA Report *Tomorrow's Company* (1995) has clearly indicated several grounds for optimism about the future, the evidence for which is set out in the preceding chapters.

There is clearly a rapidly growing number of companies embracing key aspects of the inclusive approach:

▌ More and more businesses are acknowledging their responsibilities to stakeholders in their statements of purpose.

▌ More and more are not only publishing statements of their mission, vision and values, they are doing so after consulting their employees and other stakeholder groups.

▌ Company reports increasingly provide information on their activities under the headings of environmental and social as well as financial performance. Much work is being done to develop better standards and tools for measurement purposes.

▌ Investment funds based on selectivity on the grounds of sustainability or social responsibility are growing fast and generally performing well.

▌ Some of the largest pension funds and fund managers are flexing their muscles and engaging companies in dialogue.

▌ Alternative indices of stock market performance focusing on sustainability are being developed.

▌ The growth of public concern is reflected in both growth in the number of NGOs and the size of their membership. There is increasing collaboration between them and companies. The increasing accessibility of information via the Internet is helping bring this about.

▌ Another welcome development is the setting up of independent monitoring agencies in respect of working conditions in developing countries. There is a related growth in the adoption of responsible sourcing practices in relation to such commodities as tea, cocoa and coffee.

▌ There exists a new emphasis on training and development for leadership as distinct from training in the tools and techniques of management.

▌ Changes in company law, especially ones relating to governance and reporting, are being actively debated and enacted.

▌ Overall, the debate has shifted its focus from 'Why adopt the inclusive approach?' to 'How can we do so most effectively?'.

On the downside, it is probably true to say that the inclusive approach is a long way still from being mainstream among companies outside the top few hundred. Although it is difficult to produce evidence in support, it does seem the case also that company chairpersons and chief executives are, in many instances, taking a permissive attitude to the process of becoming more inclusive, rather than seeing it as a core element in their business strategy. It is slightly worrying to see so many new appointments such as Director of Social Responsibility, as if CEOs are in effect saying, 'There is now somebody whose task it is to look after things such as our stakeholder engagement and our community relationships – I can get on with running the business'.

WILL THE INCLUSIVE APPROACH BE SUSTAINED?

At the time of writing (September 2001), the fragility of the global economy is once more evident. Even before the terrorist outrages in New York and Washington the threat of recession was growing. All the Western economies were experiencing problems such as falling share prices, lower company profits, plant closures and downsizing and company failures. The big question is whether the inclusive approach will survive difficult times or whether it will be abandoned as short-term pressures increase. Companies, in their struggle to survive recession, might abandon the very practices that are designed to ensure their long-term survival. The answer largely depends, of course, on how far top management is really committed to the inclusive concept. As has happened with training and development departments in the past, if the new departments concerned with such matters as stakeholder relations are seen as dispensable and peripheral to the business, then they will not last very long. The new armies of consultants working in this field will disappear as rapidly as they have grown up.

If, on the other hand, there is real commitment from the top, resulting from visionary leadership, then the inclusive approach will stand the test of hard times – as it has indeed during past recessions in such 'built to last' companies as those which have been profiled earlier.

My own view is that there are now so many powerful forces pushing for change that it is inevitable. A powerful social movement has been set in motion. Recession may slow its progress but will not halt it. We are witnessing the early stages of the emergence of a new form of capitalism, one in which concern for social justice and for the environment are seen as goals ranking in importance alongside shareholder value. John Elkington (2001) uses the metaphor of 'The Chrysalis Economy' to describe what he calls the economic equivalent of an 'extraordinary natural process of metamorphosis' as the old economy mutates into a 'dematerializing, bit-driven new economy'. He goes on to say that 'Only if today's Corporate Locusts and Caterpillars can become Corporate Butterflies and Honeybees can we have any chance of creating truly sustainable forms of capitalism'. My own expectation is that such a form of capitalism will be more rather than less successful in wealth creation than that which existed at the end of the 20th century. As it matures, however, we shall be using somewhat different definitions of 'wealth' from those we have used in the past.

Appendix

Standards and guidelines

The late 1990s also saw the emergence of a number of organizations consisting of alliances of business organizations or of business, NGOs and governments and the establishing of standards and guidelines for sustainable development policies and practices, stakeholder engagement and measurement and reporting practices. The result is an abundance of ideas and processes, which can lead to confusion. Nevertheless, there is a wealth of advice and prescription from which newcomers to the field can select according to their needs. The most important agencies and the guidelines or principles they offer are described below.

THE BELLAGIO PRINCIPLES

In 1987, the World Commission on Environment and Development (Brundtland Commission) called for the development of new ways to measure and assess progress toward sustainable development. In November 1996, an international group of measurement practitioners and researchers from five continents came together at the Rockefeller Foundation's Study and Conference Center in Bellagio, Italy to review progress to date and to synthesize insights from practical ongoing efforts. The principles set out below resulted and were unanimously endorsed.

These principles serve as guidelines for the whole of the assessment process including the choice and design of indicators, their interpretation and communication of the result. They are interrelated and should be applied as a complete set. They are intended for use in starting and improving assessment activities of community groups, non-government organizations, corporations, national governments and international institutions. The principles are set out below:

1. Guiding Vision and Goals. Assessment of progress toward sustainable development should be guided by a clear vision of sustainable development and goals that define that vision.

2. Holistic Perspective. Assessment of progress toward sustainable development should:

   ▨ include review of the whole system as well as its parts;

   ▨ consider the wellbeing of social, ecological and economic subsystems, their state as well as the direction and rate of change of that state, of their component parts, and the interaction between parts;

   ▨ consider both positive and negative consequences of human activity, in a way that reflects the costs and benefits for human and ecological systems, in monetary and non-monetary terms.

3. Essential elements. Assessment of progress toward sustainable development should:

   ▨ consider equity and disparity within the current population and between present and future generations, dealing with such concerns as resource use, over-consumption and poverty, human rights, and access to services, as appropriate;

   ▨ consider the ecological conditions on which life depends;

   ▨ consider economic development and other, non-market activities that contribute to human/social wellbeing.

4. Adequate Scope. Assessment of progress toward sustainable development should:

▪ adopt a time horizon long enough to capture both human and ecosystem timescales, thus responding to the needs of future generations as well as demands for short-term benefits;

▪ define the space of study large enough to include not only local but also long-distance impacts on people and ecosystems;

▪ build on historic and current conditions to anticipate future conditions – where we want to go, where we could go.

5. Practical Focus. Assessment of progress toward sustainable development should be based on:

▪ an explicit set of categories or an organizing framework that links vision and goals to indicators and assessment criteria;

▪ a limited number of key issues for analysis;

▪ a limited number of indicators or indicator combinations to provide a clearer signal of progress;

▪ standardizing measurement wherever possible to permit comparison;

▪ comparing indicator values to targets, reference values, ranges, thresholds, or direction of trends, as appropriate.

6. Openness. Assessment of progress toward sustainable development should:

▪ make the methods and data that are used accessible to all;

▪ make explicit all judgements, assumptions and uncertainties in data and interpretations.

7. Effective Communication. Assessment of progress toward sustainable development should:

▌ be designed to address the needs of the audience and set of users;

▌ draw from indicators and other tools that are stimulating and serve to engage decision makers;

▌ aim, from the outset, for simplicity in structure and use of clear and plain language.

8. Broad Participation. Assessment of progress toward sustainable development should:

▌ obtain broad representation of key grass-roots, professional, technical and social groups, including youths, women and indigenous people – to ensure recognition of diverse and changing values;

▌ ensure the participation of decision makers to secure a firm link to adopted policies and resulting action.

9. Ongoing Assessment. Assessment of progress toward sustainable development should:

▌ develop a capacity for repeated measurement to determine trends;

▌ be iterative, adaptive and responsive to change and uncertainty because systems are complex and change frequently;

▌ adjust goals, frameworks and indicators as new insights are gained;

▌ promote development of collective learning and feedback to decision making.

10. Institutional Capacity. Continuity of assessing progress toward sustainable development should be assured by:

▌ clearly assigning responsibility and providing ongoing support in the decision-making process;

▌ providing institutional capacity for data collection, maintenance and documentation supporting development of local
assessment capacity.

For more information see the Web site iisd.ca/measure.1.htm.

THE CAUX ROUND TABLE

The Caux Round Table was founded in 1986 by Frederik Philips,
former President of Philips Electronics, and Olivier Giscard d'Estaing,
Vice-Chairman of INSEAD, as a means of reducing escalating trade
tensions. It is concerned with the development of constructive
economic and social relationships between the participants' countries,
and with their responsibilities toward the rest of the world.

At the urging of Ryuzaburo Kaku, Chairman of Canon Inc, the
Round Table has focused attention on the importance of global corporate responsibility in reducing social and economic threats to world
peace and stability. The Round Table recognizes that shared leadership is indispensable to a revitalized and more harmonious world. It
emphasizes the development of continuing friendship, understanding
and cooperation, based on a common respect for the highest moral
values and on responsible action by individuals in their own spheres
of influence.

The Caux Round Table believes that the world business community
should play an important role in improving economic and social
conditions. As a statement of aspirations, this document aims to
express a world standard against which business behaviour can be
measured.

The principles are rooted in two basic ethical ideals: *kyosei* and
human dignity. The Japanese concept of *kyosei* means living and
working together for the common good, enabling cooperation and
mutual prosperity to coexist with healthy and fair competition.
Human dignity refers to the sacredness or value of each person as an
end, not simply as a means to the fulfilment of others' purposes or
even majority prescription.

The General Principles seek to clarify the spirit of *kyosei* and human
dignity, while there are also specific Stakeholder Principles concerned
with their practical application.

General Principles

Principle 1.   The Responsibilities of Businesses: Beyond Shareholders Toward Stakeholders. Businesses have a role to play in improving the lives of all their customers, employees and shareholders by sharing with them the wealth they have created. Suppliers and competitors as well should expect businesses to honour their obligations in a spirit of honesty and fairness. As responsible citizens of the local, national, regional and global communities in which they operate, businesses share a part in shaping the future of those communities.

Principle 2.   The Economic and Social Impact of Business: Toward Innovation, Justice and World Community. Businesses established in foreign countries to develop, produce or sell should also contribute to the social advancement of those countries by creating productive employment and helping to raise the purchasing power of their citizens. Businesses also should contribute to human rights, education, welfare and vitalization of the countries in which they operate.

Principle 3.   Business Behaviour: Beyond the Letter of Law Toward a Spirit of Trust. While accepting the legitimacy of trade secrets, businesses should recognize that sincerity, candour, truthfulness, the keeping of promises and transparency contribute not only to their own credibility and stability but also to the smoothness and efficiency of business transactions, particularly on the international level.

Principle 4.   Respect for Rules. To avoid trade frictions and to promote freer trade, equal conditions for competition, and fair and equitable treatment for all participants, businesses should respect international and domestic rules. In addition, they should recognize that some behaviour, although legal, may still have adverse consequences.

Principle 5.   Support for Multilateral Trade. Businesses should support the multilateral trade systems of the GATT/World Trade Organization and similar international agreements. They should cooperate in efforts to promote the progressive and judicious liberalization of

Principle 6.   trade and to relax those domestic measures that unreasonably hinder global commerce, while giving due respect to national policy objectives.

Principle 6.   Respect for the Environment. A business should protect and, where possible, improve the environment, promote sustainable development, and prevent the wasteful use of natural resources.

Principle 7.   Avoidance of Illicit Operations. A business should not participate in or condone bribery, money laundering, or other corrupt practices: indeed, it should seek cooperation with others to eliminate them. It should not trade in arms or other materials used for terrorist activities, drug traffic or other organized crime.

For more information see the Web site www.cauxroundtable.org.

THE GLOBAL SULLIVAN PRINCIPLES

In 1977, the Reverend Leon Sullivan launched the original Sullivan Principles. Over the years, these have developed into the Global Sullivan Principles for Corporate Social Responsibility.

New 'Global Sullivan Principles' for corporations were announced at the UN on 2 November 1999. Sullivan worked with a group of multinational corporations from three continents and a business association from Latin America to create the Principles. Input and support were sought and received from a broad group of NGOs, intergovernmental organizations and national governments.

The objectives of the Global Sullivan Principles are to support economic, social and political justice by companies where they do business; to support human rights and to encourage equal opportunity at all levels of employment, including racial and gender diversity on decision-making committees and boards; to train and advance disadvantaged workers for technical, supervisory and management opportunities; and to assist with greater tolerance and understanding among peoples, thereby, helping to improve the quality of life for communities, workers and children with dignity and equality.

For more information see the Web site www.globalsullivan principles.org.

AMNESTY INTERNATIONAL

Amnesty International publishes Human Rights Guidelines for Companies offering a basic framework for developing human rights policies. It provides a checklist of principles based on internationally accepted human rights standards that are embodied in a range of UN conventions and protocols.

It also publishes a short booklet intended to provide the trustees of UK Occupational Pension Funds with terms of reference to respond to recent regulatory changes and to the growing concerns of pension scheme members about the social impact of their investments. The guidelines explain how taking ethical factors into account is consistent with the legal responsibilities that trustees have towards their scheme's members.

For more information see the Web site www.amnesty.org.

THE WORLD BUSINESS COUNCIL FOR SUSTAINABLE DEVELOPMENT

The World Business Council for Sustainable Development (WBCSD) is a coalition of some 140 international companies united by a shared commitment to sustainable development, ie environmental protection, social equity and economic growth.

Its members are drawn from 30 countries and more than 20 major industrial sectors. The WBCSD also benefits from a thriving global network of national and regional business councils and partner organizations.

The WBCSD was formed in January 1995 through a merger between the Business Council for Sustainable Development (BCSD) in Geneva and the World Industry Council for the Environment (WICE), an International Chamber of Commerce (ICC) initiative, in Paris. It is concerned with such issues under the heading of corporate social responsibility as:

- human rights;

- worker rights;

- environmental impact;

▌ community involvement;

▌ supplier relations;

▌ monitoring.

Recognizing that transparency and dialogue are key elements to successful management of the issues, WBCSD organized a stakeholder dialogue in September 1998. Participants at the dialogue represented a wide range of civil society. Many felt that business could move significantly from a narrow focus on responsibility to shareholders towards a greater sense of responsibility to society at large. More stakeholders would be influential in shaping the content of corporate responsibility. As companies developed and used that influencing process their sense of corporate responsibility would become deeper and more robust, and would reduce their exposure to liabilities.

The dialogue emphasized the following:

▌ the role of leadership in promoting a set of core corporate values;

▌ the need to ensure that corporate responsibility is part of the overall business strategy;

▌ the value of the WBCSD endorsing corporate responsibility as a philosophy;

▌ the importance of 'getting the process right', ie via transparency and consultation.

A first report, *Meeting Changing Expectations: Corporate Social Responsibility*, was issued in March 1999. The report:

▌ outlines business thinking on CSR issues;

▌ provides good practice examples of how companies have dealt with some of the issues;

▌ defines the issues and explores the gaps between stakeholder and business expectations;

▌ stimulates further high-quality learning contributions for a subsequent publication.

To include greater input from non-OECD countries in the work, the WBCSD conducted several stakeholder dialogues with various interested parties in Africa, Asia and Latin America throughout 1999. Using the WBCSD's global network of national and partner Business Councils for Sustainable Development, the dialogues provided an important source of ideas, by bringing in different views and approaches.

Following this, the WBCSD has put forward guidelines for stakeholder engagement. 'The essence of corporate social responsibility is to recognize the value of external stakeholder dialogue.' The two crucial questions to be answered are to whom should a company talk and why. It suggested that stakeholders should be screened by asking three questions:

▌ Legitimacy. Is a particular stakeholder group representative of issues that are relevant to the business and accountable to people who have a legitimate interest in the way the company does its business?

▌ Contribution/influence. Does the stakeholder group have a contribution to make towards helping the business run more responsibly? Does it have a significant influence on the business and/or other stakeholders?

▌ Outcome. Is the engagement likely to have a productive outcome in the long run?

WBCSD suggests using a matrix with key stakeholders listed on one axis and issues on the other. (The issues include such matters as values, governance processes, accountability, disclosure, human rights, employee's rights and working conditions, product quality and safety, impact on communities, impact on environment etc.) The cells of the matrix can then be completed to indicate areas of strong, moderate or little impact.

The matrix can also be used as a basis for identifying appropriate measurements or indicators for monitoring the company's performance in terms of its social impact. For example, in the cell which relates the stakeholder group 'suppliers' to the issue 'impact on local communities', an appropriate indicator would be the proportion of supplies drawn from local suppliers.

For more information see the Web site www.wbcsd.org.

CERES

CERES is 'the leading US coalition of environmental, investor, and advocacy groups working together for a sustainable future'. A community of forward-looking companies has committed to continuous environmental improvement by endorsing the CERES Principles, a 10-point code of environmental conduct.

The CERES Coalition is a network of over 70 organizations, including:

I environmental advocates such as Earth Island Institute, Friends of the Earth, Green Seal, National Wildlife Federation, Natural Resources Defense Council, Rocky Mountain Institute, Sierra Club, Union of Concerned Scientists, and World Wildlife Fund;

I investors, advisers and analysts representing over $300 billion in invested capital, including the Calvert Group, Friends Ivory & Sime, Interfaith Center on Corporate Responsibility, Kinder, Lydenberg, Domini & Co, the New York City Comptroller's Office, Presbyterian Church (USA), Shorebank, and Trillium Asset Management;

I public interest and community groups, including AFL-CIO, Alternatives for Community and Environment, Center for a New American Dream, Co-op America, Council on Economic Priorities, Fair Trade Foundation, New Economics Foundation, and Redefining Progress.

The 50-plus companies endorsing the CERES Principles include American Airlines, Bank of America, Baxter International, Bethlehem Steel, Coca Cola USA, Bethlehem Steel, Ford Motor Company, General Motors, ITT Industries, Nike, Northeast Utilities, Polaroid, and Sunoco and The Body Shop International.

For more information see the Web site www.ceres.org.

THE GLOBAL REPORTING INITIATIVE

The Global Reporting Initiative (GRI) was established in late 1997 with the mission of developing globally applicable guidelines for reporting on economic, environmental and social performance, initially for corporations and eventually for any business, governmental, or non-governmental organization (NGO). Convened by the Coalition for Environmentally Responsible Economies (CERES) in partnership with the United Nations Environment Programme (UNEP), the GRI incorporates the active participation of corporations, NGOs, accountancy organizations, business associations and other stakeholders from around the world.

The GRI's *Sustainability Reporting Guidelines* were released in draft form in London in March 1999. The GRI *Guidelines* represent a global framework for comprehensive sustainability reporting, encompassing the 'triple bottom line' of economic, environmental and social issues. Twenty-one pilot test companies, numerous other companies, and a diverse array of non-corporate stakeholders commented on the draft *Guidelines* during a pilot test period during 1999–2000. Revised *Guidelines* were issued in June 2000.

By 2002, the GRI aims to be established as a permanent, independent, international body with a multi-stakeholder governance structure. Its core mission will be maintenance, enhancement and dissemination of the *Guidelines* through a process of ongoing consultation and stakeholder engagement.

For more information see the Web site www.globalreporting.org.

CSR EUROPE

CSR Europe is an inclusive organization that welcomes as members all companies investing in Corporate Social Responsibility in Europe. It is a business-driven network with the mission to help companies achieve profitability, sustainable growth and human progress by placing corporate social responsibility in the mainstream of business practice.

With over 40 company members and 15 National Partners, CSR Europe achieves this objective in the following ways:

- serving over 50,000 business people and partners annually through print and online publications, best practices and tools;

- offering business managers learning, benchmarking and tailored capacity building programmes;

- including CSR issues in stakeholder dialogue and focusing particularly on the European Institutions.

CSR Europe today collaborates with over 15 different organizations in more than a dozen European countries. These National Partner Organizations (NPOs) promote Corporate Social Responsibility at national, regional and local level.

The NPOs together with CSR Europe:

▮ provide expert products and specialized services to the business community;

▮ identify ways for all organizations to benefit from the knowledge and experience of their peers;

▮ engage in joint projects and programmes that result in streamlined efforts to advance socially responsible business practices.

The CSR Matrix makes it possible to check the performance of a wide range of companies. The horizontal axis covers: Social reports, Thematic reports, Codes of Conduct, Web information, Stakeholder consultation, Internal communication, Standards and labels, Awards and events, cause-related marketing and Web press releases.

The vertical axis includes Mission values and vision, Workplace climate, Social dialogue, Human Rights, Community involvement, Local economic development, Environment, Marketplace, Ethics and Others.

For more information see the Web site www.csreurope.org.

ISO 14001

One outcome of the United Nations Conference on Environment and Development, or Earth Summit, Rio de Janeiro, Brazil, 1992, was the launch of ISO 14001, an international standard that addresses environmental management and pollution prevention. Prior to the conference, representatives approached the International Organization for Standardization (ISO), asking them to participate and create international environmental standards. ISO announced at the conference that they would undertake this effort. Thus, ISO 14001 was conceived to help achieve sustainable development.

The ISO 14001 standard specifies requirements for establishing an environmental policy and environmental objectives, determining environmental aspects and impacts of activities, products and services. Thus, 'by establishing and maintaining an environmental management system that meets the ISO 14001 standard, companies will be implementing a strong and effective environmental management program'.

Organizations are required to implement an environmental management system (EMS) in accordance with standards as set forth in the ISO 14001 specification; it requires organizations to establish an environmental policy for determining environmental aspects and impacts, and to reduce impacts in order to solve the environmental problems.

For more information see the Web site www.bsi-global.com.

SA 8000

SA 8000 is a system that defines a set of auditable standards and an independent auditing process for the protection of workers' rights. It covers child labour, forced labour, health and safety, collective bargaining, discrimination, disciplinary practices, working hours, compensation and management system. The standards incorporate those of International Labour Organization treaties, the Universal Declaration of Human Rights and the UN Convention on Rights of the Child. SA 8000 provides a common standard for companies seeking to assure the fundamental rights of workers.

SA 8000 provides a framework for the independent verification of the ethical production of all goods, made in companies of any size, anywhere in the world. Its use enables a company to demonstrate its commitment to best practice in the ethical manufacture and supply of the goods they sell.

The SA 8000 standard was created in 1997 by The Council of Economic Priorities Accreditation Agency (CEPAA), subsequently changed to Social Accountability International (SAI). CEPAA was the sister organization of the Council on Economic Priorities (CEP), based in New York. CEP, founded in 1969 by Alice Tepper Martin, formerly a securities analyst and labour economist, has been rating companies on issues such as environmental stewardship and treatment of employees since 1975. Social Accountability International (SAI) accredits independent auditing firms to monitor compliance with SA 8000.

For more information see the Web site www.cepaa.org/sa8000.

THE SIGMA PROJECT

The UK Sustainable Development Strategy included a government commitment to sponsor the creation of a sustainability management system. In July 1999, the SIGMA project was launched, with funding from the Department of Trade and Industry's Sustainable Technologies Initiative.

The UK's Sustainable Development Strategy, published in May 1999, defines sustainability in terms of four objectives:

▌ social progress which recognizes the needs of everyone;

▌ effective protection of the environment;

▌ prudent use of natural resources;

▌ maintenance of high and stable levels of economic growth and employment.

The SIGMA project is a partnership between three organizations with expertise in the different aspects of sustainability:

▌ British Standards Institution (BSI);

▌ Forum for the Future;

▌ The Institute of Social and Ethical Accountability (AccountAbility).

These three organizations made up the SIGMA Project Steering Group during Phase 1 of the project. The project steering group has now been expanded to include partners from a range of interest groups. Both the Department of Trade and Industry (DTI) and the Department of the Environment, Transport and the Regions (DETR) are also actively involved. For Phase 2 of the project, the Department for International Development (DfID) and the Department for Education and Employment (DfEE) will also be represented on the Project Steering Group.

The project's overall aim is to create a strategic management framework to assist organizations on the path to sustainability. Progressive companies already have considerable experience in tackling these issues, but the lessons learnt need to be drawn out and translated into a generic framework that can be applied across industry as a whole.

In the early 1990s, the UK developed the world's first environmental management system – BS 7750. In the same way, the SIGMA project aims to create the next-generation tools and standards for managing sustainability that will eventually be adopted at European and international level.

The key outputs of the SIGMA project will be a sustainability management system and a sustainability toolkit. The management system will assist organizations to balance competing interests and focus on targets and performance improvements. The system will enable organizations to take a strategic view of sustainability issues and integrate non-financial issues into decision-making processes. The emphasis will be on simplicity, practicality and integration. The toolkit will supplement the management system giving guidance on how organizations can manage and integrate specific issues such as social capital and environmental accounting and will be developed using best practice, research and practical experience. In particular, it will integrate existing standards into the SIGMA management system.

The system will seek to provide an integrated framework for strategic and operational management through the following core processes:

▮ mission, organizational values and principles;

▮ baseline setting;

▮ impact and risk assessment;

▮ strategic planning and policy development;

▮ integration of social, economic and environmental aspects of business activities;

▮ innovation, learning and culture change;

▮ stakeholder engagement, communication and feedback;

▮ governance, internal controls and accountability;

▮ compliance;

▮ management programmes;

▌ documentation and record keeping;

▌ performance measurement, including the use of appropriate indicators and benchmarks;

▌ audit verification and management review;

▌ reporting and disclosure;

▌ continual improvement.

The SIGMA project is divided into two phases. Phase 1 ran from July 1999 to April 2000 and consisted of:

▌ a comprehensive survey of existing tools and standards in the environmental, social and economic fields, followed by a gap analysis to identify where new work is required;

▌ the recruitment of a consortium of 20–25 organizations to experiment with new tools and standards as they are developed;

▌ initial consultations with a wide range of stakeholders who will be invited to input directly into the project;

▌ a seminar for participating organizations and key stakeholders to review progress so far, and map out the programme for Phase 2.

Phase 2, running from May 2000 to April 2002 consists of:

▌ the commissioning of fresh research from a variety of NGOs and research bodies;

▌ the live piloting of new and existing tools and systems by the organizations recruited during Phase 1;

▌ the establishment of committees and working groups to undertake the formal development of new tools and standards;

▌ the dissemination of the project's findings through a series of publications and seminars.

For more information see the Web site www.projectsigma.com.

AA1000

AccountAbility (The Institute of Social and Ethical Accountability) was founded in 1996 as an international membership organization, based in the United Kingdom. It aims to improve the accountability and performance of organizations worldwide. AccountAbility is a professional body committed to strengthening the social responsibility and ethical behaviour of the business community and non-profit organizations. It addresses this mission by: promoting best practice social and ethical accounting, auditing and reporting; and developing standards and accreditation procedures for professionals in the field.

AccountAbility's members are drawn from experts and leading practitioners in the field of accountability. Current membership comprises around 400 members in 40 countries.

New guidance for organizations faced with managing ethical challenges was launched in November 1999 by the Institute. The AA1000 standard provides both a framework that organizations can use to understand and improve their ethical performance and a means for others to judge the validity of ethical claims made. It was launched at AccountAbility's third international conference on social and ethical accounting, auditing and reporting, held in Copenhagen.

Before now, companies that wanted to take control of their destiny by proving themselves ethical were 'feeling their way in the dark', said AccountAbility Council Chair, Simon Zadek. 'The AA1000 standard provides organizations with a process that has been agreed as "best practice" by experts from around the world. More importantly, however, it gives internal and external stakeholders reassurance that there is real substance behind an organization's actions – that it's more than PR.'

The professional qualification is double-faceted. It comprises the accreditation of training providers and individuals seeking qualifications. Both students and accreditation seeking organizations will be expected to comply with the Institute's Code of Conduct, which the panel is also currently developing.

At the time of writing, the Institute was developing a new standard – AA2000. This builds on and extends the AA1000 framework, moving from achieving transparency on to developing organizational learning and innovation, engaging with stakeholders, integrating management systems, securing verification and assurance and developing effective governance approaches.

For more information see the Web site www.accountability.org.uk.

THE CENTRE FOR TOMORROW'S COMPANY

In its publication *Sooner, Sharper, Simpler* (1998), The Centre for Tomorrow's Company proposed a scorecard to test the extent to which a company's annual report was inclusive. The main headings in the scorecard were as follows:

▌ Purpose and values. Does the company clearly state its purpose and values?

▌ Success model as a basis for measurement. Does the company make use of a clear model such as the balanced business scorecard to demonstrate linkages between aspects of performance and financial results? Does it include measures of such things as learning, knowledge management, etc?

▌ Progress in key relationships. Does the company give a clear account of the progress it is making in developing its relationships with its stakeholders, including reports of dialogues and other forms of stakeholder engagement?

▌ Licence to operate. Does the company demonstrate that it is adding value to the community, thus enhancing its licence to operate?

▌ The annual report as part of a total communication process. Does it offer the reader opportunities to acquire further information and to engage in a dialogue?

▌ An account of the Board's Stewardship over time. Does the report chart progress over time with regard to key indicators? Does it include forward-looking indicators?

▌ Clarity. Does the report use plain English, graphics and layout to good effect?

For more information see the Web site www.tomorrowscompany.co.uk.

THE COPENHAGEN CHARTER

The Copenhagen Charter, a management guide to stakeholder reporting, was launched at the third international conference on social and ethical accounting, auditing and reporting, 1999, and was published jointly by Ernst & Young, KPMG, PricewaterhouseCoopers and the House of Mandag Morgen.

The basic assumption underlying the Charter is that the processes of stakeholder dialogue and reporting must be embedded throughout the organization, in the mission, vision and values of the company, and in management and corporate governance systems. The mission, vision and values are both the foundation of the reporting process and the outcome of it, in that stakeholder reporting enables management to test that they meet stakeholders' expectations. The process is envisaged as a feedback loop involving the following steps:

- statement of vision and values;

- identification of key stakeholders and critical success factors;

- dialogue with stakeholders;

- determination of Key Performance Indicators and adaptation of management information system to incorporate these;

- monitoring performance;

- action plan to improve performance;

- prepare, verify and publish report;

- consult stakeholders about performance and revisit vision and values.

For more information see the Web site www.copenhagencentre.org.

References

Anderson, C (1997) Values-based management, *Academy of Management Executive*, **11** (4), pp 25–46

Anderson, R (2001) A lesson from America, in *Sustainable Development*, Director Publications, London

Argenti, J (1996) Are you a stakeholder? *Strategy*, Issue 9

Aspen Institute (2001) *No More Grey Pinstripes*, Aspen, CO

Atkinson, A A, Waterhouse, J H, Wells, R B (1997) A stakeholder approach to strategic performance measurement, *Sloan Management Review*, Spring, pp 25–37

Bass, B M (1989) Assessing the charismatic leader, in *The Frontiers of Leadership*, ed M Syrett and C Hogg, Blackwell, Oxford

Bell, D (1972) *The Coming of Post Industrial Society*, Penguin Books, London

Bennis, W (1997) *Organizing Genius*, Addison-Wesley, Reading, MA

Block, P (1993) *Stewardship*, Berrett Koehler, San Francisco

Brown, J A C (1963) *The Social Psychology of Industry*, Penguin Books, Harmondsworth

Brown, M (1999) The invisible advantage, *Directions*, Ashridge Management College, Berkhamsted

Cairncross, F (1997) *The Death of Distance*, Orion Publishing, London

Carson, R (1962) *The Silent Spring*, Houghton Mifflin, New York

Centre for Tomorrow's Company (1998) *The Corporate Reporting Jigsaw*, CTC, London

Centre for Tomorrow's Company (1998) *Sooner, Sharper, Simpler*, CTC, London

Centre for Tomorrow's Company (2001) *Twenty First Century Investment. An agenda for change*, CTC, London

Centre for Tomorrow's Company/GPL (2001) *Leading and Managing in the New Economy*, CTC, London

Ciulla, J B (1999) The importance of leadership in shaping business values, *Long Range Planning*, **32** (2), pp 166–172

Club of Rome (1972) *The Limits to Growth: A report of the Club of Rome's project on the predicament of mankind*, Universe Books, New York

Collins, J (2001) Level 5 leadership, *Harvard Business Review*, **79** (1), January, pp 67–76

Collins, J and Porras, J (1995) *Built to Last*, Century, London

Company Law Review Steering Group (2000) *Modern Company Law for a Competitive Economy*, consultation document, Department of Trade and Industry, London

CSR Europe (1999) *Best Practices on Corporate Social Responsibility: United Kingdom*, CSR Europe, Brussels

CSR Europe (2000) *A European Assessment of 46 Companies' Performance on Social and Employment Issues*, CSR Europe, Brussels

Day, G (1999) Aligning organization structure in the market, *Business Strategy Review*, **10** (3), pp 33–46

De Geus, A (1997) *The Living Company*, Nicholas Brealey, London

Drucker, P (1969) *The Age of Discontinuity*, Heinemann, London

Drucker, P (1986) *The Frontiers of Management*, Heinemann, London

Drucker, P (1992) Leadership – more doing than dash, in *Managing for the Future*, Butterworth-Heinemann, London

Durkheim, E (1893) *The Division of Labour in Society*, The Free Press, New York, 1984

Edvisson, L (1997) Developing intellectual capital at Skandia, *Long Range Planning*, **30**, pp 366–373

Elkington, J (1997) *Cannibals with Forks*, Capstone, Oxford

Elkington, J (2001) *The Chrysalis Economy*, Capstone, Oxford

Evans, P (1992) Developing leaders and managing development, *European Management Journal*, **10** (1), March, pp 1–9

Fukuyama, F (1995) *Trust: the Social Virtues and the Creation of Prosperity*, Hamish Hamilton, London

Goldenberg, P (1997) *Shareholders v. Stakeholders: The Bogus Argument*, IALS Lecture

Goyder, M (1998) *Living Tomorrow's Company*, Gower, Aldershot

Goyder, M (1999) Value and values: lessons for tomorrow's company, *Long Range Planning*, **32** (2), pp 217–24

Goyder, M (2000) Connected economy, disjointed society, *Insight*, vol 2 no 5 p 455

Greenleaf, R (1982) *The Servant as Leader*, Robert K Greenleaf Center, Indianapolis

Handy, C (1992) The language of leadership, in *The Frontiers of Leadership*, ed M Syrett and C Hogg, Blackwell, Oxford

Handy, C (1997) *The Citizen Corporation*, Seminar Paper, Birkbeck College, London

Heifitz, R A (1994) *Leadership Without Easy Answers*, Harvard University Press, Cambridge, MA

Hertz, N (2001) *The Silent Take-over*, William Heinemann, London

Hobsbawm, E (2000) *The New Century*, Little, Brown and Company, New York

Hooper, A and Potter, J (1997) *The Business of Leadership*, Ashgate, Aldershot

Howe, M (1990) *The Origins of Exceptional Abilities*, Blackwell, Oxford

Industrial Society (1999) *Liberating Leadership*, Industrial Society, London

Jones, H (2001) Responding to stakeholders concerns in the New Economy: Nike's experience, in *Perspectives on the New Economy of Corporate Citizenship*, ed S Zadek *et al*, The Copenhagen Centre, Copenhagen

Kennedy, A (2000) *The End of Shareholder Value*, Orion Business, London

Kinsman, F (1989) *Millennium*, W H Allen, London

Klein, N (2000) *No Logo*, Flamingo, London

Korten, D C (1996) *When Corporations Rule the World*, Earthscan, London

Kotter, J (1990) What leaders really do, *Harvard Business Review*, May/June, pp 154–67

Kotter, J and Heskett, J (1992) *Corporate Culture and Performance*, The Free Press, New York

Kotter, J P (1988) *The Leadership Factor*, The Free Press, New York

Lank, E (2000) Workers fed knowledge in café community, *Human Resources*, February

Law, A (1998) *Open Minds*, Orion Business, London

Le Carré, J (2001) *The Constant Gardener*, Hodder & Stoughton, London

Lomberg, B (2001) *The Skeptical Environmentalist: Measuring the real state of the world*, Cambridge University Press, Cambridge

MacMillan, K and Downing, S (1999) Governance and performance: goodwill hunting, *Journal of General Management*, **24** (3), Spring, pp 11–21

Mansley, M and Dlugolecki, A (2001) *Climate Change – A Risk Management Challenge for Institutional Investors*, USS, London

Manz, C C and Sims, H Jr (2001) *The New SuperLeadership*, Berrett-Koehler, San Francisco, CA

Mathur, S and Kenyon, A (1997) *Creating Value*, Butterworth-Heinemann, London

Mayo, A and Lank, E (1994) *The Power of Learning. A Guide to Gaining Competitive Advantage*, Chartered Institute of Personnel and Development, London

McCall, M, Lombardo, M and Morrison, A (1988) *The Lessons of Experience*, Lexington Books, Lexington, MA

Monks, R (1998) *The Emperor's Nightingale*, Capstone, Oxford

National Council for Education in Management and Leadership (2001) *Leadership Development: best practice guide for organizations*, London

Neely, A (1998) *Measuring Business Performance*, Economist Books, London

Nevins, M and Stumpf, S (1999) 21st century leadership, *Journal of Strategy and Business*, 3rd quarter

New Economics Foundation (2001) *Stakes not Shares*, NEF, London

Nicoll, D (1986) Leadership and followership, in *Transforming Leadership* ed J D Adams, Miles River Press, Alexandria, VA

OECD (1999) *The Economic and Social Implications of E Commerce*, OECD, Paris

Pascale, R (1991) *Managing on the Edge*, Penguin, London

Pfeffer, J (1998) *The Human Equation*, Harvard Business School, Cambridge, MA

Pfeffer, J (2000) *The Human Equation*, Harvard Business School Press, Boston, MA

Plender, J (1997) *A Stake in the Future*, Nicholas Brealey, London

Putnam, R (2000) *Bowling Alone*, Simon & Schuster, New York

Reich, C A (1970) *The Greening of America*, Allen Lane The Penguin Press, London

Reichheld, F F and Teal, T (1996) *The Loyalty Effect*, Harvard Business School, Cambridge, MA

Royal Society of Arts (1995) *An Inquiry into the Nature of Tomorrow's Company*, London

Sadler, P (1993) *Managing Talent*, FT Pitman, London

Schein, E (1992) *Organisation Culture and Leadership*, Jossey Bass, San Francisco, CA

Schwartz, P and Gibb, B (1999) *When Good Companies do Bad Things*, John Wiley, New York

Senge, P (1993) *The Fifth Discipline – The Art and Practice of the Learning Organization*, Century Business, London

Spears, L (1995) Servant leadership and the Greenleaf legacy, in *Reflections on Leadership*, ed L C Spears, John Wiley and Sons, New York

Sternberg, E (1999) *The Stakeholder Concept: a Mistaken Doctrine*, Foundation for Business Responsibilities, London

Strategic Planning Society (1997) *Interview with John Neill*, SPS Newsletter, London

SustainAbility (2000) *The Global Reporters*, London

SustainAbility (2001) *The Power to Change: Mobilising Board leadership to deliver sustainable value to markets and society*, London

Svendsen, A (1998) *The Stakeholder Society*, Berrett-Koehler, San Francisco, CA

Taylor, M and Godfrey, J (1999) *Forces of Conservatism*, Institute of Public Policy Research, London

Tichy, N M and Devanna, M A (1986) *The Transformational Leader*, Wiley, New York

Turner, A (2001) *Just Capital*, MacMillan, London

University of Sussex Science Policy Research Unit (1973) 'The Limits to Growth Controversy Special Issue', *Futures*, **5** (1), February

Vogt, W (1948) *Roads to Survival*, William Sloane Associates, New York

Waddock, S and Graves, S (1997) Quality of management in quality of stakeholder relations, *Business and Society*, **36** (3), September

Warburton, J and Cardoza, N (2001) A true ethical dilemma?, in *Directions*, Spring, Ashridge Management College

Warburton, P (1999) *Debt and Delusion*, The Penguin Press, London

Waterman, R (1994) *The Frontiers of Excellence*, Nicholas Brealey London

Wilson, A and Gribben, C (2000) *Socially Responsible Investment and Pension Funds*, Ashridge Centre for Business and Society, Berkhamsted

Wilson, I (2000) *The New Rules of Corporate Conduct*, Quorum Books, Westport, CT

Wolfensohn, J D (2001) Foreword, in *The New Economy of Corporate Citizenship*, ed S Zadek *et al*, The Copenhagen Centre, Copenhagen

World Conference on Environment and Development (1987) *Our Common Future*, Oxford University Press, Oxford

Zadek, S (2001) *The Civil Corporation*, Earthscan, London

Index

NB: numbers in italics indicate tables